"It might be thought impossible to write anything new on the Elizabethan age except in the narrow sphere of minute and detailed research, but Mr. Smith has called on the depth of his learning and knowledge to produce a brilliant synthesis of English and European history which can be compared only with G. M. Young's classic essay on Victorian England. Certainly it stands head and shoulders above any other book on Elizabethan England published in the last ten years.

By beginning in the fifteenth century he demonstrates the strong medieval elements in Tudor rule and sixteenth-century English life; by taut, perceptive surveys of France, Holland and Spain and their respective rulers and leaders he places Elizabeth's reign in its true Continental perspective, and besides all this he finds the space to produce vivid and stimulating studies of particular topics, the best perhaps, being his deflationary study of the Elizabethan hero as a paranoic. By the exercise of great literary skill all these disparate elements are woven into a fabric of great strength and beauty : the result, a real work of art"

J. P. Kenyon in *The Observer*

Lacey Baldwin Smith is Professor of English History at Northwestern University, Illinois. *The Elizabethan Epic* is a Book Society Choice. Previous works by Professor Smith include *Tudor Prelates and Politics* and *A Tudor Tragedy* (also a Book Society Choice)

Lacey Baldwin Smith

The Elizabethan Epic

Panther History

The Elizabethan Epic
A Panther Book

First published in Great Britain
by Jonathan Cape Limited 1966

Panther edition published 1969

Published by special arrangement
with the editors of *Horizon*
magazine

to my wife

Printed in England by
C. Nicholls & Company Ltd.,
The Philips Park Press, Manchester,
and published by Panther Books,
3 Upper James Street, London W.1.

Contents

List of Illustrations

Acknowledgments

The author and publishers are grateful to the following for permission to reproduce the illustrations:

The Trustees of the British Museum (medals and coins on plate 2; plates 5 and 8)

The National Portrait Gallery (front cover illustration; portrait of Henry VII, plate 3; plate 6)

The Mansell Collection (portraits of Henry III and Henry IV, plate 3)

The Museo del Prado (plate 10)

A. F. Kersting, A.I.I.P., F.R.P.S. (plate 1)

M. Jean Arlaud (portrait of Calvin, plate 3)

Introduction: THE ELIZABETHAN AGE

The Elizabethan Age

EVERY schoolboy knows that the Elizabethan age was history's finest hour, a rare moment when the magic of a Virgin Queen conjured up a generation of heroes who dared all and claimed England and the world as their rightful stage. It is unnecessary to prove twenty million schoolchildren wrong. Raleigh's gallantry in the face of a mud puddle, the classic calm of Drake finishing his game of bowls before setting forth to destroy the Spanish Armada, the calculated villainy of Philip of Spain surrounded by his family coffins, the evil eye of Catherine de Medici presiding over the debauched and vicious Valois court of France, and finally the splendour of England's Goddess Queen adored by all her subjects – all these are Anglo-Saxon lore. Philip and Catherine, William the Silent and Henry of Navarre, Suleiman the Magnificent and Ivan the Terrible sang no treble to Elizabeth's bass. Yet legend need not be wholly devoid of truth. The second half of the sixteenth century belonged to Gloriana. "Both in her life and her death she was appointed to be the mirror of her time," and the age properly bears her name: "Blessed Elizabeth of famous memory".

Elizabeth stood at a focal point of history, the *femme fatale* of Europe. Ivan the Terrible of Russia, though he mocked her as "a poor lady" victimized by a community of boorish shopkeepers, offered his bloody hand in marriage to the Queen's young cousin, Mary Hastings, and

urged Elizabeth to grant him asylum should the need arise;
the King of Poland begged her aid against Russian aggres-
sions into Europe and warned her that Ivan was "the enemy
to all liberty under the heavens"; the Netherlands sought
her protection and offered her their kingdom if only she
would consent to be their queen; Protestants in every corner of Europe viewed her as their Deborah; and Philip of
Spain came to the agonizing conclusion that she was possessed by the devil and had to be destroyed for the sake
of Christian souls as well as for the security of Spain. So
often was the Queen's life pulled "even out of the lion's
jaws in despite of Hell and Satan" that one is almost temp-
ted to agree with the loyal Elizabethan who firmly announced that "indeed the Lord hath vowed Himself to be
English".

Naming an age is one thing, understanding and dating it
another. On what basis is it possible to comprehend an era
that roasted heretics at the stake, axed and mutilated men
who held unorthodox political views, condoned and practised slavery, administered various forms of punishment
ranging from boiling alive to ear-clipping and branding,
but yet retained an image of man just below the angels
and proclaimed a new philosophy that called "all in
doubt"? When and where did the Elizabethan age commence? With her accession in 1558? With her birth in 1533?
With the forces of revolution that created the magic of a
Shakespeare, the dreams of a Raleigh, the pride of an Essex, the scepticism of a Montaigne, and the vision of a
Bacon or a Copernicus? Or must the essence of the century
be sought in the medieval past, in the spirit that produced
the granite theology of a Calvin, the religious imagination
of a Loyola and the militant faith of Puritans and Jesuits?

On all sides existed contrast and contradiction. Raleigh
was as interested in theology as in discovery; Queen Bess
spent hours translating devotional literature and writing
prayers; and for every Elizabethan who sought "new
worlds for gold, for praise, for glory", another warned that
"peace with God is the true cheerfulness of heart". Standing in silent but unforgotten splendour was an endless succession of decades receding into the medieval gloom.
Everywhere the past remained in evidence as a living ideal

or as a fossilized reality. Renaissance zest for life, "wild, indecent and improvident", existed side by side with medieval contempt for this world. Machiavelli and Copernicus
may have been the harbingers of the future, yet most Elizabethans preferred the ancient cosmic order in which both
man and God observed "degree, priority and place".
Elizabethans were joyfully aware of their humanity but
deeply sensible of their morality. They stood upon what
seemed to many to be the threshold of a new dawn in
which man dared all and might achieve all. The literature
of the century abounded with works of practical advice,
ranging from Machiavelli's instructions on how to be a
successful prince and Henry Peacham's rules for becoming
The Compleat Gentleman to Thomas Heywood's less ambitious counsel on *How a Man May Choose a Good Wife
from a Bad*. The Elizabethan man sensed in himself the
power of creation. At the very least he proclaimed the
world to be "a great Volume and man the Index to that
Book". The whole world, wrote Gabriel Harvey to Edmund Spenser in 1580, was seeking "after News, new
Books, new Fashions, new Laws, new Officers, and some
after new Elements, and some after new Heavens and Hells
too". But in the midst of this boisterous and bloody life
remained death – "an eternal gnawing" of man's conscience. Marlowe for all his religious scoffing still placed
Dr. Faustus where most Elizabethans firmly believed him
to be – in Hell.

> Faustus is gone: regard his hellish fall
> Whose fiendful fortune may exhort the wise,
> Only to wonder at unlawful things,
> Whose deepness doth entice such forward wits
> To practise more than heavenly power permits.

The age of Elizabeth both in England and on the continent was a century of extremes of anguish and delight.
Philip of Spain arrived in London to marry Mary Tudor
in 1554 garbed in surcoat, doublet and hose of crimson
velvet set off with gold chain and silver filigree, yet he
ended his life surrounded by unrelenting black. It was a century of immoderation in religion, in commercial practices

and in the enjoyment of life. Don Juan and Dr. Faustus were record-breakers. "Their very wanting is excessive," and Don Juan's one thousand and three seductions in Spain alone stand as the symbol of a society determined to excel even in warranting perdition. Conversely, the thunderous denials of the pleasures and foibles of this world were equally excessive. Beauty was branded as "a wind-blown bladder" and worldly love as "the food of cloying concupiscence" that leaves no leisure to guard against sin.

In the midst of such contrast and variation, all that can be said with certainty is that the image of the future was sharper in 1560 than it had been in 1460; that the scent of optimism was more pervasive than the odour of despair; and that the Elizabethan age was acutely conscious, if not of its own modernity, at least of a sense of history, of having come out of the medieval past. Some men applauded the process; others deplored it and begged for a return; but everyone recognized change. On the eve of the sixteenth century Erasmus of Rotterdam voiced the two discordant themes of the coming era. In one breath he mourned: "Where now is gladness, where tranquillity of heart? Everything is full of bitterness and trouble; wherever I turn my eyes, I see nothing but what is melancholy and cruel." In the next moment his heart was filled with gladness and he extolled "this age of ours which promises to be an age of gold if ever there was one". Elizabethans could never quite make up their minds which prediction had in fact come true.

In order to capture the flavour of Elizabethan Europe, to comprehend how Renaissance dynamism could have lived in the same body with medieval melancholy, it is necessary to delve back into the decades before 1558 or even 1533, to sketch in the medieval profile, of which part was fading but much lingered on to characterize the Elizabethan age.

One

Medieval Twilight:
The Odour of Despair

"I APPEAL", said Charles VII of France, "to the sharp end of my sword." As the medieval world slowly dissolved, Europe of the fifteenth century fell prey to a barbarism, sacrilege and selfishness in which man's inhumanity to man knew no limits and all men made appeal to the sharp end of their swords. It has been said that the century produced no attractive figures except John Huss in Bohemia, Savonarola in Florence and Joan of Arc in France, and it is an interesting commentary upon the age that it should have burned all three of them. On all sides the alchemy of change and the shock of catastrophe were generating despair and foreboding, inducing men to forsake and pervert the old standards. In poetry and art, in actions and aspirations, in sermons and chronicles, despondency prevailed. As early as the fourteenth century, Eustache Deschamps set the tone for most of late medieval Europe when he sadly posed a question, still unanswered when Elizabeth mounted the throne in 1558.

> Why is our life so cruel and dark
> That men no longer speak to friend?
> Why does evil so clearly mark
> The monstrous government of men?
>
> Compare what is with what is past
> And see how fraud and sorrow stand.

> While law and justice fade so fast
> That I know no longer where I am.

Compared with what was past, the fifteenth century presented a spectacle of royal murders, clerical corruption, international anarchy and spiritual neurosis. Medievalism was slowly dissolving into mouldering feudalism and obsolescent formalism, devoid of meaning and vitality. Traditionally the medieval ideal had been one of universalism, balanced by diversity. Christendom was seen as a seamless cloak, a single corps in which the universal Catholic Church and the Holy Roman Empire shared the two swords of Christ – the spiritual and the temporal authorities.

Religious unity had at one time been a reality, but political union had never been more than a myth, the phantom of the Roman *imperium* living on in the moribund body of the Holy Roman Empire. By 1400 medieval Christianity was in disarray. The Holy Roman Empire had become a spectre in which real power rested not with the emperor but with a myriad of principalities scattered throughout Germany, the Low Countries and Northern Italy. Each prince, prelate and imperial town possessed sovereignty within the Empire, and the emperor, chosen by the seven electors of Germany, was little more than a cipher burdened with endless duties but exercising only nominal rights. By 1485 the memory of imperial authority had faded to the point that, when the Emperor offered to invest Ivan III of Russia as King within the Empire, the Tsar wrote back politely but firmly that there was no need. The Holy Roman Empire had become a soulless and artificial relic of the past held together by hollow pomp and gaudy circumstance. It amounted to little more than its mechanical representation on the clock outside the church of Our Lady in the imperial city of Nuremberg. At noon two puppet trumpeters raise their tiny horns, a drummer boy beats out the measure, and seven resplendent effigies, representing the electors of Germany, parade in front of the Emperor, bowing their heads in acknowledgment of his august presence.

Spiritually the Christian world was also in chaos. Religious unity had disintegrated into the degrading spectacle of rival popes, one at Avignon, the other in Rome, each claiming for himself the keys to the kingdom of heaven and each thundering dire anathemas and maledictions at any Christian who dared accept the authority of his rival. The Great Schism of Catholicism lasted thirty-seven years, from 1378 to 1415. Significantly Europe divided along national lines, England and Germany siding with Urban VI in Rome, and France and Scotland following Clement VII at Avignon; a sure sign that the medieval ideal of universality was giving way to international anarchy in which God was French or German, English or Scottish. On all sides, medieval institutions survived but the spirit that had once sustained them withered and died. Kings continued to rule but subjects complained that "the law serveth for naught else but to do wrong"; the chivalric creed persisted but the feudal knight, encased in iron, became a military anachronism; the cleric retained his privileged position in society but his flock learned to use such expressions as "fat as a canon", "lazy as a monk", and "lewd as a Carmelite". In Crown, baronage and Church, the fifteenth century experienced a failure of leadership.

From Germany to England, from the Low Countries to Spain, the dynasties of Europe were afflicted with incompetence, insanity and sudden death. The medieval concept of kingship had incorporated three ideals – piety, justice and courage. The king was the pillar of piety, the fountain of justice, and the model of bravery. He lived apart, using his private wealth to sustain his regal office. He ruled by law, defending and recognizing the rights of his subjects, and he dedicated his energies to the defence of the Holy Church, championing the true faith against the infidel. Such a king had been Louis IX of France, and both Church and state agreed that he deserved the name of saint.

If Saint Louis stood for the ideal of medieval kingship, reality in the fifteenth century was clean contrary. In France the realm fell prey to internal discord, foreign invasion and governmental paralysis. When Charles V died in 1380, the crown passed to a twelve-year-old minor who moved rapidly from adolescence into insanity. At twenty-four Charles VI, known for obscure reasons as the "well-beloved", went mad, and the kingdom was exposed to a surfeit of wicked uncles. From the moment Charles took control of the government, he proved to be a monarch of inordinate passion: immoderate in work, in generosity, in war and in pleasure. The expenses of his court rose from 94,000 to 450,000 livres, and during the periods of his madness, officially termed the "king's absences", the land was torn by bitter rivalry between the princely houses of Burgundy and Orleans. Baronial slander, blackmail, and mutual recriminations ultimately led to bloodshed and civil war when in 1403 the King's brother, the Duke of Orleans, arranged the murder of his uncle, the Duke of Burgundy. Four years later the tables were reversed when Burgundy's son ambushed and struck down his cousin of Orleans. For thirty years France bled; neither 'the fear of God, nor love of our neighbours, nor anything else" was sufficient to restrain Frenchmen from doing violence to one another.

The shattered skull of Burgundy became "the hole by which the English entered France", for a lunatic king and a quarrelling nobility offered England the chance to regain her lost province of Normandy and to initiate a second bout of the Hundred Years War. The war between the two kingdoms was a horror story punctuated with appalling atrocities, guerrilla tactics and broken promises, both sides fighting to the point of total exhaustion. The little village of Neville-sur-Saône was sacked six times in three years by the mercenary troops hired by each side. By 1435 the town of Limoges had been reduced to five inhabitants and the diocese of Rouen had fallen from fifteen thousand to six thousand. The mercenary troops, hired for summer campaigning and left to their own vicious devices during the winter months, resembled wolves more than men. It was said that "they leave nothing in the houses they pillage, not a hen, not a chicken, not a cock ... They beat the owner of the house while they devour his goods and if there is a girl in the house, she must come to them, and they take her without her poor father's daring to say a word". Only the walled towns offered a measure of defence for the peasants who toiled in the fields with one ear cocked for the tolling church bells that signalled the presence of plundering troops. Even the pigs and cattle, it was said, became so accustomed to the sound that they scurried to safety of their own accord whenever the alarm sounded.

France finally cast out the "goddams", as the English were called, but her success had less to do with royal leadership than with the mounting weakness of her enemy. England was handicapped in 1422 by the succession of a nine-month-old sovereign, who ruled off and on for the next fifty years with varying degrees of pious incompetence. Ever since 1399 when Richard II, the last of the direct Plantagenet kings, had been deposed and murdered by his cousin, Henry Duke of Lancaster, the kingdom had suffered from the curse of disputed succession. Baronial feuding among the great magnates was momentarily set aside when Henry V led his barons to victory at Agincourt, but once the conqueror died in 1422 leaving an infant son to the tender mercies of avaricious relatives, and once the tide of victory in France ebbed into defeat, England dissolved into party discord and civil war. Defeat in France was the signal for strife to begin at home, for, as one French commentator put it, "upon their return into England [from France] not one of the English lords thought of lessening his estate; and the whole revenue of the kingdom was not sufficient to satisfy them all. Wars arose among them for command and authority, which lasted a long time." The Wars of the Roses between the Red Rose of the house of Lancaster and the White Rose of the house of York lasted by one computation until 1471 when Edward, Duke of York, made good his claim to the throne and ruled as Edward IV. By another calculation, the wars endured until 1485 when Yorkist Richard III fell at Bosworth field and Henry Tudor, the grandfather of Queen Elizabeth, snatched his crown from a legendary thorn bush.

The decade that saw in England the murder of Richard II in 1399, and in France the assassination of Louis of Orleans in 1407 by his Burgundian cousin, Jean sans Peur, found in Germany the deposition of a drunken and sadistic emperor who had already reigned twenty-two years. The Emperor Wenceslas was an alcoholic who was relieved of his imperial office in 1400 when, among other escapades, he shocked even his hardened age by roasting his cook on a spit for having spoiled his dinner. The paralysis of regal

leadership throughout Europe was never more vividly revealed than when Wenceslas and Charles VI of France
met in an effort to heal the religious schism of Christendom. The meeting in 1398 had to be conducted by under-
lings since the Emperor was too drunk and Charles too
mad to confer. The conference did nothing but increase
the number of Europe's woes; instead of ending schism,
it added a third pope to the controversy, converting a
duality of pontiffs into an "accursed threesome". For ten
years after 1400 the German empire was torn by disputed
elections and by three warring emperors corresponding to
the three rival popes. Later in the fifteenth century the
electors chose an emperor who may have suited the realities of political power but who was a pale shadow of the
imperial ideal of the medieval past. Frederick III (1440–
93) reigned for fifty-three years and was a Kaiser who,
in the words of one contemporary, "sits at home, garden-
ing and catching little birds, the poor creature".

Elsewhere in Europe royal dynasties were cursed by the
same madness and violence. The Kingdom of Castile
learned four times over the dreary truth of the warning:
"Woe to the land whose king is a child." Of the seven kings
who reigned following the death of Sancho IV in 1295,
four were children; Ferdinand IV came to the throne at
nine, Alfonso XI at one, Henry III at eleven and John II
at two. The very names of the kings of Castile are brutal
evidence of the barbarism, reprisals, poverty and injustice
that plagued the Iberian peninsula. There were Peter the
Cruel, Henry the Invalid, John the Ailing and Henry the
Impotent, more aptly called the Degenerate. Castile, like
England and the Empire, suffered the prolonged rule of a
well-meaning but ineffectual monarch, Juan II, who announced at the close of a reign of forty-eight years that he
would have been happier had he been born the son of a
poor artisan. The humanist Lucio Marineo Siculo painted
a picture of almost total anarchy in Spain. The kingdom,
he said, was worn out by a multitude of murderers, adul-
terers and thieves who scorned the law, both human and
divine, shamelessly violated wives, virgins and nuns, and
"cruelly assaulted and robbed tradesmen, travellers and
people on their way to fairs".

Fortune's wheel, from which princes fell with alarming regularity, was no more secure for queens than kings. René of Anjou, after a frustrated lifetime aspiring to the crowns of Sicily, Hungary and Jerusalem, married his sole surviving child to England's imbecilic monarch, Henry VI, and Margaret's life became the model for a treatise upon fortune's "inconstancy and deceptive nature". She was caught up in the turmoil of civil war and party strife during the English Wars of the Roses, regularly losing or regaining her crown and the control of her royal husband, until finally the Red Rose of her house of Lancaster suffered total defeat at Tewkesbury in 1471. Her only son died or more probably was murdered upon the battlefield, her husband was quietly assassinated in the Tower of London, and the Queen herself was imprisoned for five years until she was turned over to Louis XI of France, who set her free only after she had renounced all claims to her father's estates and inheritance.

Only in the Low Countries was the scene different. There the dukes of Burgundy had constructed a vast and formless realm through the accident of feudal inheritance. In contrast to France or England, the dukes' rambling possessions, especially that "Florence of Flanders", the wealthy city of Bruges, were accounted an earthly paradise. The dukes of Burgundy – Philip without Fear, Philip the Good, Charles the Bold (better translated "the Rash") – were the first nobles of Europe, calling themselves dukes by the grace of God and aspiring to the title of king. Their chivalric Order of the Golden Fleece was the most coveted knightly association in Europe, for it was limited to twenty-four *gentils hommes de nom et d'armes et sans reproche.* But even in the rigid magnificence of the feudal court of Burgundy, financed by the trade and wealth of the Low Countries, the House of Burgundy did not escape the taint of madness. The last duke, Charles the Rash, was well named. Introverted, fanatic, and stubborn, he symbolized the worst and most unyielding aspect of the feudal spirit: insatiable pride. As one moderate observer of his habits put it, he was "very splendid and pompous in his dress and in everything else, and, indeed, a little too much". In the end, his reckless ambitions, boundless greed, and

unreasoning hatred for the king of France, to whom he owed
feudal fealty, destroyed him. His death in 1477 and the de-
flowering of his feudal army, which impaled itself upon
the pikes of Swiss mercenary troops, revealed that medieval knighthood was as moribund as feudal monarchy.

Never was the contrast between official theory and
reality so marked as in the gulf that existed between the
ideals and actions of the feudal nobility. The knight remained the social paradigm of the century, but his military
reason for being had vanished in the face of royal
law, government bureaucrats, Swiss pikemen, English long-
bows, and that costly but "final argument of kings", the
cannon. At one time, the mounted feudal knight and his
retainers had been the effective, if unruly, instruments by
which kings, princes and emperors had been able to maintain a reasonable degree of security. Above all else the
knight had been a warrior, and the ethics and structure of
feudalism had been geared to his military activities. The
virtues of his caste were those of the hero; he was expected
"to protect the church, to fight against treachery, to reverence the priesthood, to fend off injustice from the poor,
to make peace in his own province, to shed his blood for
his brethren, and, if need be, to lay down his life" for his
overlord. Reality was quite otherwise. One fifteenth-
century critic of the knightly order branded it as a vicious
veneer, "a nutshell without a kernel" which was "full of
worms". The medieval knight may have been well suited to
private brawls and religious crusades, but the advent of
gunpowder made killing so easy that it was no longer the
work of experts, except possibly the metallurgist. Yet war
remained in the estimation of knighthood a glorious thing,
and chivalric heroes sought to perpetuate their species by
encasing themselves in arrow- and musket-proof steel armour. In the end, however, technology proved their undoing. Clothed in iron and too cumbersome to fight on foot
or even to mount a horse without the aid of a derrick, the
feudal knight was struck down by English archers at Agincourt in 1415 and by hired Swiss pikemen at Morat in
1476. More and more the medieval warrior had to leave
war to kings and mercenaries who fought for money, not
for diversion or glory.

As knightly existence lost its military significance and political purpose, it gained in ceremony and formality. The chivalric code went to seed, becoming mere politeness and extravagance. Men wore shoes with beaks so long that they could scarcely walk; women adorned their heads with peaked caps two feet high; and ostentatiousness of attire became the mark of a bottomless exchequer and even of nobility itself. Cloaks were pieced together from three thousand sable skins; the Duke of Orleans used seven hundred pearls to embroider a song upon his sleeve; and the aristocratic captain of the Paris watch in 1418 did his rounds in the company of a small brass band. The fact that such fanfares scared away every malefactor within miles of the city seems to have been of little concern to a nobleman more anxious to advertise his social status than to apprehend criminals. Much of this pageantry and posing was a mask for covetousness, cruelty and calculation. The knightly order was more than once dismissed as "mere disorder", and throughout Europe the picture of the overmighty magnate, proud, predatory, and irresponsible, claiming a privileged place in society as his ancestral birthright, became the symbol for violence, mismanagement and anarchy. In the end it was a well-worn proverb that "the nobles make promises and the peasantry keep them". Bad faith, broken vows and tricky arguments to avoid moral commitments seemed so much a part of the aristocratic order that Philip Commines, chamberlain to the Duke of Burgundy and counsellor to the King of France, sadly concluded in 1477 that "the want of faith is the source of all mischiefs and villainy". Commines's estimation of high society was remarkable only in that he did not place the blame upon the Church. Most men were at pains to point out that "the greatest scourge" and "the source and germ of all disorders" were the men within God's Church who, ignorant and defiant of Church law, had raised themselves to high pastoral office.

Of all the concerns of medieval life, death remained the most important, for life was a vale of tears a divine pilgrimage upon which the wanderer ventured until he reached the final fork leading upwards to salvation or downwards to damnation. Sin, Satan and suffering, as well as saintliness, were everywhere present. The dark places of the earth were foul with demons and the air was filled with little devils "as numerous as the dust-particles in a shaft of sunlight". Marsh gas and thunderbolts, floods and pestilence, famine and wild beasts belonged to the domain of Lucifer, who laboured to capture men's souls and frustrate God's design. In the midst of the chilling unknown, and in a world surrounded by perpetual pain and accustomed to death which struck at the infant in his cradle and at half the wives in childbirth, God's Church stood as a sentinel against evil and offered to man the hope of salvation. Of all medieval institutions the Church was the most universal, the most intimate and the most beloved. From birth to death it enveloped every human act with meaning and richness, and always it held out to mankind the picture of paradise. Faith, hope and charity were the pillars of its doctrine, and it assured to all men, irrespective of rank or profession, that God's mercy was available to one and all. The medieval Church was in accord with Chaucer's Wife of Bath, who firmly believed that "God calls His folk to Him in many ways".

The essence of medieval Christianity was the doctrine of hope and moderation: hope of salvation and moderation in life. "Man," said St. Thomas Aquinas, "is called by nature to live in society that he may not only live but live the good life." The good life was in effect the exercise of moderation and charity in the affairs of this world and the constant hope that God's mercy would bring man safely into the next world. For the man who lived by these standards, the gates of heaven were for ever open. In the attainment of such an ideal the role of the Church was vital. As yet the skyscraper had not replaced the church spire as the symbol of man's aspiration, nor had the insurance company encroached upon the cathedral as the bastion of man's defence against an uncertain future. Not only did the Church maintain a tight hold upon the keys to the kingdom of heaven, but it also kept a sharp eye on man's actions on earth. Men woke, slept and worked to the knelling of bells. They were baptized, confirmed, married, confessed and shriven within the universal fold of the

Church. Their wills were proved, their charity administered, their children taught, their minds shaped and their transgressions judged by clerics. Great and small, prince and pauper were expected to render account to God's vicar on earth, and every act, from the bureaucrat's financial peculations to the peasant's petty adulteries, was judged in terms of man's ultimate purpose on earth – the drama of his salvation and damnation. A careful regulation of the economic impulses of society was as essential to man's spiritual welfare as it was to his material well-being. There was a righteous price in commerce, based on considerations of morality, as well as an economic price reflecting the mechanical laws of supply and demand. Gluttony and lack of moderation, whether in capitalistic ventures, usurious rates of interest, baronial pride, or monarchical sharp practices, were condemned as being cancerous to society and dangerous to the soul's salvation. Nothing burned more fiercely in a medieval Christian hell than pride, the mother of egotism, greed and treason, and "the whole puddle and sink of all sins against God and man".

The Church taught that man should exercise a series of exquisite checks and balances, since all forms of imbalance and immoderation were regarded as being the antithesis of the good and moral life. Men were urged to render unto both God and Caesar; to counterpoise good works and charitable acts with faith in God's grace; to offset what was economically feasible with what was morally right; and finally to balance a full and useful life on earth with the knowledge that death, not life, was the ultimate lot of man. To translate such an ideal into reality and to administer her responsibilities, the Church maintained a complex bureaucratic machine with its heart in Rome and its financial and legal arteries spread throughout the length and breadth of Christendom. At its height the Church attracted to it the best brains and the most dedicated service in Europe, while its way of life and the ideals it preached became the central core of Christian civilization.

By the fifteenth century the Church had expanded mightily, but its way of life had long since ceased to correspond to its ideals. Whether the medieval *ecclesia* had

ever attained a total fulfilment of its spiritual and ethical
aspirations is questionable, but certainly during the twilight
years of the feudal era the Church learned the ironic truth
of the proverb: "Nothing fails in religion like success."
In becoming rich, autonomous, privileged and complacent,
the Church began to forsake the virtues which had origin-
ally been the source of its strength, and the medieval world
learned to despise the unpreaching prelate "loitering in his
lordships", the tricky ecclesiastical lawyer extracting the
last penny from his legal fees, and the papal tax collector
bent on fleecing God's flock. It was not so much that
churchmen were more corrupt than royal servants or aristocratic brigands. It was merely that the ecclesiastical body
was judged by a higher standard. The ignorant peasant
was a source of humour, the slothful priest was scandalous;
the profiteer in commerce was secretly admired, the greedy
cleric was shocking; the Machiavellian bureaucrat was
honoured, the conniving clergyman was condemned. By
the standards of any age the Catholic Church was found to
be woefully lacking. Ideally priests and prelates were the
curators of souls and the representatives of a higher way of
life; in fact they were lawyers, tax collectors and financiers.
The papal curia developed the most expert and tenacious
bureaucracy in Europe and became the biggest business in
Christendom, but in doing so it fell victim to all the temptations of worldly success. As Abbot Samson of St.
Edmondsbury in England "appeared to prefer the active to
the contemplative life, and praised good officials more than
good monks", so popes and prelates gave greater attention
to financial debits and credits than to their spiritual ledgers.
Whether the Vatican by 1499 had in fact become "the
sewer of the world" is debatable, but certainly religion and
morality were parting company, the former degenerating
into a business and the latter becoming a means for extracting money for the licence to sin. The story is told of
Cardinal Borgia that, when he was criticized for selling
pardons for criminal offences, he replied that "God desires
not the death of sinners but that they should pay and
live".

The monk who received word of the birth of a son on
the day that he was elected abbot, and who announced:

"Today I have twice become a father; God's blessing on it," was hardly in a position to condemn the venial sins of his flock. Denys de Moulins, Bishop of Paris, who in 1441 extracted the last measure of his legal and financial rights and filed fifty lawsuits in a single year, could scarcely criticize the uncharitable practices of tight-fisted laymen. The monks of St. Denis, who in 1422 claimed the rich pall covering the coffin of Charles VI and who fought in the streets of Paris during the funeral procession with the salt-weighers of the city who also claimed the prize, were in no position to censure human greed and pettiness. Alonso Carrello, Archbishop of Toledo, who fluctuated wildly between extremes of bloodthirsty bragging and infantile sulking and who was more at home in feudal armour than clerical surplice, or his colleague of Santiago, who raped a young nun, were in no position to castigate baronial violence. Eventually such clerical corruption bred contempt both for ecclesiastics and for the ideals for which the Church stood. An elegant and lavish feast became known in the fifteenth century as a "prelate's dinner"; it was said mockingly that celibacy differed from wedlock only in that laymen had to make do with a single wife while clerics had ten; and the reputation of the Church sank so low that it became a current joke that if a man desired "to offend God beyond all other sinners" he should become an episcopal officer or tax collector.

Ideally the Church was unified and universal, the keeper of Europe's conscience and the curator of Christian souls. In reality, it presented to the world the picture of religious schism in which popes and even saints squabbled over the keys to paradise, and Christians wondered whether Urban at Rome was the rightful heir to St. Peter's throne and Clement at Avignon was the anti-Christ, as St. Catherine of Siena stated, or whether the situation was reversed, as St. Vincent claimed. In the face of such spiritual strife, there seemed to be no certainty in life, and men whispered abroad that nobody could be saved while the Great Schism endured.

On all sides there was growing evidence that a spiritual cancer was crippling the Church, profaning its ideals and making a mockery of its aspirations. The image of the

Madonna and Child, symbolizing the infinite compassion of the Virgin and the innocence of the Christ Child, was a cherished Christian theme, but by the fifteenth century that ideal had degenerated into a mere artistic convention, a meaningless and profane pose in which ladies of high fashion sat for their portraits holding naked children in their laps. In the hands of Jacques Foucquet (1415–85) the Virgin became a fashionable whore surrounded by cherubs that looked like red imps. Legend says that the lady was Agnes Sorel, mistress to Charles VII of France! Even Hans Memling, one of the greatest of the Flemish religious painters, did an altarpiece in which he portrayed the face of St. Barbara as Margaret Duchess of Burgundy, the sister of Edward IV of England. She was dressed in the height of fashion, her eyebrows carefully plucked, her temples shaven, and her head adorned with a brightly jewelled turban. One of Memling's disciples went further, profaning the Assumption of the Virgin by representing the Mother of God as a nude Venus. Moralists complained with some cause that "nowadays, there is not an altar but a harlot stands thereon ... What sort of piety does this breed in a young cleric when he prays his *confiteor*, and sees these pretty statues in front of him?"

Everywhere distortion, weariness, apathy and corruption were evident, and the ideals of the Church appeared more and more to be at variance with reality. It was increasingly clear to clerics and laymen alike that it was impossible in the world of the fifteenth century to live according to the Christian precepts of moderation and piety. Instead, all elements of society were "running after those trades and occupations that will bring the most gain", and all the clever heads of Christendom, it was said, were engrossed in activities which were so saturated with dishonesty that no honourable man ought to be engaged in them. The Church assured its flock that the surest path to damnation was that taken by the proud and intemperate man, yet immoderation seemed the only path to material riches and well-being. "Riches", warned the Church fathers, "exist for man, not man for riches," and the moneylender and the extortionist, the dishonest merchant and the fraudulent financier were assured of a warm welcome in hell. "Take ye not interest from loans" was clear to all, yet the voice of conscience was dead. The papacy was the greatest financial institution in Europe and regularly committed the sin of usury. The de Medicis of Florence amassed a fortune of over half a million gulden by selling their souls for lucre, yet two members of their clan wore the papal tiara. It was all too clear, as one medieval cynic remarked about usury: "He who takes it goes to hell, and he who does not goes to the workhouse." Christians simply had to choose, and by the fifteenth century they were unwilling to impose upon themselves the self-restraints and self-sacrifices necessary to translate the ideals of society into reality. Instead they were content to "leave the present world to men of business and the devil".

The calamities of late medieval society seemed to be without end, and men warned that disease, death, suffering and war were manifestations of God's wrath directed against a depraved and corrupt Church and against those individuals who had allowed the devil to enter into their lives. It seemed that the voice of Cassandra spoke nothing but the truth, for in 1349 death struck in proportions that annihilated hope and came close to destroying society itself. Accurate figures for the mortality of the bubonic plague are impossible in an age which was happily free from statistical bias and was horrified by the sight of agony which inevitably ended in common graves hastily dug for the plague victims. Possibly one-quarter to one-half of Europe died in an epidemic during which there remained neither priest nor grave-digger to attend upon the dead and dying. With terrifying perversity the Black Death struck down the healthiest and most vigorous elements within society, concentrating on men between the ages of twenty and thirty. Somewhere between forty and sixty per cent of the clergy succumbed; entire villages were wiped out; and one educated guess presents the total mortality at twenty million persons. The only people who seemed to have survived were the soldiers, for throughout the long-drawn-out struggle between England and France there were always men to be found who were willing to loot and to plunder. Economically as well as statistically the plague came close to destroying Europe. Trade stagnated and incomes for every

section of society began to wither. The nobility faced
economic ruin as their rents from land slowly decayed and
as their peasants demanded higher and higher wages and
greater and greater freedom. Merchants and artisans were
caught up in a vast depression cycle of contracting markets
and increasing violence, and barons and peasants, artisans
and bankers were alike in their willingness to risk political
gangsterism and economic sharp practices to save what
little remained.

In the midst of internal crisis came the shock of invasion
from the East. For centuries Europe had been secure;
Christianity had been the aggressor not the defender, and
the boundaries of Christendom had been pushed forward
at the expense of the followers of Allah. In 1361 Sultan
Bayazid, the Flash of Lightning, destroyed the last of
Europe's crusading armies and took a great oath that he
would not rest till the altar of St. Peter's Cathedral had
been transformed into a stall for his stallion. A century
later, the Sultan's oath seemed on the verge of fulfilment,
when, on May 29th, 1453, the imperial city of Constantinople fell to the Ottoman Turks and a militant Muslim faith
turned Santa Sophia into a mosque. The fall of Constantinople meant the loss of the largest city in Christendom
and the end of the Roman Empire. The body of the last
direct successor of Augustus was found under an immense
pile of corpses and was recognized by the imperial eagle
embroidered in gold upon his shoes. More important, the
capture of the city opened Eastern and Southern Europe
to the expansion of the Muslim faith. Athens fell in 1458;
Italy was invaded and Otranto taken and put to the sword
in August 1480.

Popes and bishops regularly preached the desperate need
for a new crusade against the infidel, but the response was
apathetic, for, as one future pontiff sadly noted, "Christianity has no head whom all will obey." The Christian world
was too torn by internal strife to react against the Muslim
aggressor, and the medieval crusading spirit had long since
died. Kings, princes and merchants talked much of a
crusade, but their words were as meaningless as their vows
were hollow, and their crusading zeal was limited to one of
the most extraordinary extravaganzas in the history of

chivalry. In 1454 Philip Duke of Burgundy held a magnificent Feast of the Pheasant at the city of Lille. The knights of the Golden Fleece, dressed in vermilion velvet and cloth of gold, were entertained at lavishly decorated tables: on one stood a church complete with ringing bells and singing choir, and on another was a pie in which twenty-eight musicians played. The climax of the banquet arrived when a fair damsel, sitting upon an elephant led by a giant dressed as a Saracen, entered the great hall. The symbolic meaning was clear: the Holy Church was in chains to the infidel, and the lady herself appealed to the knights of the Golden Fleece to liberate the *ecclesia* and free Constantinople. Philip and his knights were presented with a pheasant bedecked with gold and precious jewels, whereupon the Duke and his company rose and in the name of the pheasant vowed to take up the sword in defence of the true faith. Not a member of this chivalric company had any real intention of going on a crusade, and in the end what saved Europe was the death of Mohammed II and the voluntary withdrawal of Turkish troops from Italy.

Dowager duchesses, moralists and educators are notorious pessimists, bewailing the decline of standards and castigating the passing of "the good old days". In the fifteenth century, however, there appeared to be both truth and urgency to the warning that "there is no reverence and no obedience". Even the shrewd and practical Philip Commines remarked that everywhere men were failing to accept God as their refuge and were having recourse to arms. Europe was in panic, in a state of shell-shock, the repercussions of which lasted long into the Elizabethan age. As the medieval world stood upon the threshold of a new century, all that contemporaries could see was the misery of life, the cold of the night, and the heat of the day. From the curses directed against the lice and fleas that made life hideous for all, to the cries of the victims of the Black Death, a "thick fog of lamentation" lay heavy upon Christendom. In the face of the disgusting death reserved for those tortured by the plague and for those unfortunate enough to fall into the hands of flayers and bandits, Christians asked themselves what kind of God of mercy could bring such suffering to his flock and what terrible sins

humanity had committed to warrant such punishment.
"God", cried Fernando del Pulgar, "is angry with humanity which is rotten."

Surrounded by inordinate death, senseless destruction
and awful suffering, a life of moderation seemed to be impossible, and men looked to fanaticism, ceremonialism and
neuroticism as the only way out of their fear and disillusionment. Some men turned their backs upon the old
way of life and took refuge in worldly excesses and material
success. "If," said Cosimo de Medici, "St. Peter is to keep
the keys ... to the tree of knowledge as well as those of
the gates of heaven and hell ... nine-tenths of us would
prefer to go to Beelzebub at the beginning, instead of having to do so at the end." In the Low Countries, where the
profits of commerce and sin could still be enjoyed to the
full, fat burghers who had "no God but their belly and
their money-bags" were almost as successful as Cosimo in
his Florentine palace. They were content to concentrate
on their account-books and drown their consciences in
beer and schnapps.

Others, generally the less successful, condemned the life
of Florence and Bruges as vicious and depraved, and turned
instead to religious fanaticism. Hell, "where there is no
voice but of weeping, no face but of the tormentors",
drove men of tender conscience to all sorts of emotional
extremes – masochistic religious practices, witchcraft, diabolism, superstition and mysticism. Satan covered the world
with his black wings and men sought in a variety of fantastic ways either to escape his clutches or to join his ranks.
Flagellant monks, garbed in black, bearing red crosses and
ceaselessly chanting their prayers, wandered the highways
and byways of Europe. They denounced the evils of humanity and renounced the Church's path to salvation
through the sacraments, claiming that self-flagellation was
the true communion, for only when the blood of man
was joined to that of Christ could the sinner find redemption. Religious sensationalism of every variety was on the
increase. In 1429 Friar Richard thundered dire warnings
every day for a week from five in the morning till mid-
afternoon. He urged his Parisian audience, who numbered
between five and six thousand, to burn their lewd books,

cast away their rich apparel and renounce the evil in their lives. Though churchmen struck out against the religious extremists whose depiction of hell "milked an old woman to tears" or made "her blood run cold", spiritual emotionalism and the appeal to the imagination became the dominant motif of late medieval religious expression. At the monastic hospital of Isenheim, which specialized in the care of syphilitics, Mathias Grünewald was commissioned to paint his greatest altarpiece. The Christ that he portrayed was even more diseased than the inmates of the hospital. Twisted, bleeding and decayed, the Saviour's body hung in agony. To those afflicted with incurable venereal disease which inevitably ended in madness and death, the sight of the dying Christ and the imaginative and sensual witnessing of His suffering were the only reliefs available.

Emotional ecstasy went further: it moved into black magic, sorcery and perversion. In the general breakdown of morality and moderation there were some who argued that if there was no escape from damnation then they might as well invoke the devil and enjoy his company. Alchemy and astrology were old and recognized professions, but a new urgency entered the efforts of men of letters and of wealth who sought furiously for the philosopher's stone of knowledge, the well of eternal youth, and the magic of transmuting base metals into gold. The most notorious of them was Gilles de Rais, colleague of Joan of Arc, Marshal of France, humanist and sorcerer, who practised the black arts, worshipped the devil, kidnapped and butchered one hundred and forty children in ritualistic murders, and after eight years of satanic orgies was finally detected and in 1440 burned at the stake.

Diabolism and witchcraft were extreme varieties of the spiritual malaise that had settled upon Europe and of the growing desire for more potent emotional experience, but nothing revealed more clearly the degree to which old standards had lost their hold over society than the decline of orthodox religion itself. More and more religion was viewed as a means of propitiating an ill-natured deity. If most men refrained from seeking defence against calamity through the outright worship of the devil, the great majority nevertheless firmly believed that "a candle offered to St. Lowye" would protect their cattle from disaster and that a gift made to the Virgin would stave off evil. For the late medieval world, religion was a variety of magic: the scrupulous and absolute fulfilment of the teachings of the Church was a magic ritual which bestowed power upon the performer. As the peasant burnt a candle for St. Lowye, so King Louis XI of France endowed chapels and monasteries. When the Lord faltered in His bargain, as He so often did, and failed to reward the faithful with material success, both king and peasant were justifiably enraged. Fear and suffering made men reckless to find some means of controlling the evil that abounded in the world, and in their desperation they turned to superstition. King Louis XI could never bring himself to wear again the clothes in which he had received bad news, and he once ordered the destruction of the part of the forest in which he happened to be riding when he heard of the death of a newly born son.

The desire to warrant salvation in the midst of sin and to propitiate the anger of a vengeful god by any means possible led men not only into supersition but also into the elaboration and repetition of the rituals within the Church itself. As the old ways became less certain, they were more often repeated, and a form of galloping mechanization seized the medieval Church. If the collecting of relics, the saying of prayers, and the burning of candles were desirable, then it seemed to follow that the more candles offered up and the more relics collected, the greater man's chance of salvation. At Wittenberg Frederick the Wise of Saxony was seized by exactly such a quantitative approach to religion and became an avid collector of relics. By 1509 he had gathered a museum of holy treasures which included four hairs from the Virgin's head, three pieces from her gown, four from her girdle and seven from her veil, a wisp of straw from the manger, a piece of gold presented by the Wise Men, a lock of Jesus's beard, a thorn from His crown, a morsel of bread consumed at the Last Supper, and a nail certified to have pierced the Saviour's hand. In all, there were 19,013 sacred bones stored in the castle church. No wonder Savonarola thundered that "all fervour and inward worship are dead, and ceremonies wax more numerous, but have lost their efficacy".

As the dead weight of repetition increased, confidence declined. The old standards had lost their efficacy but no new ones had risen in their stead. There remained nothing to do but to forsake religion completely and turn to the devil, or to repeat endlessly the old ritual in the hope that quantity would somehow make up for quality. In architecture, in dress, in vows and sermons, exaggeration, elaboration and proliferation predominated. Sermons became marathons; vows grew longer and more ornate but always had some tricky qualifications that prevented their fulfilment; clothing became flamboyant and erotic, as grotesque cod-pieces for men and low-cut bodices for women emphasized the sensuality of the age. Architectural design as well as religious ceremonies tended to become all form and no soul. Ornamental details and ostentatious magnificence began to replace the simplicity of the early Gothic perpendicular outline. Technical perfection was attained in the ceiling of Henry VII's chapel at Westminster, but the very richness of art, novelty of form and labyrinth of detail obliterated the totality of the conception. Cathedrals became houses of light, not of God, monuments to man's architectural inspiration, where humanity worshipped its own ingenuity and not God's mercy.

As inward worship withered, fascination with mortality increased. Familiarity with death did not of necessity generate fear if reasonable hope of salvation remained and if life were sufficiently sweet to obscure the approach of death. In a later age, Elizabethans would find that "the general mortality of the age" kindled not a morbid terror of death but a passionate preoccupation with living, but in the fifteenth and early years of the sixteenth century the same mortality engendered necrophilia, the fascination with death and the act of dying. The ugly process that turn all to "earth, ashes, dust and worm's meat" and devours "thy beautiful face, thy fair nose, thy clear eyes, thy white hands, thy goodly body" was feared and yet revered. The equality and the unexpectedness of death caught and held the medieval mind. Places of execution – Tyburn, where Marble Arch now stands, or the giant gibbet of

Montfaucon in Paris – became centres of entertainment and
a source of perverse fascination. Montfaucon with its colon-
nade of gibbets and iron-grated grave pit, into which the
blackened bodies were ultimately thrown, was a picnicking-
place for young gallants who took their girls to the execution
grounds for an evening of "good cheers and devilment".

The most famous and revered sight in Paris was the ancient Cemetery of the Innocents where possibly a million
paupers, mostly plague victims, were buried in nameless
graves. By the thirteenth century the cemetery had been
walled in and a cloistered arcade constructed where Parisians promenaded of an evening. The walls were lined with
shops and vendors' stalls, and within the cloistered walk,
resting on open shelves, were great piles of human bones
and skulls. As the cemetery filled up, the bodies were moved
to make room for new arrivals and were placed on the
shelves of the arcade. Here the bones slowly decomposed
into dust and were eventually swept on to the pavement
where the living walked and joked and speculated upon
the grim dance in which not even the dead found rest.
Later in the century (1424) the *Danse Macabre* was painted
upon the cloister wall. There in stately elegance was depicted the endless dance of death in which a skeleton dragged pope, peasant and priest into the grave. Death held
the hand of an abbess fresh from hearing mass; he seized
the scholar in the midst of his books; he awaited the emperor rejoicing upon his throne; he welcomed the usurer
clinging to his gold; and he led the blind man to his destruction. Standing in the middle of the cemetery was Death
himself, a cold stone figure with raised arm and tightly
clenched fist – the ultimate conqueror. Day after day immense crowds were drawn to this place where the odour
of corruption prevailed. Louis XI of France presented the
Church of the Innocents with "a whole Innocent" encased
in a crystal coffin; lumps of earth from the cemetery were
thrown into the graves of those who could not be buried
in its hallowed grounds; and visitors from every corner of
Europe came to view and pay their respects to Death.

Among those who came to behold the charnel house
and the thirty scenes of the *Danse Macabre* was John Lyd-
gate of Bury St. Edmunds, and in 1460 he reproduced the

sequence in the cloister of Pardon Church next to St. Paul's Cathedral in London. All Europe was anxious to imitate and embellish this theme of irony, mortality and despair. The greatest of the dances of death was completed by Hans Holbein the younger in 1526. His prints were published in 1538 and such was their popularity that they went through eleven editions before 1562, while between 1555 and 1573 no less than five plagiarized versions appeared on the market. Possibly there were a hundred imitations of the Holbein Dance published during the sixteenth century. Holbein, however, represented the end as well as the culmination of late medieval preoccupation with death. Elizabeth and her world were still touched with necrophilia; the graveyard scene remained a stock dramatic ploy, poor Yorick found as little rest as the Innocents of Paris, and John Knox took pleasure in warning Mary Queen of Scots that "foul worms will be busy with this flesh, be it never so fair and tender". Yet by mid-century the tone had begun to change. The Cemetery of the Innocents slowly lost its hold and was all but forgotten, its stores and stalls were closed and its crowds dispersed. Eventually it was destroyed in the name of progress when in 1667 the walls with their macabre dance were pulled down to make way for a new and improved road. In England the end came earlier; the cloisters next to St. Paul's were torn down in 1549, a victim of the new Protestant faith.

In the midst of decay there lingered the breath of hope; the generation that erected the monument to Death in the Cemetery of the Innocents also produced the statue of René of Châlons. René commissioned his wife to have an effigy made of him as he would look three years after death. The form is that of the familiar and grotesque cadaver, yet there is an exalted quality about the pose, for the old warrior is holding up the one element of his humanity which is still untouched by corruption and death – his soul. Expectation of life in the sixteenth century was no greater than it had been a hundred years before, but reaction to death was changing, for new impulses and new ideas were slowly lifting Europe out of the despair and depression of a dying civilization. The scent of optimism was growing stronger as the fifteenth century gave way to the sixteenth.

Two

Medieval Twilight:
The Scent of Optimism

"HISTORY", said Tolstoy, "would be an excellent thing if only it were true." The picture of despair, the sense that "all people go wandering about without any goal and without knowing what is happening to them" is only one side of the fifteenth-century profile. The Cimmerian darkness of despondency contained the hint of a new dawn; in the midst of chaos lay hope of new order. Imperceptibly the archaic feudal image of depraved clerics, indolent monarchs, unruly barons, club-fisted usurers, and ranting fanatics receded, and a new outline began to emerge. Old bottles were filled with new wine, ancient dynasties were fortified with new blood, and failing economic pursuits were replaced by new and vigorous enterprises. In state, church and business, men of novel views and aggressive practices took over from those who lacked confidence in the future.

The harbingers of change were feared and hated because they advocated exactly those practices and doctrines most deplored by the defenders of the medieval way of life. On all sides the antithesis of the Christian doctrine of moderation seemed to be triumphant: excessive interest in money in the form of capitalistic schemes, inordinate and unscrupulous power exercised by the "New Monarchs", immoderate religious sensibilities in the persons of Martin Luther and his disciples, and, above all, a satanic view of life in which man became not only the measure of all things but the equal of God Himself. In Italy, Leon Battista Alberti (1404–72) announced that "men can do all things if they try" and Michelangelo was called *divino*. Man's ultimate conceit, and to the medieval mind his unforgivable blasphemy, was reserved for the German painter, Albrecht Dürer, who in 1500 portrayed himself as Christ. The medieval doctrines of balance and moderation which had died in the communal graves of the plague victims and in the anarchy of war and economic recession were never resurrected. Instead, immoderation in government, in business and in mortality triumphed and was accepted as the norm of the new way of life.

To describe the new spirit as secular is to misrepresent its flavour, the essence of which was individualism. In church, state, art and economic organization men were breaking with the corporate society of the medieval past. In religion, Martin Luther set private judgment "against the faith held by all Christians for a thousand years". In economics, Cosimo de Medici knew that the Church's laws against usury and unethical commercial practices did not apply to him for he had "God the Father, God the Son, God the Holy Ghost in his books as debtors". In government, kings demanded a monopoly of power in which the rights and privileges of chartered towns, the ancient nobility and the Universal Church were sacrificed upon the altar of the divine-right monarch who claimed *raison d'état* as the highest justification for action. That supreme egotist and sublime craftsman Benvenuto Cellini inadvertently voiced the spirit of the new morality when he worried more over the position of a magnificent diamond than over the representation of God the Father in an immense ceremonial button which he was creating for Pope Clement VII. There was nothing modest about Cellini's description of his artistry: "I had laid the diamond exactly in the middle of the work, and over it I had represented God the Father sitting in a sort of a free, easy attitude which suited admirably well with the rest of the piece, and did not in the least crowd the diamond."

The shrinking markets of the fifteenth century and the growing rigidity of the old guild system accelerated the process whereby a more rational, efficient and competitive system of business enterprise was adopted. The medieval guild, with its corporate and monopolistic economic structure, which protected the artisan from his more predatory competitor and the public from shoddy merchandise, had deteriorated into a self-perpetuating and niggardly routine, incapable of change and so encumbered with petty regulations as to make efficient production almost impossible. More and more individual artisans – cloth manufacturers, mining operators, tanners, importers of silks and spices – broke away from the older restrictions and went into business for themselves in defiance of the guild codes, the Church laws against usury, and the traditional system of ethics. They moved to the new centres of trade and prospered, because they lived by the standard that "conscience is a pretty thing to carry to church", but he who "pursueth it in fair market or shop may die a beggar". Business shifted to Antwerp and Augsburg, where freer trade regulations and sharper mercantile practices transformed the hardworking craftsman into a prince of commerce and finance. The acquisitive spirit in Northern Europe may have hesitated at linking God and economic success in quite the same fashion as did Francisco di Marco Datini who inscribed each of his account books with the words "in the name of God and of profit", but Jacob Fugger of Augsburg lived to write one of the most arrogant epitaphs ever conceived:

To God, All Powerful and Good! Jacob Fugger of Augsburg, ornament to his class and to his country, Imperial Councillor under Maximilian I and Charles V, second to none in the acquisition of extraordinary wealth, in liberality, in purity of life, and in greatness of soul, as he was comparable to none in life, so after death is not to be numbered among the mortals.

The first Fugger, Hans, was a weaver by trade and an innovator by taste. He moved to Augsburg in 1367 and set himself up in the manufacture of fustian, a new kind of cloth combining cotton and flax. When he died he was worth 3,000 florins; by 1517 the family had so prospered that it was able to lend Charles of Spain 543,000 florins with which to purchase his imperial title. From weaving, the Fuggers went into silver mining, invested money in the Portuguese spice trade with the Far East, and finally ended as the international bankers of Europe with offices in Antwerp and Rome. By 1536 their ledgers showed a balance of 3.8 million gulden, and "fuggering" had become a synonym for usury. At the apogee of their influence, it was recorded that "the names of Jacob Fugger and his nephews are known to all kingdoms and lands; yea, among the heathen also. Emperors, Kings, Princes and Lords have sent to treat with him, the Pope has greeted him as his well-beloved son and embraced him, and the Cardinals have risen up before him ... He is the glory of all Germany."

A revolution had in fact taken place, for what had once been branded as "a vile and sordid love of money" was now "entertained as the truest wisdom". Christopher Columbus could greedily avow before those Most Catholic Monarchs of Spain that "gold is most excellent – with gold is treasure made; he who has it can do whatever he wants". Of course, not all men were as open in their cupidity as Columbus, and moralists continued to parrot the old view of society in which the commercialist had no legitimate part:

> God has shapen lives three,
> Boor and knight and priest they be.
> Devil made the fourth and he
> Drives the trade of usury.

Spaniards in the fifteenth century were wont to make a virtue of necessity, and the Bishop of Burgos in 1434 claimed that the measure of a man's honour was to be found in the quality of his beautiful deeds and not in the store of his money. Riches, he said, were "not to be argued into this matter (as the English argued them); for if we should mete out the precedences according to riches, Cosimo de Medici, or some other very rich merchant, mayhap would come before some duke." The world, however, was passing the good Bishop by, and England and much of northern Europe soon learned to admire the lines that stated:

> Some men of noble stock were made,
> Some glory in the murder blade,
> Some praise capital science or an art;
> But I like honourable trade.

The ethics of honourable trade went further than the
frantic activities of wool chapmen, scavengers and appren
tices skipping from shop to shop or even the privileged
wealth of the Fuggers. In England, and to a lesser extent
in the Low Countries and France, the spirit of commerce
had percolated down to the gentry, who began to discard
their feudal outlook and judge nobility in terms of "the
abundance of worldly goods". Whether the lesser landed
aristocracy of the medieval past had in fact lived up to the
knightly ideal of a true gentleman – "to profit many, to
do good to the country, to maintain the poor, to relieve the
succourless, to nourish the weak, to cherish their needy
tenants" – is doubtful. On the other hand, a growing number of sixteenth-century landowners seemed to have been
swept up by the zeal of an acquisitive society and lived by
the motto:

> As riseth my good
> So riseth my blood.

Younger sons of landed stock went into trade and merchants sought to transform the profits of commerce into
landed wealth. In doing so they brought to the control of
land a business spirit which viewed the management of
estates as a mercantile venture, and as early as 1434 Englishmen had acquired the reputation of being a race "vainglorious of money". The swan-song of medieval religious
standards was sung, and the full measure of commercial
respectability in town and shire was attained, when Dean
John Colet in 1510 chose to place the management of St.
Paul's School in the hands of solid London "citizens of
established reputation", because he had lost confidence in
the good faith of priests and noblemen. There was, he
said, "nothing certain in human affairs, yet he found the
least corruption" in men of business.

Similar changes were taking place in the chanceries of
kings who were as anxious to "modernize" their kingdoms
as financiers were to calculate the risks and profits from
illegal traffic in usury. It has been said of King Louis XI
of France that he represented the worst side of the fifteenth century: cold, deceitful and suspicious. He viewed
both God and man as purchasable commodities and was

so cautious that when he imported a particularly holy hermit from Italy, he insisted on testing the saintliness of his acquisition by placing before him the temptations of the flesh. Yet the very qualities that earned Louis the sinister description of "the universal spider" were exactly those attributes that brought success to his reign and won for him a place among the "New Monarchs" of Europe, who were taking the first hesitant steps towards converting their medieval kingdoms into sovereign national states. Nothing justified knavery like prosperity, nothing succeeded like success. Upon the thrones of England, France and Spain sat monarchs who made up in success what they may have lacked in legitimacy or the traditional virtues of medieval kingship. As one writer put it, they may have believed in the old piety but "they acted, perforce, like a gang of disingenuous cannibals". The insanity and turpitude that had dogged royal leadership and the centrifugal forces that had been tearing the feudal monarchies asunder began to diminish during the final decades of the fifteenth century. Louis XI of France, Henry VII of England, Ferdinand and Isabella of the United Kingdom of Spain were strong-minded sovereigns determined to be masters in their own realms, and they brought to their offices the two essentials of success that had already been applied to the counting-house: hard work and calculation.

Debate continues to rage as to whether the "New Monarchs" were in fact as new as historians once thought them or whether they were simply modelling themselves upon older medieval sovereigns who also had worked to establish the financial solvency of their crowns and had endeavoured to liberate royal government from the spiritual interference of ecclesiastics and the political meddling of over-mighty magnates. Yet something new had been added. There existed a degree of efficiency in government which had been unknown to the feudal world. Under the "New Monarchs" law enforcement loomed higher than strict legality; the reality of power was more highly regarded than political theory; and the duties of subjects were of greater concern than the rights of peers, priests and principalities. The institutional forms remained centuries old but a new spirit had entered them. Success was in the air; and as the calculating commercialist and the enterprising landlord were successful, so also were the "New Monarchs". In England, for the first time, a king was praised not for his heroism or his piety but for those achievements attained by "acts of peace alone without sword or bloodshed". Henry VII was "full of notes", and with infinite care he initialled each page of the exchequer accounts, amassing a comfortable surplus in the treasury. Attention to the details of government and an astute understanding of the importance of finance applied to Louis XI as well as to Henry VII. Both monarchs knew the truth of the advice that in peace as well as in war "three things must be made ready: money, money, and once again money", and both were willing to pay the price of success: the scorn of the old nobility who despised their bourgeois tastes, the hatred of all who feared and envied their authority, and the endless hours of work that stood behind their achievement. "I think", Philip Commines said of Louis, "that if all the good days he enjoyed during his life, days in which he had more pleasure and happiness than hard work and trouble, were carefully numbered, they would be found to be few; I believe one would find twenty of worry and travail for one of ease and pleasure."

Though the "New Monarchs" were men of great stature and industry, the secret of their success was revealed by Erasmus when he said that "there is nothing I hate so much as civil war, to which I prefer peace on the hardest conditions". In England, France and Spain the only conditions under which government could function were Draconian, and monarchs demanded and achieved a measure of obedience that no feudal sovereign had ever enjoyed. In France the tradition of immensely powerful and independent ducal families, who coined their own money and disregarded the king's law, was finally smashed when Charles of Burgundy was destroyed by a combination of his own insistence upon anachronistic medieval standards and the persistent craft and duplicity of the French king. By the year of Louis XI's death in 1483, not only had the duchy of Burgundy been reunited to the French crown but so also had Anjou, Maine and Provence. Feudal nobles, chartered towns, and rebellious provinces had to learn that "obedience is best in each degree". No matter how unjust, brutal and costly, the prince's will had to be accepted as law. The burden of taxation steadily rose under Louis XI, who successfully increased his non-feudal revenues from 1.2 million to 4.7 million livres, and he enacted more legislation than any sovereign since the days of Charlemagne. Yet the price appeared small to Frenchmen who admired, even if they did not love, a king who argued that "the notable cities of Christianity have become great ... not by exploits of arms but by good government".

In England the same steps were taken when Henry VII and his son insisted that the only peace that might prevail was the king's peace, the only justice that should be allowed was royal justice, and the only loyalty that mattered was devotion to the crown. The divine right of aristocracy slowly receded before the divinity that "doth hedge a king", and the old nobility reluctantly learned that the meanest servant of the crown had "sufficient warrant to arrest the greatest peer of this realm". Private armies, private justice and private war had to give way if Englishmen were to live under a single law. Henry's income, like his royal cousin's in France, rose from £52,000 to £142,000, and the royal tax collector confronted the king's subjects with the dilemma of Morton's Fork: those who lived lavishly were persuaded to part with their gold because such high living was evidence of their ability to contribute generously to the king's exchequer; conversely, those who lived in poverty were also relieved of their money on the grounds that their frugality was proof of great savings, a portion of which should be offered to support the kingdom.

Events in Spain followed a somewhat different path. No tradition of Iberian unity had ever existed. Disunited as England and France may have been, the theory of feudal unity remained. In England of the fifteenth century, royal justice may have been perverted by the great barons, but it remained royal. In France, the dukes of Burgundy may have regarded themselves as divine-right rulers, but they did fealty to the kings of France. In contrast, Spain was not reunified, it was liberated. The common memory of the peninsula was not political union but a Christian crusade against the infidel. The accident of dynastic marriage joined two of the three major kingdoms together when in 1469 Isabella, Queen of Castile, and Ferdinand of Aragon were married. Though Ferdinand was as ruthless and calculating as any monarch of Europe and Isabella as hard-working, the forces that underlay Spanish union were spiritual, not political. More important than the need for internal security and good government was the demand that the citadel of the faith be strengthened and prepared for its final apotheosis and the ultimate achievement of God's design – the conquest of Granada. The law was codified and enforced, the hundred and fifty mints throughout Spain were reduced to five, the currency was standardized, and the historic tariff barriers within the realm were abolished. The aristocracy were forbidden their cherished symbols of independence – the birthright to include a crown in their coats of arms, the licence to be preceded by a macebearer, and the right to build castles. Above all else, the nobility were persuaded to part with the lavish grants and sinecures which they had been able to extort from countless feudal kings, and the Catholic Monarchs found themselves thirty million maravedis richer than their predecessors. Significantly, however, the argument that induced the aristocracy to disgorge such sums and to accept correction was the plea that the money and the discipline were necessary for the Christian conquest of Granada.

In England the instruments by which the Crown extended its authority and unified the realm were the king's courts of Chancery and Star Chamber, which directed royal justice against the over-mighty and cast the mantle of governmental protection over the weak. In France the same end was achieved by the laborious construction of a royal bureaucracy, but the Catholic sovereigns of Spain worked largely through the Church and the Inquisition. Purity of faith and orthodoxy of thought were everywhere on the increase throughout Europe, but in Spain, where the infidel remained secure in the mountains of Andalusia, they became the very essence of "Spanishness". Formerly both Jews and Muslims had been tolerated, but with the fall of Granada in January 1492 a new era of spiritual purity and religious unity commenced. In the spring of 1492, two hund-

red thousand Jews were expelled and ten years later the
Moors suffered a similar fate. Even after Jew and Saracen
had turned Christian in order to escape persecution and
exile, the fear remained that Satan had not been banished
but had gone underground to practise his evil in secret
cellars and remote mountain villages. Failure to work on
Saturday or even a dislike of pork was enough to arouse
suspicion, and thousands of Christian converts were inter-
rogated and condemned by the Inquisition. In Spain the
unified sovereign state and militant crusading Catholicism
were forged in the same furnace.

However much the means may have varied, by 1500 a
new phenomenon had materialized in Europe: the sovereign national state. Feudal kingdoms had been mere com-
posites of rights, liberties and privileges, united only by
frail ties of allegiance to the king. Man's first loyalty had
rested with his village, his profession, his overlord and his
Church. On occasion feudal monarchs had been inspired
leaders of men, but rarely, except possibly in England, did
they view themselves as the regal symbol of state. Change,
however, was everywhere apparent. The medieval world
had looked upon government as a necessary evil at best;
the sixteenth-century man was now beginning to suggest
the strange and alien notion that it might be a positive
good. Slowly an image of society was evolving in which
the state was viewed not as a composite of feudal boxes
but as a totality, a living organism with a will and justification of its own. The ambassador no longer spoke for his
province or for his profession but for the common good.
The business of the ambassador, said one Venetian civil
servant, was to "do, say, advise and think only whatever
may best serve the preservation and aggrandizement of
his own state".

The truth was no longer to be sought for in God's laws
or in Christian morality; it could now be created to suit
the needs of the state. "The opinion of the world", said
Henry VIII, "is often stronger than the truth," and public
opinion was a commodity which the sixteenth century
quickly learned could be moulded to conform to the pur-
poses of national policy. In the name of *raison d'état* and
in defiance of Christian opinion, Francis I of France could

ally himself with the infidel Turk even as Suleiman the Magnificent was hammering at the gates of Vienna. In the name of state diplomacy, a Scotish archbishop was assassinated by order of a Christian king of England. In the name of the welfare of the state, an English bishop so far forgot the existence of a higher law as to argue that "in matters of state individuals were not to be so much regarded as the whole body of the citizens".

The more "the whole body of the citizens" was heralded as the altar upon which private and feudal rights had to be sacrificed, the more men and women sang the praises of their own land and noted their neighbour's defects. National consciousness, a sense of Englishness, Spanishness or Frenchness, was relatively new to the sixteenth century, but dislike of strangers was a common characteristic of the medieval world. The traveller from southern France who ventured as far north as Paris found Parisian French almost incomprehensible; Englishmen spoke a babble of dialects; neighbouring villages eyed one another with suspicion; and Frenchmen were convinced that Englishmen were born with tails. The birth of the state converted man's inherent prejudice for his family, his village and his faith into a larger loyalty, so that by 1500 travellers were complaining that Englishmen think "there are no other men than themselves, and no other world but England; and whenever they see a handsome foreigner, they say that 'he looks like an Englishman'." England had been transformed into "this other Eden, demi-paradise", while Spain, with its religious preoccupation, was becoming a land in which all men should seek to die "because of the faith there, which is so Catholic, so firm, and so true".

The indispensable conditions of statehood – linguistic unity and pride – were rapidly developing in Spain, England and France during the fifteenth century. The first grammar of any modern language was presented to Queen Isabella in 1492, and Spaniards were so convinced of the superiority of their tongue that they boasted that "one can more rightly fear its descent than hope for its elevation". Englishmen were even more extreme in their defence of their native language, and one devotee asserted that his Anglo-Saxon tongue might not be "as sacred as the

Hebrew or as learned as the Greek", but it was "as fluent as the Latin, as courteous as the Spanish, as court-like as the French, and as amorous as the Italian". The babble of tongues throughout Europe was less multifarious by the sixteenth century, but more distinct, as London English, Parisian French, and Castilian Spanish predominated over rival sounds and each became the medium through which the state sang the praises of its own national uniqueness and virtues.

The "New Monarchs" helped to create the idea of the state and a sense of nationalism by the extension of royal law and the enforcement of royal justice in every corner of their realms, and by their insistence that neither divine nor historic law stood higher than the dictates of state survival. Quite deliberately the sovereigns of Europe were attempting to absorb provincial and family loyalties into a higher devotion directed towards their own august persons. The sixteenth century would have denied vigorously the reputed boast of Louis XIV of France that *"l'état, c'est moi"*, yet "New Monarchs" everywhere were insisting that "what pleaseth the prince has the force of law". The preservation of the state demanded the divinity of kings, for only by elevating the authority of sovereigns to immoderate and unheard-of heights could feudal factionalism and discord be abolished.

The moment the "New Monarchs" associated themselves with national prejudice and Bluff King Hal and Gloriana became the symbols for all that was best and English, or Francis I became for all Frenchmen, *"mon Roi, mon Seigneur, mon César et mon fils"*, then sovereigns became not kings to be obeyed but idols to be worshipped. Subjects had to learn to make a distinction between "their own fond follies and the king's most worshipful pleasure". Lord, commoner and clergyman owed their first duty to the Crown, and the full measure of Tudor authority was voiced when it was said of Bishop Fox that to "serve the king's turn [he] would agree to his own father's death". The "New Monarchs" demanded the destruction of one of the most sacred and essential elements of the medieval formula, the balanced obligation offered to both God and Caesar. Erasmus may have been overstating the case but

he spoke little more than the simple truth when he said
that before the threat of princes "the people tremble, the
senate yields, the nobility cringe, the judges concur, the
divines are dumb, the lawyers assent, the law and con-
stitution give way, neither right nor religion, neither justice
nor humanity avails". The very existence of the sovereign
national state necessitated a double standard between kings
and mere mortal men, and the distinction was trumpeted
from every pulpit of the sixteenth century. The Elizabethan
world agreed with Robert Greene who argued:

> Why, Prince, it is no murder in a king,
> To end another's life to save his own:
> For you are not as common people be,
> Who die and perish with a few men's tears;
> But if you fail, the state doth whole default,
> The realm is rent in twain in such a loss.

New nations, "New Monarchs", new financiers were
symptomatic of a new spirit. Optimism was in the air, in
government, in commerce, and even in religion, and Erasmus in 1517 confidently predicted a future in which true
Christian piety, sound scholarship and public peace would
soon prevail. An increasing and articulate coterie of
scholars, artists, magistrates, and popes were beginning to
look away from the *Danse Macabre* and turn instead to
the dance of life. In Venice, where a golden shower of
ducats had produced a society in which artists, scholars,
courtesans and merchants were judged by the single standard of talent, Albrecht Dürer suddenly discovered that he
was a gentleman while back at home in Germany he was
still "a parasite". For a moment in the early years of the
sixteenth century it appeared as if the rich vitality of
Renaissance Italy was moving northwards, bringing with it
a view of the world in which the individual was held up as
the highest expression of divine wisdom. In man were to be
"found all and every ratio and proportion by which God
reveals the innermost secrets of nature". In England and
France, the second generation of the "New Monarchs"
seemed to herald a new age in which "the heavens laugh,
the earth exalts, and all things are full of milk, of honey,
and of nectar!"

The spirit that transformed the youthful courts of Henry VIII and Francis I into pavilions of Renaissance brilliance was heavily classical in flavour, deeply humanistic in its insistence upon the worth of man, childishly naive in its expectations, and blatantly defiant in its denial of the medieval view of man's proper role in the divine order of things. The sins that the medieval world had most warned against – the exaltation of the individual and man's ability to fashion himself and his society into whatever shape he pleased – were the very virtues that the humanists most loudly extolled. Where the past had preached against pride, the Renaissance praised the virtuosity and creative genius of human talent in every field. Where the medieval Church had thundered against the dangerous imbalance of total preoccupation with the affairs of this world, the early sixteenth century applauded the universal man who explored eagerly every aspect of life. Where man's humility in the face of the mysteries of life and death had once been acclaimed, now it was condemned. The individual was urged on to dare all, to test all, to inquire into the secrets of heaven and hell, to play the man and say with Webster's Bosola: "I'll be mine own example."

In Italy and in parts of Northern Europe, men agreed that it was "undoubtedly a golden age which had restored the light of the liberal arts that had almost been destroyed: grammar, eloquence, painting, architecture, sculpture, music". In France, Budé sang paeans to sacred truth which, he claimed, was beginning "to shine forth from the filth of the sophist school". In the Low Countries, Erasmus of Rotterdam begged to be rejuvenated for a few years so as to enjoy the approaching golden age of learning. In Germany, Ulrich von Hutten sang: "Oh world, oh letters, it is a delight to live." In Dante's *Inferno*, the bottom pit of hell contained three men encased in ice, Cassius, Brutus, and Judas, the three supreme egotists who had set themselves above their overlords, but by the sixteenth century Brutus had become "an honourable man".

More than a touch of naivety existed in the midst of such enthusiasm, for all things seemed possible and all matters were of equal interest. In 1486 in Italy, Pico della Mirandola announced publicly that he was willing to enlarge upon all human knowledge, which, at the age of twenty-three, he had reduced to nine hundred theses. In 1517 a Monsieur de la Vernade imported the first crocodile ever to be seen in Paris and presented his trophy to the Church of St. Anthony where it was fixed upon the wall.

The youthful boastings of Pico and the sacrilegious conversion of God's Church into a museum dedicated to man's insatiable curiosity and collector's instinct seemed to many men to be presumptuous and dangerous. The need for faith and spiritual authority remained. Humanism with its pedantic overtones and naive individualism proved to be distasteful to those of non-intellectual appetite and limited purse. It was all very well for Erasmus to purge the Church with laughter, to wash away abuse with mirth and to expose the foibles of society to friendly ridicule. Humanity took itself far too seriously, and the weight of clerical corruption was too heavy to be lifted by mere laughter. Christian humanists deplored the apathy and hollowness of a ritualistic religion, and Erasmus asked whether man should adore "the bones of Paul preserved in a shrine and not adore the mind of Paul made manifest in his writings'. But scholarly reform within the Church lacked the strength to do more than reveal the sickness of Christendom; it could not cure it. It was Erasmus himself, the prince of all humanists, who confessed the underlying weakness of the reforming scholar when he sadly acknowledged that not everyone had "the courage to be a martyr. I am afraid if I were put to the trial, I should be like Peter".

The medieval *ecclesia* faced no danger from humanism: the enemy lay closer to home, within the Church itself. The path of religious revolution was not cut with the sharp razor of humanistic scholarship but with the heavy sword of Martin Luther's spiritual despair. The fear that he would never be able to warrant salvation became for Luther the path to a profound truth: in total despondency lay new hope. It was this discovery that gave him, and others like him, the strength that Erasmus lacked.

Luther was no child of the Renaissance. He was born of peasant stock in Thuringia in 1483, where men of piety still said their paternosters and attended mass. He was a young man of deep religious sensibilities who united a persistent conviction of his own damnation with a pressing sense of God's dreadful omnipotence and ruthless justice, and like a good son of the medieval Church he turned in 1505 to the Augustine monastery at Erfurt to seek religious solace. By a life of fasting, prayer and self-discipline and by the meticulous observation of every detail of the monastic rule, he sought to find salvation. "True it is," he confessed, "I was a good monk and ... if ever a monk got to heaven by monkery, it was I." The endless repetition of monkery failed in its purpose, and his sense of guilt remained until one day in 1515 he happened to ponder anew the words of St. Paul (Romans i 17): "The just shall live by faith." Thereupon he knew himself to have been reborn and the endless night of doubt and anguish receded; Luther had "gone through open doors into paradise". The path to heaven was through the doctrine of justification by faith alone. The old medieval balance between good works and faith was demolished. It was unnecessary to light candles, renounce life, retreat into a monastery, or endow chapels, for the excellent reason that heaven could not be bought with pious works. Man was saved by God's infinite mercy, and humanity could in no way warrant, merit or purchase salvation; all it could do was to have faith in divine charity.

The implications of the new doctrine were revolutionary. Against the claims of the medieval Church to an absolute control of the channels by which God's grace was dispensed to man, Luther proclaimed that individuals were saved by their own faith without benefit of sacrament or cleric. Against the Church's assertion of a monopoly of the roads to salvation, Luther set up the priesthood of all the faithful in which there was no distinction between a priest and a layman. Against the Church's insistence that God spoke only through the ecclesiastical hierarchy of popes, bishops and priests, Luther maintained the right of the individual, inspired by his faith, to comprehend God's Word as revealed in Scripture.

Luther did not learn his theology all at once. From the monastery he was called to the new university of Wittenberg, where he lectured on the Bible and slowly formulated his religious views. It was only in 1517 that the sequence of events commenced which ultimately led him to challenge the entire edifice of medieval Catholicism and to destroy for ever the spiritual unity of Christendom. The episode involved one of the most flagrant abuses of good works and one of the most startling examples of the sterile mechanization and soulless ceremonialism into which the medieval Church had slipped. The papacy of Leo X was in need of silver to construct that magnificent monument to Renaissance grandeur, the new Cathedral of St. Peter. In order to raise the money, the Pope turned to the international banking house of the Fuggers, and, by way of collateral, issued a bull of indulgence whereby the faithful might purchase, for the price of a single silver coin, remittance of the pains of purgatory. The Fuggers supervised the collection, and John Tetzel, a Dominican monk, acted as chief vendor and canvassed Germany, assuring his listeners that:

> As soon as the coin in the coffer rings
> The soul from purgatory springs.

When Tetzel approached Wittenberg, Luther struck out against the belief that remission of sin could be bought, and on October 31st, 1517, he posted upon the collegiate church door his Ninety-Five Theses, offering to debate the purpose of the indulgences ,their spiritual value, and the Pope's authority to issue them.

Unexpectedly a personal and somewhat academic vendetta became the signal for spiritual revolution. Luther was acclaimed a hero by those who resented German money being sucked into the building of the "insatiable basilica" of St. Peter in Rome, and by those who wished to rid the Church of its commercialism, ritualism and sterility. Every effort to discipline the wayward monk produced stronger words of defiance, until Luther stood in open rebellion against the entire Catholic edifice. At the imperial diet at Worms in April 1521, he voiced the final logic of his heresy: "Unless I am convinced by Scripture and plain reason – I do not accept the authority of popes and councils, for they have contradicted each other – my conscience is captive to the Word of God. I cannot and will not recant anything, for to go against conscience is neither right nor safe. God help me! Here I stand, I cannot do otherwise.' To the Emperor Charles V, who sat listening to Luther's presumptuous challenge, it seemed intolerable that "a single monk, led astray by private judgment", should have set "himself against the faith held by all Christians for a thousand years or more" and should have impudently concluded "that all Christians up till now have erred". But Pope and Emperor, medieval Church and Empire reckoned without "the marvellous comfort and quietness" that Luther's message held for all who felt close upon them the fires of damnation or who could find no relief in the bosom of the Catholic *ecclesia*. Luther's books sold everywhere and six hundred copies of his Ninety-Five Theses were sent to France, Spain and England, where men of similar heart, plagued by the same sense of despair, either followed in his footsteps or sought their own brand of spiritual solace in defiance of established authority and ancient formulas.

In religion, in politics, in commerce and in the governments of men, the warm breath of change surged and swelled, and by 1533, the year of Elizabeth's birth, the main outlines of modern Europe were clearly discernible. But even as Elizabeth and her generation stood upon the threshold of modernity, the ghost of medievalism lingered on, fettering the minds of men, and holding captive their imaginations. Scratch an Elizabethan deeply and a medieval man lay revealed. Sir Thomas More has been called the father of political science, the first man to apply human reason to the study of a sane and realistic society, yet More placed duty to God above obedience to the state and sacrificed his life for the medieval concept of a unified Christendom. Quite deliberately he turned his back upon the new age where the acquisitive capitalistic spirit, the monolithic and godless national state, the exaltation of the individual, and the clamour of religious discord were the order of the day.

The troubled mind of the fifteenth century was obviously receding, but ambivalence nevertheless remained. The Frenchman Jean Bodin was able to discover clearly the nature and limits of the secular sovereign state, and to perceive that the curse of inflation which afflicted the sixteenth century had little to do with human avarice or moral evil but was the result of gold and silver from the New World glutting the money market. Bodin was able to divorce fiscal theory from religious morality, yet he wrote in defence of witchcraft and carried the title of "Satan's Attorney General". The attraction of the Cemetery of the Innocents was passing, but the human body in various stages of decomposition remained popular in tombstone art, and Gloriana in the quiet of her study voiced the persistent doubt that lingered in every Renaissance heart when she asked: "What have I rendered to Thee? Forgetfulness, unthankfulness and great disobedience. I should have magnified Thee. I have neglected Thee. I should have prayed unto Thee. I have forgotten Thee. I should have served Thee. I have sinned against Thee. This is my case, then where is my hope?

Everywhere the medieval heritage died hard, and the new impulses in society faced constant challenge from the past. Feudal castles still stood, ties of blood and lordship remained strong, and man's image of society continued to be medieval. Throughout Europe the official view of the social order was static, closed, hierarchical and religiously inspired. The Elizabethan state was no human contrivance constructed to advance the material well-being of man. It remained a divinely ordained structure into which individuals were born with prescribed duties and fixed status. The favourite political metaphor of the age was the beehive in which all members knew their place and over which the queen and her aristocracy ruled. From Madrid to London, from Paris to Rome, the sixteenth century insisted upon "a head to rule, priests to pray, counsellors to counsel, judges to judge, noblemen to give orders, soldiers to defend, farmers to till, tradesmen to do business and artisans to take care of mechanical matters".

The much-proclaimed sovereign national state was as yet no Leviathan, and though it demanded the loyalty of its subjects on the grounds of conscience as well as necessity, it still lacked the machinery to make its claims effective. During much of the sixteenth century Parisians were "so ready to uproars and insurrections that foreign nations wondered at the patience of the Kings of France". Royal patience, however, was unavoidable, for twelve thousand royal officials endeavoured rather ineffectually to govern fifteen million Frenchmen, a figure which represents a ratio of one official for every twelve hundred and fifty inhabitants, or one bureaucrat for every sixteen square miles. By modern standards and proportions, which work out at one official for every seventy Frenchmen and fifty-six bureaucrats for every sixteen square miles, France was scarcely burdened with an over-abundance of government. The era of private armies and feudal revolts was far from over. Over-mighty subjects still retained vast military and economic resources and did not hesitate to appeal to clan, custom and feudal privilege. In England the feudal north in 1570 made a last bid to return to "the good old days", and in France the realm was engulfed in dynastic, regional and religious wars which lasted for over a generation.

The myth of European political unity still excited the imagination; the fatuous dignities of the Holy Roman Emperor were still held in awe; and the European family of states was still subject to divine governance. Medieval theory and modern reality stood at total variance with one another, but most men continued to live the dream of what had once been, and they desired a return to the days when there had been but one truth, one faith and one Church. The existence of two absolute truths – one Catholic, the other Protestant – meant not toleration but religious controversy, in which the faithful were urged to sacrifice all other concerns to the defence and aggrandizement of their particular brand of orthodoxy. The clash of loyalties to God, to man, to state, to family and to feudal overlord imposed strains upon society as great as those that had existed in the fifteenth century and produced equally violent extremes of despondency and delight. In France, the Low Countries and parts of Germany, society dissolved into civil war and religious bloodshed; in Spain, the state became the hallowed instrument of Catholic truth; and in Geneva, an equally belligerent Protestant orthodoxy prevailed. In England alone, a more moderate political and religious behaviour triumphed through the magic of a Virgin Queen.

Three

Sin and Schism

ELIZABETH may not have been born in sin, but she was certainly the child of schism, and her sex was a bitter disappointment to a parent who had risked his crown and kingdom to father a legitimate male heir. From the moment of her conception, the princess's sex and legitimacy were crucial factors in the course of European history.

Elizabeth was born into a world which viewed her birth and continued good health as the cardinal stumbling-block to the spiritual reunification of Christendom and the extinction of the Protestant heresy. Most of Europe, and possibly even a majority in England, regarded her as the product of adultery, a royal bastard incapable of lawful inheritance. Only a few militant Protestants greeted her arrival with fervent prayers of thankfulness, and even they were aghast that the future of their faith should be tied to the frail life of a girl child. As for her father, that massive Titan of a sovereign, who joined in his royal person the savage pride of a Lucifer and the irresistible charm of a Falstaff, he was outraged that God and fortune had made him ridiculous by presenting him with still another heiress to his kingdom.

The story of Elizabeth's birth goes back to the year 1527, when Henry VIII was afflicted by three related emotions: mounting concern over his Queen's advancing years and continued barrenness; the prick of religious conscience for having married his deceased brother's wife; and a violent sexual attraction for a young lady of the court, who obstinately insisted that sharing her sovereign's crown was a prerequisite to sharing his bed.

As a young man, Henry had fulfilled his father's death-bed request that he marry Catherine, daughter of Isabella and Ferdinand of Spain and widow of Prince Arthur. Special papal dispensation had been arranged so that the young King might violate the Book of Leviticus, which clearly stated that "if a man shall take his brother's wife, it is an unclean thing ...; they shall be childless." Marriage with Catherine had not been totally barren and the Queen had done her best. Five children had been born but only a daughter survived, a fact which was regarded by most learned and politic men as a sure invitation to disputed succession and civil war. By 1527 Catherine was an ageing and rotund forty-two, and her husband, who was six years her junior, began to ponder, despite papal assurances to the contrary, whether he was not in fact an incestuous king and the victim of Heaven's displeasure. Whether the events that culminated in the most celebrated divorce suit in history stemmed from Henry's tender conscience or his far from tender infatuation for the ebony-eyed, white-skinned and intelligent beauty, the Lady Anne Boleyn, is more a matter of personal opinion than historical fact capable of proof. What is clearer is that the case was presented to the world as a question of political necessity: no matter what the price, England had to have a legitimate male heir to secure the succession and save the kingdom from civil war fought by the advocates of the King's legitimate daughter, the Princess Mary, and those of his illegitimate son, the Duke of Richmond.

Every consideration seemed to call for a divorce, a step which was not unique in the annals of dynastic history. Wives of royalty promised to be "bonair and buxom in bed and at board" and when they went so far as to forget their wedding vows, it was accepted procedure that they should be put away for someone who was capable of providing that most precious of assets in an age of high infant mortality – a son and heir. In a world that made exceptions for kings and princes and looked kindly upon the matrimonial requirements of sovereigns, Henry anticipated no problem in the matter of obtaining a divorce. The Pope

had obliged him by making it possible to marry Catherine
in the first place, so now, eighteen years later, it was expected that His Holiness would grant his faithful son and
Defender of the Faith his wish. In this pleasant and easy
solution to domestic matters, Bluff King Hal reckoned
without his wife's Spanish pride, her European relatives,
and the conscience of Christendom.

The fact that the King's "Great Matter", as Henry's
divorce was referred to in the chanceries of Europe, took
six interminable years to run its course is evidence not so
much that Henry had the patience of Job but that the pace
of diplomacy in the sixteenth century was leisurely in the
extreme. The world of Henry VIII and Elizabeth still
thought in terms of distances that took weeks and months
to cover and foreign policies in which ambassadors spent
a large portion of their waking hours jogging painfully
along in sluggish mule-trains. Diplomatically London and
Paris were at best two days' journey apart, and during the
winter months official dispatches might take over a month
to get through. Madrid and Rome were over a fortnight
distant, and the news of Elizabeth's death in 1603 took a
week at breakneck speed to reach an expectant James in
Edinburgh.

The fastest, but at times the most dangerous, mode of
transportation was by sea, and Mediterranean galleys,
oared by countless slaves and helped by a favourable
breeze, might achieve one hundred and twenty-five miles a
day. The great galleons, propelled only by sail but capable
of surviving in the grey waters of the Atlantic, were con-
siderably slower, but they could still beat equestrian speeds
that occasionally achieved eighty-five miles in a day. The
great disadvantage of ocean travel lay in contrary winds,
high waves and unpredictable currents. At the Straits of
Gibraltar, for instance, where the Atlantic rushes into the
Mediterranean at a rate of five to six knots, ships had to
wait for weeks for a wind strong enough to carry them
through into the ocean. Whether it was Henry waiting for
information from his ambassadors in Rome, Elizabeth expecting word of the Armada, or Philip of Spain planning
his moves in the game of international cold war, news
travelled at a pace unimaginably slow.

Europe of the sixteenth century consisted of six major powers all of which claimed the special attention of the deity but none of which allowed spiritual concerns to interfere seriously with questions of state. Henry of England displayed the title of Defender of the Faith; Francis I was the Most Christian King of France; His Holiness, the Pope, possessed the keys to the kingdom of heaven; Suleiman, the Sultan of the Ottoman Empire, was caliph of all true believers; and finally Charles V was both Emperor of the Holy Roman Empire and His Most Catholic Majesty of Spain. Of all the sovereigns of Europe, the Emperor Charles and the Sultan Suleiman were the most powerful. The Ottoman Turks had penetrated the bulwark of Christendom, overrunning Hungary, razing the Christian churches of Buda and replacing them with mosques, and slaying at Mohácz the Emperor's brother-in-law, the twenty-year-old King of Hungary. Six times Suleiman led his armies to the very gates of Vienna, and in sight of the imperial city he died in his seventieth year. The Sultan's strength was in large measure relative to his opponent's embarrassment of possessions, for Charles's ramshackle empire imposed upon him so many obligations that he could never marshal his full military potential against the infidel.

The vast empire of the Habsburgs was the result of dynastic accident, and historic proof of the effectiveness of the maxim by which the Habsburgs lived: "Others wage war, but you, happy Austria, make marriages." From his paternal grandfather, the Emperor Maximilian (1494–1519), Charles inherited the Habsburg possessions in Austria and the Low Countries. Through his mother, mad Joanna, daughter of Ferdinand and Isabella, he was heir to the kingdom of Spain and the riches of the New World. The imperial dignity, to which he was elected in 1519, the military might of the Spanish infantry, the wealth of the silver mines of Peru, and the economic prosperity of the Netherlands were united under a single hand, and Charles was told in all seriousness that God had given him the extraordinary grace of raising him above all other kings and princes and had placed him "on the road to universal monarchy". The imperial shepherd, however, discovered, that for every sheep he gathered to the fold there lurked a wolf, and each new title brought added obligations. Had the Emperor ever been able to isolate his enemies, to crush the Lutheran heretics in Germany, to curb the independence of the great princes of the empire, to surround and destroy Valois France, and to cast out the forces of Allah from Europe, the dream of "gathering Christendom together beneath a single shepherd" might have been achieved. As it was, Charles spent a lifetime preserving the status quo, fighting delaying actions, and hurrying from Milan to Antwerp and back to Madrid in an effort to contain the French, repulse the Turks, prevent the spread of heresy, and save what he had inherited. In one area alone was he successful: France was thrown out of Italy and the whole peninsula fell under imperial domination, a matter of supreme importance to the success of Henry's "Great Matter", for only the Roman pontiff could grant the divorce. With Spanish and Imperial troops at his doorsteps, Clement VII decided "to live and die an Imperialist".

Unfortunately for Henry, the wife he proposed to divorce was the aunt of the man who controlled the wealth of the Indies, the markets of the Netherlands, the armies of Spain and the conscience of the Pope. Worse still, Catherine at forty-two proved to be something more than a dowdy spouse with spreading hips and domestic tastes, content to count her sovereign's laundry and preside over his household. Beneath a placid surface lay hidden the furious pride and unbending obstinacy of her Iberian blood. The Queen was "no English woman but a Spaniard born", and she set her heart and soul against any idea of divorce. Her royal husband might have as many concubines as he desired, but no common lady-in-waiting would ever replace her as rightful queen and no child of sin would displace her daughter as legal heir to the Tudor throne. Humility and loyalty were the words of her motto, but Henry quickly learned that her humility was to God, her loyalty to her blood, and in her determination to thwart her husband's matrimonial plans she called upon the influence of her family and the dynastic pride of her nephew, the Emperor Charles.

For six years, Henry applied persuasion and coercion to his wife and used the weapons of war and diplomacy upon Charles and Clement VII, but by 1532 time and patience were running out. In September Anne Boleyn's resistance, substantially weakened by her elevation to the peerage as Marchioness of Pembroke with an annual income of a thousand pounds, gave way. By December she was pregnant, and on January 25th, 1533, Anne and Henry were secretly married. If the child was to be legitimate and the father saved from bigamy, only seven months remained in which to accomplish the divorce. From January on, the pace of events increased, culminating in spiritual revolution and the defiance of the Christian world.

Archbishop Warham died in August 1532, and in his place was appointed Thomas Cranmer, a Cambridge don with a gift for translating the fire of religious faith into the majesty of the English language. With Cranmer's elevation the shape of revolutionary things to come was clearly present, but a frightened Pope, still anxious to placate Henry yet unwilling to grant him a divorce, blessed the appointment, and the new Archbishop was legally installed in March of 1533. The new prelate was ready and willing to grant his king a divorce, but any decision rendered in the Archbishop's court would be exposed to review and reversal in Rome. Therefore, in April the irrevocable step was taken; by the Act in Restraint of Appeals the legal fabric binding England to Rome was cut and the court of the Archdiocese of Canterbury decreed to be the highest spiritual forum for Englishmen. In May Henry was ordered to appear before a tribunal of his own kingdom, presided over by a prelate of his own creation. The decision surprised no one, and the King was set free to announce publicly his marriage to Anne and to crown her Queen on June 1st, 1533. With studied care the stage had been prepared, new statutes passed and old laws violated, a Spanish queen sacrificed and a new one created, all in anticipation of a legitimate male heir. It was almost too much to bear when on September 7th, 1533, the prince born to Anne Boleyn turned out to be Elizabeth Tudor.

The Catholic world guffawed and perceived evidence of divine judgment; Anne was despondent and Henry indignant at this trick of fate. Comfort, however, could be taken from the fact that the child was healthy and the new Queen fertile, and the forty-year-old monarch had no doubts about his own fecundity. More children would follow. The immediate problem was to complete the break with Rome and create a Church of England that would be independent of the Pope but not of the King. The new *ecclesia* must be free of foreign interference, and, more important, its authority and fiscal perquisites transferred to the Crown. By the second Act of Annates, in 1534, the financial links with Rome were severed and the revenues redirected into the royal coffers. New legislation gave Henry the right to make ecclesiastical appointments, and in November 1534 the constitutional revolution reached its climax in the Act of Supremacy whereby the King assumed the title of "Supreme Head of the Church of England". Henry was, in his own words, "Pope, King and Emperor" in England.

Transfer, not reform, was the theme of the English Reformation. The vicar of Christ at Rome had been displaced by God's lieutenant on earth in London. The revenues, powers and privileges of His Holiness had been conferred upon His Grace, the sovereign King of England. The Church of England remained Catholic and orthodox, for the man who assumed the mantle of spiritual authority was no heretic. All "his devout subjects" were "as obedient, devout, Catholic and humble children of God and the Holy Church as any people be within any realm of Christendom". Henry had abolished the pope but not popery, and those who desired the reform of the Church as well as the transfer of papal authority from the Vatican to Westminster were disappointed in a monarch who wanted "to sit as anti-Christ in the temple of God", and they suspected with some justification that "the rich treasures, the rich income of the Church, these are the gospel according to Harry." The structure of Henry's Church was still thoroughly Catholic in form and doctrine. Canon law remained valid, spiritual violators were put to public penance, the rights and powers of the Church to excommunicate were still held in awe, ecclesiastical courts continued to hear divorce cases and handle the probate of wills, and the archbishop retained authority to grant special dispensations for those who infringed upon the laws of God. The only difference was that the source of all of this authority was now the king and not the pope.

Henry had achieved the means to his end, but the end itself – a legitimate male heir – continued to elude him. The situation at home was made easier in January 1536 when Catherine died, possibly of murder or deliberate neglect but more probably of heart disease. Henry's reaction was to thank God and to make much of the infant princess Elizabeth. He celebrated his wife's death by a court ball which he attended "clad all in yellow from top to toe". Though much was made of the royal babe, time was running out, for Anne Boleyn was proving herself to be as barren of male offspring as her predecessor. Again the King was touched in his conscience for fear that his second marriage was displeasing to God. Proof of divine wrath seemed manifest when, on January 29th, Anne miscarried of a dead baby boy as a consequence of finding her husband in the embraces of one of her maids-in-waiting, the demure and affable Jane Seymour. By May, the Queen had been accused of high treason and adultery; on the 19th of the month she was executed; and eleven days later Henry married Jane Seymour. On October 12th, 1537, Henry was granted his wish, for the new Queen fulfilled her nuptial vows and gave birth to Prince Edward.

The old King married thrice more, once for reasons of diplomacy, once for love, and once to find a companion in his advancing years and a nurse for his diseased and dying body, but with Edward the number of his children was completed: Catholic and Spanish Mary, Protestant and English Elizabeth, sickly and legitimate Edward. In the end Henry willed his throne as if no breath of scandal had touched his dynasty: first to Edward, then to Mary and finally to Elizabeth, and if the children of his own body should die without issue, the crown was bequeathed to the offspring of his younger sister, Mary Duchess of Norfolk.

Throughout Henry's reign, the tide of religious passion in England and Europe had been steadily rising, engulfing Christendom in the strife and bloodshed of religious discord. With almost apocalyptic speed, Lutheran ideas spread, breeding social and spiritual revolution. By 1547, Prussia, Denmark, Sweden and Brandenburg had gone over to the new heresy, England was schismatic, and the Netherlands and northern France were hearkening to the

stern word of God as revealed by John Calvin. The fact
that reform spoke not with a single voice but in a babble
of warring tongues, each claiming a monopoly of the truth,
was of little comfort to men of the old school who be-
wailed the existence of a world filled with error and who
knew not where to flee. The Lutheran poison had done its
work, and every new Protestant faction seemed more quarrelsome and sententious than the last. Luther at Wittenburg,
Bucer at Strasbourg, Zwingli at Zürich, Calvin at Geneva,
and the Anabaptists at Münster thundered militant threats
in which all was fair as roses or black as pitch. In every
country the leadership of the Protestant movement seemed
to be falling into the hands of fervent and aggressive reformers, who sought not to countenance life but to remodel
it into a community of saints. "Zely people", who were sustained by their faith even in the face of a martyr's death,
fought as the soldiers of the Lord.

In England, Henry as Supreme Head and Defender of
the Faith faced a growing and exultant minority of saints,
righteous in their spiritual strength and adamant in their
stand against evil, who saw the break with Rome as the
prelude to the establishment of the kingdom of heaven on
earth. To such men, the pope was the devil's disciple and
the Roman Church was Mistress Rose of Rome, the painted
whore of Babylon. In their stern eyes, popery was as pernicious as the pope, and the cry went up to "get rid of the
poison with the author". As long as Henry lived, the call
went unheeded, but on his death, England was caught up
in a religious maelstrom.

Princess Elizabeth was thirteen when her father died in
the early morning of January 28th, 1547, and the control
of the state passed to her brother, a precocious child of
nine, and to his naive if well-meaning uncle, Edward Seymour, Duke of Somerset. The princess's formal education
as a woman of the Renaissance was the work of tutors
appointed by her father, but her training in statecraft commenced the day the old King died. Under Edward and
Mary, she learned exactly what it meant to be a Tudor
heir and the truth of the saying: "Slippery is the place next
to kings". The miracle of Elizabeth's future success in re-

straining religious passions and preserving the unity of the realm, and the tragedy surrounding the reigns of her brother and elder sister, are intimately related. A decade of indecent Protestant fanaticism under Edward and Catholic bigotry under Mary presented to the Princess and all England a lesson in what religious hatred and social violence could do to a kingdom.

The man most responsible for the failure of Edward VI's reign was Edward Seymour who, as the sovereign's uncle, was appointed Lord Protector of the Realm and Governor of the King's Person. The new *alter rex* endeavoured to substitute sweet reason and tolerance for the old King's Draconian measures, and the results came close to tearing the country to pieces. The moment the government indicated its willingness to discard Henry's *via media* of Catholicism without the pope, the clamour for religious revolution rose to deafening proportions. The ale-house and the tavern, the royal household and the bishop's palace became arenas of religious strife where the holy mass was referred to as a jack-in-the-box and the time-honoured words of the consecration – *Hoc est corpus* – were translated hocus-pocus. The Lord Protector's solution was the introduction of a massive and comprehensive religious conformity which aimed at bringing into a single fold a determined Protestant minority, made more radical by the addition of continental reformers, and a Catholic faction, made more desperate by the growing force of heresy. The Prayer Book of 1549 tried to satisfy all parties and ended by alienating both faiths, for it deliberately obscured the central issue of dispute: the question whether the mass was a sacrifice in which the body and blood of Christ were actually present and resacrificed for the benefit of mankind, or whether it was a commemorative service bringing to mind the memory of Christ's sacrifice and redemption. Written by Archbishop Cranmer in 1549 and reflecting the richness of his language and the softness of his compromise, the Prayer Book was a literary masterpiece but a religious debacle. It irritated reformers who demanded that in religion it was "more proper to call a spade a spade than throw ambiguous expressions before posterity," and it drove the conservative shires of southern England into open revolt, the peasants calling for a return to the good old days of Henry VIII.

The Lord Protector was no more successful in satisfying the ambitions of his family than in uniting his sovereign's kingdom. Edward Seymour had a younger brother, Thomas, "fierce in courage, courtly in fashion, in personage stately, in voice magnificent, but somewhat empty in matter". While the elder brother was aloof and tactless, the younger was ruthless and charming; while the Lord Protector had greatness, title and wealth thrust upon him, Thomas Seymour had been left with a single crumb of high office – Lord High Admiral of England. Thomas was critical of his brother's policies, covetous of his authority, and infuriated by the lordly bearing of a man who was his own flesh and blood. The Lord Admiral's ambitions were built upon his personal magnetism, his charm with the ladies, and his way with small boys, especially young Edward VI. He offered himself as a suitable husband for either Elizabeth or Mary and when the King's council dismissed the suggestion, he secretly married the Dowager Queen, Catherine Parr. His wife did not long survive her nuptials, dying a year and a half later in childbirth. Seymour next cast his net at Elizabeth and Edward. The way to the King's heart was through his pocket-money and he tried to turn Edward against his uncle by showing that the Lord Protector had kept him "a beggarly king" and had treated him like a small boy. To Elizabeth he made advances even while Catherine lived, entering her bedchamber in night-gown and bare legs and romping with his royal stepdaughter. After his wife's death, the romping took on more serious overtones, and he again began to hint at marriage.

What Seymour's ultimate plans were – kidnapping the King, replacing his brother, leading an insurrection, or marrying Elizabeth – remains a mystery. The results, however, were clear: they destroyed both the Lord Admiral and his brother and placed Elizabeth's life in jeopardy. In self-defence, the Lord Protector was forced to act, and on January 18th, 1549, he ordered his brother's arrest. A full-scale investigation was conducted into the relationship between the Lord Admiral and Elizabeth, and the Princess was grimly reminded that "she was but a subject". If nothing else, the future Queen learned discretion, and when Thomas Seymour was executed in March she remarked: "This day died a man of much wit and very little judgment."

The death of the Lord Admiral was a prelude to the fury of factional discord and backstairs politics that eventually swept the Lord Protector from his office and to the execution block. In 1550 a palace revolution took place in which the Protector's rival, John Dudley, later created Duke of Northumberland, seized control of the council and the King's person. Historians have rarely had a good word to say about Dudley. He was a questionable Catholic by conviction, a ruthless Protestant by politics and an insatiable dynastic by instinct. Under the Duke, full-scale plunder of the *ecclesia* began, and extreme Calvinistic Protestantism was officially fostered. Religious reformers and tough court politicians had one idea in common: clerical wealth and property were harmful to the spiritual vigour and purity of God's Church. Religious righteousness and economic self-interest made it highly desirable to relieve the princes of the Church of as many lordships as possible. Northumberland therefore found it profitable to support the extreme Protestant argument that the mass was purely a commemorative service, that priests were biblical and moral teachers, that altars should be replaced by tables, and that the Church should be returned to its pristine ceremonial purity. By the new Ordinal of 1550, the divinely ordained priest became a parson appointed by government patronage, and the wind of religious change reached gale force in 1552 when a revised version of the 1549 Prayer Book was issued ending any pretence at compromise with Catholicism.

How long a worried realm, still attached to the ancient ritual and outward trappings of Catholicism, would have tolerated doctrinaire radicalism in religion and the brazen plundering of the Church is difficult to surmise, But in 1553 the rock on which Northumberland's power rested turned to sand. He was suddenly informed by the royal doctors that Edward VI was dying of consumption and had less than six months to live. The Duke had tied his star to a priggish and humourless sixteen-year-old monarch, who

had never had a chance to live a normal childhood, and
to an advanced variety of Protestantism which was popular
in London and almost nowhere else. Dudley was feared,
but loved by no man, not even by reformers who saw him
as "an intrepid soldier of Christ". In the face of a Catholic
Mary who was the next in line of succession, he embarked
upon the desperate gamble of kingmaking. The Tudor
throne was too strong to usurp, but Northumberland hoped
that the succession could be altered and Henry's will set
aside. He convinced the dying Edward to strike a blow for
God and for Northumberland by declaring Princess Mary
to be illegitimate and incapable of lawful descent and willing his imperial crown to Lady Jane Grey, grand-niece of
Henry VIII and the Duke's daughter-in-law.

The night of Edward's death was dark and stormy, and
men whispered that Henry's grave at Windsor had cracked
open and that the old King had risen up in ghostly wrath
against those who dared upset his will. Northumberland's
desperate calculations reckoned without Henry's dead hand
and without the loyalty that the Tudor dynasty had gathered to itself. When Edward, "tormented by constant
sleeplessness" and spewing forth sputum "livid, black, fetid
and full of carbon", finally died, England rallied to Catholic Mary who claimed her throne by God, by inheritance
and by right of blood. Forsaken by the council in London
and by his own army, the Duke surrendered and even went
so far as to apologize for the arrogant presumption that
had led him to defy the divinity of kings and the will of
Henry VIII.

Mary was a Catholic but she was also a Tudor, and except
in the austere and jaundiced eyes of a Protestant minority
she was of unimpeachable descent, claiming her throne by
parliamentary statute and divine succession. She was her
father's daughter, which was sufficient for most men, and
though John Knox, safe in the Calvinistic citadel in Geneva,
thundered against the monstrous regiment of women,
Englishmen were willing to risk feminism in high office
and Catholicism on the throne in order to escape the nightmare of factionalism, strife, party dissension and "the

dolorous experience of the inconstant government" of Edward's reign.

With the forces of factionalism utterly destroyed and the Duke of Northumberland safely in the Tower, Mary proved the truth of the Henrician Reformation: that what the government demands is an article of faith for Englishmen to be believed "for life and death". The new monarch was no daughter of the Renaissance. The soft glow of Catholic humanism, the laughter of Erasmus's *Praise of Folly* and the tolerance of More's *Utopia* had long since blistered and died in the face of Mary's Spanish pride and granite conviction. Mary joined the unyielding determinism of Catherine of Aragon with Henry Tudor's ruthlessness and intelligence, yet she lacked her mother's compassion and her father's tact and magnetism. The combination was disastrous, for the new Queen came to the throne with a single mission in life: to return her errant realm to the Roman fold. Of all the Tudors the small voice of conscience spoke most loudly in Catholic Mary.

The existence upon the throne of a neurotic, thirty-seven-year-old maiden was dangerous enough; what made matters more serious was that the Church which Mary so desperately desired to restore was, in 1553, no longer the same institution which her father had defied and discarded two decades earlier. If divorce and murderous neglect of her mother had hardened Mary's heart, the fires of Protestant heresy had purged the comfortable but corrupt papacy of Clement VII. Revenge, recantation and purgation were the order of the day, and conservative churchmen who had been imprisoned under Edward VI came out of the Tower determined that reformers would soon discover that "their sweet shall not be without sour sauce".

It proved relatively easy for the government to achieve the first steps in undoing the Reformation, and the clock was quickly turned back to the days of Henry VIII. In October 1553, the Edwardian spiritual reformation was destroyed as it had been created, by Act of Parliament. An anxious and willing House of Commons reversed the divorce of Catherine of Aragon, absolved the new Queen of bastardy, repealed the Edwardian acts of uniformity and statutes determining ceremony, images and the nature of the mass. By Act of Parliament, England returned to the Henrician *via media* of Catholicism without the pope. Further than this Mary could not, and Parliament would not, go. Two barriers yet remained to block the return to Rome – the Act of Supremacy which had given parliamentary acknowledgement to the new-found spiritual authority of the prince as Supreme Head of the Church of England, and the monastic lands that had been nationalized under Henry VIII. To Mary her spiritual title was a burning crown upon her head, the work of Satan; yet Parliament politely but firmly declined to un-acknowledge the Queen as Supreme Head or make it legally possible to recognize the authority of Rome until the ultimate fate of the monastic lands had been decided. Reflecting the interests of the landed classes, the Commons refused any religious settlement which involved a return of Church funds. The soul's salvation would have to wait upon political considerations. Only after the estates of the Church had been assured to their secular owners by statutory decree was Parliament willing, in 1554, to repeal the anti-papal legislation of Henry's reign and to petition for reunion with Rome and spiritual absolution.

In foreign policy as well as in religion, Mary was determined to cast out time and return to the conditions that had made possible the marriage of her Spanish mother and Tudor father. She set her royal heart upon marrying her cousin, the heir to the Habsburg possessions, young Philip of Spain. Times, however, had changed, and English and Spanish-imperial interests were rapidly parting company. Spain and not France was emerging as the colossus of the world, the arbiter of Europe, and England's commercial competitor in the Mediterranean and Caribbean. Against the bitter opposition of Parliament, the public, and her Privy Council, Mary insisted on the match, and in July 1554 Prince Philip became co-ruler of England. The Queen had her way in religion and marriage, but within months she learned that a large and vocal segment of the population refused to follow her lead. In 1554 Kent rose up against the prospects of a Roman faith and an alien King. Led by Sir Thomas Wyatt, some three thousand Kentish

men came as close as did any rebellion to upsetting the
Tudor throne. The revolt proved conclusively that London
was the heart of England and the bastion of Tudor rule.
Mary followed the advice of the Spanish ambassador who
warned her that "if you value your crown stay in London
for once you leave, Elizabeth will be queen and the true
religion thrown out". Wyatt knocked at the gates of the
city, but when the populace, Protestant though in parts it
was, remained loyal to the daughter of Henry Tudor, his
forces evaporated and Sir Thomas suffered the fate reserved for most critics of the Tudor throne – he died on
Tower Hill at the hands of the public executioner.

Two other victims were beheaded along with the leaders
of this ill-starred venture: Lady Jane Grey, Northumberland's nine-day puppet-queen, and her husband paid the
price of Wyatt's treason. Elizabeth's fate hung by the
slenderest thread of sisterly affection, and for a moment
it looked as if the logic of *Realpolitik* would prevail. The
Princess as heir-presumptive was too dangerous to live, and
the Spanish ambassador put his finger upon the insecurity
which surrounded Elizabeth's life when he noted that she
was "greatly to be feared; she has a spirit full of incanta-
tion". Every effort was made to connect her with Wyatt's
rebellion and she was ordered to the Tower for safe-
keeping while her future was being decided. As she was led
through Traitors' Gate and up the stairs from the river
into the fortress, Elizabeth suddenly sat down and refused
to go farther. The Lord Lieutenant of the Tower appealed
to her sense of dignity and said: "You had best come in,
Madam, for here you sit unwholesomely." The Princess
answered with a simple truth: "Better sit here than in a
worse place." In the end she sat in a worse place for three
months, and such was her hopelessness that she resigned
herself to death and requested only that the sword be sharp
and the executioner be French. What saved Elizabeth was
the Queen's compassion and Philip's realization that,
should his wife die childless, his diplomatic hold over
England would depend upon Elizabeth's friendship. The
Spanish King was never one to forget the advice: "Wary is
the man who assures his own retreat."

The year 1555 was the turning point of Mary's reign.

During the first three years the Queen had hoped that spiritual absolution and the return to Rome would bring peace of mind and relief from sin to her people, and that marriage to Philip would perpetuate the Tudor dynasty in the Catholic faith. The last twenty-four months of her reign brought nothing but disillusionment, despair and defeat, and earned for Mary the infamous epithet of "bloody". To her sorrow the Queen realized that godliness and loving kindness were not sufficient to lead her flock back into the bosom of the Church. Laws would have to be written in blood; heresy would have to be put to the torch; and in the summer of 1555 the Smithfield fires were lighted. The first burnings were limited to a select few – Cranmer, Ridley, Hooper, Latimer and two others – in the expectation that the terrible fate of the leaders of Protestantism would silence the voice of heresy. Mary's government, however, badly miscalculated the faith that sustained the Protestant martyrs. It failed to realize the strength of mind and body that led Hugh Latimer to turn to Nicholas Ridley as they stood chained to the stake and say: "Be of good comfort, Master Ridley, and play the man. We shall this day light such a candle, by God's grace, in England, as I trust shall never be put out." The death of the Protestant leaders showed not the horrors of incineration but the path to glory, and gave to lesser men the strength to play the man.

Responsibility for burning three hundred Protestant martyrs must ultimately rest upon the conscience of humanity, for the explanation, if not the justification, resides in the spirit of an age which believed that "there can not be a greater work of cruelty against the commonwealth than to nourish or favour [heretics] ... who, as it were, undermining the chief foundations of all commonwealths, which is religion, make an entry to all kinds of vice in the most heinous manner". In much the same way that the twentieth century regards the use of narcotics, both Protestants and Catholics viewed heresy as an insidious social disease which could destroy the soul and lead men into rebellion and perdition. Purgation by fire was the deplorable but accepted method of extermination.

No matter how hard she laboured, Mary had not "the

favour of God, nor the hearts of her subjects, nor yet the love of her husband". Her marriage was a travesty, barren of love as well as of children. The Queen was wedded to a husband who regarded his matrimonial vows as a matter of diplomatic convenience and demanded of his wife proof of her affection by leading England into war with France on the side of Spain. Dutifully, Mary dragooned her kingdom into a war for which it was militarily unequipped and emotionally unprepared. The consequences were almost as disastrous as her religious policy. The memory of Agincourt and Crécy was blackened by defeat when the city of Calais, the last English possession in France, was lost in January 1558. It is alleged that Mary said on her deathbed that if her heart were opened up, her doctors would find the word Calais written across it. The unrelieved tragedy of her reign, however, was not the loss of Calais, which had little to bind it to England except tradition, nor the loss of her husband's love, which she had never really possessed, nor even the sterility of her loins; it was the dreadful and gradual realization that righteousness does not necessarily prevail over evil. As the rumour of her death spread on November 16th – "Hope Wednesday" her subjects called the day – Mary must have known the truth of the proverb: "The greatest curse of God to man is that he should know the truth and do it not." Mary Tudor had shown the way, but England had obstinately failed to follow. It now remained to be seen whether the realm would follow the last of Henry's children – Queen Elizabeth.

Four

The "Calm and Quiet Season"

THE bells that sounded and the fires that blazed on that dark evening of November 17th bespoke England's relief that Catholic Mary, worn out by sickness and embittered by failure, was mercifully dead. Yet "the darksome clouds of discomfort" appeared as black as ever, and Englishmen "went about their matters as men amazed, that wist not where to begin or end". The kingdom had floundered leaderless for over a decade, and in 1558 no one could see an end to discord, bigotry and quarrelling. "The wolves" were once again "coming out of Geneva and other places of Germany" where the Protestant exiles of Mary's reign had failed to learn either humility or compassion and had absorbed the acrid theological air of Calvin's Switzerland. The religious pattern of things to come remained unclear, but on one matter the soldiers of the Lord were adamant; "even the slightest vestiges of Popery" had to be driven from the land and out of men's minds. Under Northumberland, desperate and ambitious men had led the kingdom to the brink of civil war, and five years of Catholic Mary had neither softened Protestant hearts nor taught them tolerance. Now, in the cold days of November, another woman wore the crown: the monstrous regiment of women still held sway. Elizabeth inherited a throne humiliated in war, paralysed by ineptitude and sinking into spiritual and financial bankruptcy. The future remained hidden, but men predicted nothing but further agony in which Protestant zealots would replace Catholic, and Puritan martyrs would make way for papist. Throughout the realm it was agreed that "our remedy must be prayer, for other help I see none".

That the ranks were re-formed, that new life and vitality were transfused into the moribund carcase of state, and that politic and moderate men undertook the leadership of government were marvels which Elizabeth's own age attributed to the special interference of God and the divine genius of their new sovereign. God and destiny loomed large in the affairs of states when France could be catapulted into two generations of religious war by the sudden death of Henry II in 1559, and England, against all prognostications, could be saved from religious fire and political dismemberment by the magic of Elizabeth's personality and the accident that she survived disease and escaped assassination for seventy years.

Elizabeth was her father's daughter: athletic, red-haired, autocratic, inordinately vain and "of stately and majestic deportment". Time and again her subjects saw the reflection of that iron-willed and golden-headed giant in the slender person of their monarch; indeed when Londoners first beheld their Queen, they shouted: "Remember old King Henry VIII." The Spanish ambassador immediately sensed similarity and reported to his master that Elizabeth seemed to be "incomparably more feared than her sister, and gives her orders and has her way as absolutely as her father did". Later in the reign, Sir John Harington noted the same quality and concluded that "she left no doubtings whose daughter she was". Elizabeth spent a lifetime making capital of her sex, indulging her vanity, and excusing the frailty of her womanhood, but on one subject she never wavered: she had "the heart and stomach of a king" and would be master in her own house. To the Earl of Leicester, the first of the youthful heroes of her reign who aspired to her hand, she furiously raged: "God's death! my lord, I will have but one mistress and no master." Of Essex, who sought not her hand but her throne, she coldly commented after his execution: "I warned him that he should not touch my sceptre."

There were many reasons why Elizabeth never married

– political reasons, sexual reasons, historical reasons – but possibly the adroit Scottish ambassador came closest to the truth when he boldly told the Queen: "Ye think that if ye were married, ye would be but Queen of England, and now ye are King and Queen both. Ye may not suffer a commander." The decision to remain single was not easy; both public sentiment and political necessity rebelled at the idea of a queen, childless and alone. John Knox had been unbending in his views on womanhood; they were "weak, frail, impatient, feeble and foolish", and the whole world knew them to be "inconsistent, variable, cruel and void of the spirit of council". The sixteenth century also agreed wholeheartedly with Martin Luther when he said of the weaker sex: "Let them bear children till they die of it; that is what they are for." Though Tudor society was emphatic in its demand that the Queen should marry, it was not nearly so united on the subject of a proper husband. No man in the Elizabethan age would have settled for a secondary position to that of his wife, and, when the spouse was queen, a husband must needs be king. This was the insurmountable obstacle to marriage, and Elizabeth quickly learned from her affair with Robert Dudley that only in lonely virginity could she ever hope to rule her jealous subjects.

Lord Robert Dudley, as the saying went, was descended from "a tribe of traitors". His grandfather had been a ruthless and despised minion of the first Tudor king; his father, the Duke of Northumberland, had tried his hand at kingmaking; his brother, Guildford Dudley, had married Lady Jane Grey; and each had ended his life on the execution block. Elizabeth could not have given her heart to anyone better calculated to arouse the hatred and fear of every faction at court. Young, handsome and lusty, Lord Robert had been a friend of the Princess during those perilous days under Mary, and he had been created Master of the Horse almost the moment the new reign began. It was noted with alarm that the Queen tickled her young gallant's neck as she bestowed the Order of the Garter upon him, and it was rumoured that "her Majesty visits him in his chamber day and night". A more sinister piece of gossip was soon spread abroad by the Spanish ambassador; Elizabeth, he said, was only waiting for Dudley's wife to die in order to marry him, and the handsome husband was scheming to hasten that moment with poison. Suddenly, on September 8th, 1560, idle and malicious tongues had even more startling news to discuss: the lady in question had conveniently fallen down a flight of stairs and broken her neck! The coroner's inquest decided that it was an accident, Dudley's household suspected suicide, and the world whispered murder. The wind of scandal beat and rattled at the foundations of Elizabeth's shaky throne. In Paris, the English ambassador knew not what to answer when Parisians asked: "What religion is this, that a subject shall kill his wife, and the Prince not only bear withal but marry with him?"; Mary Stuart was delighted by her cousin's embarrassment and told everyone that "the Queen of England is going to marry her horse-keeper, who has killed his wife to make room for her;" and in England statesmen feared that Elizabeth would prove John Knox's dreary evaluation of womankind to be correct.

During the winter of 1560, Elizabeth stormed and stamped, threatening marriage one moment and disdaining it the next, but slowly she began to perceive that dangerous as the position of a maiden and barren queen might be, it was nevertheless safer than marriage to a man who would stir every court clique to violence and insist upon all his matrimonial rights and husbandly prerogatives. To Gloriana's "stately stomach" marriage was incompatible with sovereignty, and though Dudley always remained her "Robin", he had to make do with the title of Earl of Leicester.

The miracle of Gloriana's reign, as John Harrington wrote, was the Queen's ability "to gain obedience thus without constraint". In more modern phraseology, it was the extraordinary fashion in which Elizabeth got her own way without a standing army, without a clear and absolute title to her throne, and without even being the right sex. She was coarse, vulgar, bawdy and extroverted. She spat and picked her teeth and swore great "mouth-filling oaths". She boxed her ministers' ears and threw slippers at them in her rage, and her councillors so despaired of her ever making up her mind that they turned to prayer and the hope of miracles as England's only recourse. She could be exasperating, officious, and interfering; she corrected her councillors' reports, criticized their Latin, and drove the long-suffering Walsingham into the explosion: "I would to God her Majesty could be content to refer these things to them that can best judge of them, as other princes do." She believed in astrology, clairvoyance and black magic; her temper was uncertain, her wit cruel and her tongue razor-edged; and as she aged, her nose "somewhat rising in the midst" grew hooked as a harridan's, her sharp eyes turned dim and nearsighted, her red hair faded and gave way to a wig, and her teeth decayed and blackened.

Elizabeth took every advantage of her sex and sovereignty to indulge her wit and sarcasm, and not even the wife of her Archbishop of Canterbury was immune from her barbed and royal tongue. The Queen disliked clerical marriages on principle, and after a visit to Lambeth Palace she thanked Archbishop Parker's wife with the words: "Madam I may not call you; mistress I am ashamed to call you; so I know not what to call you; but yet I thank you." When she discovered herself to be the subject of a sermon on the sins of vanity and costly dress, she turned to her maids-in-waiting and said of the presumptuous ecclesiastic that if he "held more discourse on such matters", she would fit him "for Heaven – but he would walk thither without a staff and leave his mantle behind him". Of the two men who may have known her best during the autumn of her life, one, the devious Robert Cecil, concluded that the Queen was "more than a man, and (in truth) sometimes less than a woman", and the other, the Earl of Essex, raged that she was "cankered, and her mind as crooked as her carcase".

Yet behind the façade of gaudy vulgarity, the shallow egotism, and the feminine caprice, there lay toughness of mind, innate caution, deep humility and unmatched magnetism, for "when she smiled, it was a pure sunshine". Few monarchs ever worked at royalty as hard as did Elizabeth. The ceaseless ceremony, the endless interviews, and the exhausting spectacles in which the Queen was always the central figure were integral parts of her role as sovereign. Her ministers complained of overwork, yet Cecil admitted that it was Gloriana herself who "knew all estates and dispositions of all Princes and parties". Courtiers were dismayed by the boundless energy that not only kept their Queen dancing to tabor and pipe at the age of sixty-six but also allowed her to endure the fatigue of a royal progress throughout the realm. When some of her entourage complained, she bid "the old to stay behind and the young and able to go along with her".

The Queen knew the business of kingship. She had a marvellous memory, kept meticulous memorials, and was never frightened or bored by details, especially shillings and pence. She knew that "the greatest clerks were not the wisest men", and though she could never abide a fool, Elizabeth sensed that even the wisest man was not without his folly. With unerring eye she recognized the worth of a good servant. Her judgment of those who served her was rarely in error even when a winning smile and a well-turned calf obscured her vision. On occasion, Elizabeth "would set the reason of a mean man before the authority of the greatest councillor she had", and she never forgot the basis on which she first selected William Cecil as her Principal Secretary. "This judgment I have of you," she had said to him, "that you will not be corrupted with any manner of gift; and you will be faithful to the State; and without respect of my private will, you will give me that counsel that you think best." In lonely pre-eminence the Queen learned the trade of royalty and in anguish cried out:

> I grieve, and dare not show my discontent!
> I love; and yet am forced to seem to hate!
> I do; yet dare not say, I ever meant!

Elizabeth was nothing if not a realist, never allowing passion to overshadow wisdom and always looking "into things as they are". She coupled mildness with majesty and never hesitated to stoop to conquer. Instinctively she realized that in government the line between good and evil, honesty and corruption, was not always clear, and she warned Henry IV of France, when he judged Paris to be worth a mass and turned Catholic to ensure his throne, that it was "a perilous thing to do ill that good may come of

it!" She knew herself for what she was, a child "of corrupt
seed" and "a most frail substance" living in a "world of
wickedness, where delights be snares". The Queen was the
first to admit that she was no angel for her sins were mani-
fold, and in the quiet of her chapel she even confessed the
possibility that she was 'unworthy of eternal life, if not of
the royal dignity".

Elizabeth could be ridiculous, deceitful and vindictive,
but her humour, humility and self-criticism saved her from
becoming vicious and monstrous. She gave God credit for
pulling her "from the prison to the palace", and she confessed her "ignorance in this my calling" and her "need of
good advice and council". To God she was thankful and to
men she was merciful, for the Queen knew from youthful
experience that all men are fortune's tennis balls and that
in the bloody game of politics, "my lot today, tomorrow
may be thine." Throughout her life, Elizabeth had a sense
of mission, as if God and time were on her side. At her
coronation, she looked about her at the splendour of the
occasion and whispered: "Time has brought me hither."
Delay, procrastination, reconsideration were her greatest
assets, for the Queen was a past master of the art of biding
her time. Early in her reign, Sir Nicholas Throckmorton
warned her to walk warily and allow no party or faction
to wholly understand what she had in mind. Elizabeth
needed no such advice, for she intuitively sensed that
watchfulness, finesse, secrecy and prudence were her surest
political weapons. Presiding over a court filled with quarrelsome, hot-headed children who posed as heroic adults
and were always more willing to pay back "wrongs than
good turns", and living in an age of international hyper-
tension, Elizabeth perceived that in politics problems are
rarely solved; they are merely replaced by other more
pressing crises. Given time, men and nations could be led
into forgetfulness. The dramatic moments of her reign –
the execution of Mary Queen of Scots, the defeat of the
Armada, and the death of Essex – were events which were
thrust upon her by circumstances. Left to herself, Elizabeth invariably chose half-measures and delays in preference to rash solutions and impetuous actions. She was a
thoroughly conservative female, who shied away from new-

fangled ideas in religion, in politics and in science. Legend says that Gloriana did not even take kindly to that most dangerous of mechanical devices, the flush closet, and though she thanked the inventor, she preferred more tried and true methods of sanitation. Without royal support the contraption died out in England and had to be re-invented one hundred and seventy-five years later.

Elizabeth gloried in her nationality; she was, as she boasted, "mere English" and was confident that her subjects were all on her side, which the Spanish ambassador admitted "is indeed true". "She was Queen of the small as well as the great," and if there is a secret to her success it lay, as Sir Christopher Hatton said, in the fact that "the Queen did fish for men's souls, and had so sweet a bait that no one could escape her network". Robert Dudley was her "Sweet Robin" and her "eyes", William Cecil her "Spirit", Hatton her "Mutton" and her "Bellwether", Walsingham her "Moor", and Robert Cecil her "Pygmy". She caught each "poor fish, who little knew what snare was laid" for him.

Gloriana wooed and won her people because she was in tune with the spirit of her generation. If Mary belonged to a dying past, Elizabeth looked forward to a dynamic future. If one sister was consumed by the bright flame of conscience, the other held to the gorgeous and brilliant standards of the Renaissance in which calculation, displaced conviction, virtuosity was praised more highly than beatitude, and beardless boys carved out their kingdoms in the sky and proclaimed to the world that "Bliss was it in that dawn to be alive". No finer tribute to her achievement was ever written than the words scribbled by an Elizabethan schoolboy in his Latin textbook:

> The rose is red, the leaves are green.
> God save Elizabeth, our noble Queen.

Personality may ultimately explain the Elizabethan age, but good luck and some highly astute politics stood behind the steps taken to ensure the succession and restore peace and order to the realm. Elizabeth had one advantage: though a woman, only other women could make claim to her throne. Catherine and Mary, sisters of Lady Jane Grey, were hardly serious contenders, and Mary Queen of Scots, Henry VIII's grandniece by his elder sister, had been omitted from the succession. Moreover, Mary Stuart was the wife of the young Dauphin of France and consequently tied by marriage and sympathy to England's traditional enemy. Though good Catholics loudly denounced Elizabeth as a usurper and a bastard, her subjects accepted her as Henry's lawful daughter and heir, and her brother-in-law, Philip of Spain, defended her rights at Rome against the voice of France which urged the Pope to declare her a heretic with no legal title to her crown. Spain preferred an English queen of somewhat doubtful religious convictions to a devout Catholic monarch controlled by the Valois interests of France. That Elizabeth in part owed the peaceful succession of her throne to Philip II would become within the decade the grand irony of both their lives.

Once acknowledged queen, Elizabeth turned to men of moderation, regardless of their faith, as the prop and stay of her reign. Her council was reduced to a dozen men and purged of its episcopal members, for Elizabeth preferred laymen as her associates in government. In part the secular spirit of her administration was a matter of taste, in part it was the result of failure. As the child of Anne Boleyn, Elizabeth could be nothing except Protestant, but her faith was not the militant and burning Protestantism of the Marian exiles returning from Geneva. Instead, it was that strange spiritual mixture her father had brutally enforced, a muddled and headless Catholicism which placed heavy insistence upon outward obedience and conformity but allowed sufficient doctrinal breadth, so that both Protestant and Catholic could find a place in the spacious confusion of an Anglican edifice. The new Queen desired to make no windows into men's souls and to light no fires to consume their bodies. For Elizabeth, the essence of religion remained mystical and personal. There was, she said, "only one Christ Jesus and one faith: the rest is dispute about trifles". Politically speaking those trifles were highly combustible and dangerous to the state, and Elizabeth sought to persuade the moderates of her father's reign to undertake a second break with Rome and to reintroduce what she regarded as the safest religious solution – Henrician Catholicism. In this she signally failed.

In their salad days such men as Bishops Tunstal of Durham and Nicholas Heath of York, the Marian Lord Chancellor, had accompanied their sovereign into schism, but under Edward VI they had drawn the line at heresy and had accepted deprivation in preference to the Edwardian Prayer Books and Protestant doctrines. They had welcomed the return to Rome under Catholic Mary, and now in 1559 they refused to oblige their new Queen by sanctioning what Elizabeth demanded: the restoration of Catholicism without the pope. The episcopal conservatives had learned through bitter experience the truth of the words: –"Whatever is contrary to the Catholic faith is heresy; whatever is contrary to unity is schism ... It is the same thing, so far as schism is concerned, to do a little or to do all."

Thwarted in her desire to reconstruct the Church of her father, Elizabeth perforce turned for religious support to those of a more Protestant and obliging nature, but she avoided the radical thunder of extremists fresh from Calvinistic Geneva and endorsed the quiet voice of those who had stayed in England and had bent with the papal wind. Her new Archbishop of Canterbury embodied in his person the comfortable compromise of Elizabeth's religious settlement. Matthew Parker was no martyr. He was a loyal, obedient and efficient servant of the crown, more interested in peaceful government than in religious purity. Parker was a scholar and an antiquarian who cultivated academic obscurity. He had, however, known the Queen's mother and had been a chaplain in her house, and for this reason he felt honour bound to serve the daughter. Like his royal mistress, he detested religious extravagance such as was found in Geneva and Scotland, and he prayed long and loud that God might preserve the kingdom "from such a visitation as John Knox has attempted in Scotland; the people to be orderers of things".

In temporal matters as well as spiritual, the Queen chose cautious, professionally trained men, dexterous in the ways of politics. William Cecil was to the State what Matthew Parker was to the Church. The new Principal Secretary had

been a Protestant under Edward, a reluctant but conform-
ing Catholic under Mary, and he was a *politique* under
his new sovereign. The rise of the Cecils is the perfect
sixteenth-century success story. They started out as yeomen, who through good management, good marriages and
good political judgment rose to be country gentlemen and
minor court officials. William Cecil was born in 1520 with
a passion for hard work and an instinct for survival in the
slippery warfare of Tudor politics. He received his political
education under the Dukes of Somerset and Northumberland, but he nimbly escaped the fate of his noble patrons.
Under Mary, Cecil quietly retired into the country, and
on Elizabeth's succession became first her Principal Secretary, then her Master of the Wards, and finally in 1571
her Lord Treasurer. His reward was one of the few noble
titles conferred by Elizabeth, and William Cecil of yeo-
man stock became Baron Burghley of Stamford Burghley.
"Of all men of genius," said the chronicler William Cam-
den, "he was the most a drudge; of all men of business,
the most a genius." As a mixture of drudge and genius, he
suited the needs of his sovereign perfectly, and he became
the artful stage manager to Elizabeth's Regina. Cecil and
Parker were typical of the men who rebuilt England on the
working hypothesis that Catholics were better losers than
Protestants and were more easily controlled, since their
devotion to the Crown was greater than their sense of duty
to the Pope.

Throughout the long, bitter struggle to achieve religious
unity and workable doctrinal compromise, Elizabeth and
her ministers never forgot the Duke of Norfolk's warning
that England would not bear yet another change in religion,
for the kingdom had "been bowed so oft that if it should
be bent again it would break". The utter confusion of four
changes in religion in as many decades was revealed at
Oxford. Under Edward VI, the Italian Protestant theologian, Peter Martyr, had been appointed Canon of Christ
Church. To his new post Martyr brought not only his
learning but his wife, who died in 1552 and was buried in
the cathedral. On Mary's succession, Mistress Martyr's
remains were cast out upon a dunghill in the back garden.
When the Queen died, the canons were in haste to restore

the lady to her tomb, but were filled with indecision by the discovery of the bones of St. Frideswide, the patron saint of Oxford, which had suffered a similar fate under Edward VI. In their uncertainty, the canons wrote to Elizabeth, asking which set of bones should be honoured. There is a legend that she answered with the laconic phrase: "Mix them." Whatever her exact words, an elaborate funeral was arranged and the Catholic Frideswide and the Protestant Martyr were duly buried together. In honour of the occasion, one of the canons, with a quiet smile and a fine sense of irony, caught the spirit of Elizabeth's solution to the religious troubles of her age when he wrote:

> Papists and Protestants should now
>   In peace abide,
> As here religion true and false
>   Lie side by side.

During the spring of 1559 the Elizabethan settlement was legislated in the hope that papists and Protestants would "in peace abide". It restored the royal supremacy but softened the wording by styling the Queen "Supreme Governor", not "Head" of the Church of England. The Protestant Prayer Book of 1552 was reintroduced in slightly modified form, and obscured by the addition of language aimed at confusing the exact nature of the mass. A new Act of Uniformity was passed cutting out the tongue of discord and re-establishing the quiet of right thinking, and four years later in 1563, the final pronouncement on what an Englishman should believe was set forth by Convocation in the Thirty-Nine Articles. The old Church came to heel without a fight; the Marian bishops quietly resigned their sees; and their seats on the episcopal bench were filled with men of Protestant mettle and pragmatic flexibility. Even the militant Protestants, who persisted in regarding Elizabeth's Church as the sanctuary of "dumb dogs, unskilful sacrificing priests, destroying drones, or rather caterpillars of the Word", were silenced for the time by a Queen determined to be master in her own house.

The Elizabethan religious settlement and the ceaseless labours on the part of the Queen and her servants were aimed at a single purpose: a commonwealth composed of balanced and harmonious elements in which all men would know their place and no man would hanker after what was not rightly his. Every century and every generation has its own preconceptions and habits of thought. The twentieth century talks noisily of the equality of all men but half a century ago reference to the equality of races was rarely heard and four centuries before that, in Tudor England, the equality of man, except as a spiritual entity in the eyes of God, would have been regarded as a dangerous and preposterous supposition. The medieval concept of degree and order within the "Great Chain of Being", commencing with God and working down through the celestial hierarchy from angels and saints to men, beasts and vegetables, was the normal mental picture of God's divine structure. The universe was authoritarian, hierarchical and organic, every element playing a prescribed role and contributing to the totality of God's scheme of things. Man's society was both a part and a mirror of this grand design, and poet and Queen, statesman and courtier were at one in their view of the society recorded by Shakespeare when he wrote:

> Take but degree away, untune that string,
> And, hark! what discord follows . . .

Nothing stirred the sixteenth century so deeply as the thought of chaos and mutability, if only because the sight of disorder was everywhere present and the means of suppressing treason were so pathetically inadequate. The benefits of order, degree and balance were trumpeted from every pulpit, written into every statute and dramatized by every playwright. The favourite picture of dramatists and preachers was "the sweetness of unity, the fatness and substance of religion, the wine of obedience", and the assurance that those who rebel "against the prince get unto themselves damnation". Humility among great and small was the chief virtue of all ranks, and subjects were expected to hearken to the advice: "We should not look at what we cannot reach, nor long for what we should not have. Things above us are not for us."

The Tudor State was constantly compared to the human body in which the prince was the head that guarded the body politic from anarchy; the ministers of God were "the eyes to watch and not to wink or sleep"; the judges were the ears to hear complaints; the nobility were "the shoulders and arms to bear the burden of the commonwealth, to hold up the head, and defend the body with might and force"; and men of the lower orders were "set as inferior parts painfully to travail" for the support of those worthier than themselves. The sixteenth-century gentleman, whether he lived in Madrid, Paris or London, had a small opinion of the many-headed mob, and one and all agreed that, except for the natural leaders of society, man was "wild, without judgment, and not of sufficient experience to govern himself". This Elizabethan concept of an ordained and paternalistic commonwealth was enshrined in the Statute of Apprentices of 1563. The Act postulated the obligation of all men to toil as a social and moral duty. It assumed the existence of degree and order, and it arrayed the major occupations of the kingdom in rank of utility, moving downwards from agriculture to foreign trade. The statute tacitly presumed that town and country, court and shire were separate but interdependent parts of the total commonwealth. The structure of society was fixed and static, permitting neither a fluid labour force nor any form of social mobility, and it accepted the claims of blood, education and land as justifications for both social and political inequality in this world.

The states of Europe were everywhere as authoritarian and totalitarian as the instruments of coercion would allow. Fines were levied in England for truancy from church on Sundays; prices, wages and working conditions were regulated; beggars were whipped home to their parishes; and Elizabethans were ordered to wear hats in order to help the felt business, and eat fish on Wednesdays, Fridays and Saturdays to support the fishing industry. Spaniards were forbidden the use of all precious metal ornaments upon their clothes, and when such sumptuary legislation was ignored by the ladies of the court, Philip II tried to shame them into compliance by giving the whores of the streets the sole right to bedeck themselves in silver and silks. In

Spain, ruffs were limited to two pleats of not more than three inches in width, which could only be cut from white linen. The fine for disobedience rose from twenty thousand maravedis for the first offence to eighty thousand and a year's banishment for the third. The sixteenth-century traveller was as harassed by the officiousness of bureaucrats and the actions of government officials as any twentieth-century tourist. No one was allowed to leave England without licence; passports were issued to all persons entering or leaving the kingdom; and strict currency regulations were enforced. Travellers "upon pain of confiscation" could take no more than twenty pounds out of the country, and one visitor reported that each member of his party was obliged to give his name, the reason for his visit to England, and the place to which he was going. Moreover their valises and trunks were opened and "most diligently examined for the sake of discovering English money".

The aim of most social legislation of the century was not the welfare state, since few Elizabethans thought in terms of human well-being. The goal of society remained the maintenance of a realm fit for Christians in need of salvation and not a social-service state populated with citizens in quest of material security. The ills of society rested in man and original sin. As the tree was to be known by its fruits, so the criminal was to be known by his crimes, the glutton by his avarice, the slothful man by his poverty, the alcoholic by his drunkenness, and the traitor by his treason, for in each case the source of evil rested in man himself. What induced Elizabeth, as "the godly prince", and the aristocracy, as the natural leaders of society, to create an authoritarian state in which society endeavoured to protect the individual from his predatory neighbours was the fear of social revolution. As Sir Walter Raleigh said, the gentry were the garrisons of good order throughout the realm, and good order rested on full bellies, cheap food, steady employment, an inspected and regulated society, and the ceaseless vigil of those born and educated to rule.

At the apex of society stood the Queen, "the life, the head, and the authority of all things that be done in the realm of England". Sixteenth-century monarchy was still personal, and as the head was destined to rule the body, so the sovereign governed the state. Elizabeth was "the well-spring of all that was good and evil", the fountain of justice, the symbol of national unity, and the ultimate source of the fruits and treasures of political life. Gloriana was God's anointed lieutenant on earth, and though the Queen rarely bothered to mention the fact, no one, least of all Elizabeth, doubted that she was a god on earth. Elizabeth was addressed on bended knee; like her father she was referred to by the weighty title of Your Majesty and not by the older medieval term of Your Grace; and wherever Gloriana was in residence there was the vital centre of government and the source of all political authority. To the Queen's court came not only the representatives of foreign states and the suitors for her hand, but also all who sought wealth, power and renown. Like pale satellites to Gloriana's sun, statesmen and favourites, scamps and saints, heroes and bounders, financiers and vendors, patron-seekers and parasites, entertainers and educators were all pulled into the royal orbit, where they glittered in the reflected light of the Queen's favour.

To be banished from court was to be exiled into outer darkness, for a word spoken by the Queen was worth the riches of the Indies and a favour bestowed by Her Majesty was a greater honour than the most ancient title within the land. The favourite or minister, who by flattery, masculinity, hard work or ability controlled the approach to the throne, in effect ruled the kingdom. Elizabethan politics remained personal and intimate and consisted primarily in getting oneself and one's protégé as close to the Queen as possible. The prolonged duel between the Essex and Cecil factions during the last years of Elizabeth's reign was fought over the placement of friends and followers in positions at court where they could influence the Queen. The essential axiom of Tudor politics was not merely "out of sight, out of mind", but "out of sight, in evil mind". In the end Essex was destroyed when he was manoeuvred into accepting a position away from the court, and he wrote bitterly from Ireland to the Council in London that he could defend himself "on the breast, but not on the back" from the dagger thrusts of malicious gossip. Elizabeth's household may have been an academy of Renaissance

learning, a rich and ceremonial setting for royalty and the
political heart of the kingdom, but falsehood and greed,
callousness and spitefulness were everywhere in evidence,
and moralists and political failures agreed with Anthony
Munday's woodman, who found that:

> ... falsehoods sat in fairest looks
> And friend to friend was coy;
> Court favour fill'd but empty books
> And there I found no joy.

The court was peripatetic, elaborate and unhygienic. It
included everybody from the children of the squillery and
the grooms of the stool to the Lord Chamberlain and the
great dignitaries of the household, possibly a thousand persons in all. The most coveted positions, and consequently
the most inaccessible, were those which permitted entrée
to the Queen's chamber. Like any private household, the
court was divided along traditional lines – above-stairs and
below-stairs. The divisions corresponded roughly to the
master-servant relationship of any baronial residence. In
the case of the Queen's establishment, however, the royal
household was a public institution as well as a private
home, and the divisions were not so fixed. At one time,
Elizabeth's ancestors had kept their treasury in a chest
under their beds, like any private individual who regarded
his bed-chamber as the safest room in his house, and they
had used their servants to relieve them of their public
duties. Consequently, the domestics of the household – the
chamberlain, the steward, the butler, the marshal, the
treasurer – became state dignitaries, holding the title of
Lord Chamberlain, Lord Steward and Lord Treasurer.

Below-stairs was the preserve of the Lord Steward who
presided over a host of court servants, stretching in social
and governmental importance from the Lord Treasurer,
the Keeper of the Queen's Jewels, and the Clerks of the
Green Cloth, to the master- and apprentice-cooks and
the grooms of the stable. Above-stairs was the domain of the
Lord Chamberlain. It was a far smaller organization than
the domestic staff of the Lord Steward and was the world
of the politically élite, numbering no more than one hun-

dred and seventy-five privileged men and a dozen women. The Lord Chamberlain attended upon the Queen's person; he was responsible for the operation of her privy chamber and the organization of the ceremony that surrounded her every waking moment and which lent dignity and glamour to her life; and he controlled the appointment of those influential and ardently desired offices about the Queen – the well-born grooms and yeomen of her chamber and her ladies-in-waiting. Of all officials at court the Lord Chamberlain was politically the most important, for his were the juiciest plums of patronage.

Outside the court and the immediate entourage of the Queen, but linked closely to the royal household by overlapping personnel, was the slender structure of government by which the sovereign made her will known and through which she ruled. Tudor bureaucracy was intimate, hardworking and underpaid, and by modern standards incredibly small and understaffed. The mainspring of government in England as well as in France, Spain and elsewhere in Europe, was the council surrounding the monarch, which, wrote James I, "does watch for men when I sleep and in my absence are so careful to snip and trim the house against my return." Under Elizabeth the Privy Council was composed of twelve to fifteen ministers, who managed the realm "as if it had been the household and estate of a nobleman under a strict and prying steward". The Council handled foreign affairs, drafted official communiqués, issued proclamations that had the authority of law, and scrutinized and regulated every facet of Tudor life. Country officials such as justices of the peace, chief constables, sheriffs and lord lieutenants were appointed by the Council in the Queen's name. The price of wheat, the level of wages, the drainage of rivers, the apprehension of criminals, the supervision of the shire militia, the construction of bridges, the petitions of soldiers and sailors grown old and infirm in the Queen's service, all these and more were the daily routine of a group of men who were Elizabeth's maids of all work.

Beneath the Council were the major divisions of state: the secretariat which numbered no more than fifteen; the judicial machinery staffed possibly by fifty persons; the regional administrative organs, such as the Duchy of Lancaster with its own petty treasury and some forty officials, the Earldom of Chester, the Council of the North, and the government of Wales, in all amounting to no more than one hundred and forty-five officials; and the largest office, the treasury, with its cadre of two hundred customs officials and some sixty-five clerks of the exchequer at Westminster. Elizabeth ruled her kingdom with a bureaucracy of scarcely five hundred salaried persons, but she also had at her command an unsung and unpaid regiment of amateur officials who brought the paternalism of Tudor government directly to the shires. These were the fifteen hundred justices of the peace. Never, said Sir Thomas Smith, was there "in any commonwealth devised a more wise, a more dulce and gentle, a more certain way to rule the people". Drawn from men of birth and substance living in the counties, the justices of the peace united the two essentials of good government – knowledge of the law and an understanding of local conditions. Justices were often members of Parliament, and all of them had friends and relations among the luminaries of the court and the great nobles of the realm. They were the eyes, ears and hands of the Privy Council, informing the government of local crises, fixing wages, watching over the parish poor, supervising weights and measures, maintaining the peace, collecting parliamentary taxes and inspecting the county levies. There was nothing like them anywhere else in Europe, where kings were forced to rule through paid servants of the Crown.

If the Queen, as the heart and head of the state, was supposed to rule by divine right, the "better part" of society, the nobility and the gentry were designed by God to help her, for they were the natural leaders of society. The structure of the state was narrow and exclusive at its apex. In solitary and wealthy grandeur stood the sixty or so peers of the realm, who were worth anywhere from twenty thousand to a hundred thousand pounds and rivalled even the Queen in the lavishness of their hospitality and the magnificence of their semi-feudal households. Although the Tudor aristocrat vigorously maintained his privileged and almost divine position in society, he differed from his colleague in France in one essential quality: in England the medieval magnate had become the domesticated aristocrat. The treasured feudal tradition of baronial feuding and independence lingered on in the northern shires, but the Tudor Crown never tolerated such princely houses as the Guises and Bourbons, whose wealth and political influence allowed them to act as laws unto themselves. Below the great peers, but closely related by blood and interest, were the landed country gentlemen and their mercantile and professional cousins in trade, in law and in the Church. They numbered no more than three or four thousand persons, and most of them possessed upwards of fifty pounds a year in an age that accounted two pounds ten shillings to be a marginal but adequate income. These were the real governors of the kingdom, a select, intimate and intermarried group from whom the Queen appointed her paid and unpaid servants and to whom she offered the richest prizes of office. Elizabeth may have given unity and leadership to the kingdom, but the Crown existed only in federation with the local, regional and class interests of these natural leaders of society.

The highest authority of the realm was not the solitary voice of a wilful and capricious sovereign but the authority of that organ which spoke for all interests within the commonwealth – King in Parliament. When Elizabeth sat in the midst of her Lords and Commons and when legislation was enacted by the whole Parliament, then the kingdom spoke *ex cathedra*. The voice of the realm might in fact be that of the monarch, but constitutionally it was assumed that it was the sound of all elements singing but a single song. Parliament was the "highest and most absolute power of the realm" because "every Englishman is intended to be there present ... from the prince ... to the lowest person in England". No one knew better than Elizabeth how to play upon the heartstrings of her loyal Commons or how to produce the melody of perfect political accord. Within the mystical union of Lords, Commons and Crown, the strong voice of the Queen and her Council set the pitch and pace of government. The proper role of Parliament, especially that of the lower house, was to beseech and petition, not to command or initiate. It was true that

members belonged to the "better part" of society and were
expected to give leadership to the vulgar multitude in town
and shire, but policy belonged to the head, the prince and
the Privy Council. Justices of the peace, overseers of the
poor, sheriffs and even lords lieutenant of the county were
merely vessels through which authority was translated into local administration. When Elizabeth firmly informed a
rebellious House of Commons, which was demanding the
death sentence for Mary Queen of Scots, that "if I should
say unto you that I mean to grant your petition, I should
then tell you more than is fit for you to know", she was
stating her regal conviction that Commoners were no more
than humble petitioners.

The Queen did not know the phrase but she intuitively
sensed that political control of Parliament was dependent
upon a tight hold of the purse-strings. During the first
years of the reign, Elizabeth was parsimonious to an extreme, hoarding her regular (non-parliamentary) income
of a quarter of a million pounds a year, cutting her expenses by half, liquidating her sister's debt, building up a
slight surplus and establishing such a solid credit in Europe
that she was able to borrow at eight per cent while Philip
of Spain was charged as much as eighteen per cent. In
Elizabeth's estimation it was important that the Crown
should never have to come to the Commons, hat in hand,
to beg for money. Unfortunately, war made the Queen
insolvent, and potential bankruptcy made her dependent
upon Parliament. She did everything to avoid frequent
sessions and requests for money, and she mortgaged the
Stuart future by selling her capital in order to avoid excessive taxation. In a single year, she divested the Crown
of one hundred and twenty thousand pounds' worth of
land in order to finance her costly Irish war. In the end
the weight of financial reality proved overpowering; Henry
VII had been able to manage with an average yearly parliamentary grant of eleven thousand five hundred pounds;
his son's dependence rose to thirty thousand pounds; while
Elizabeth's reached fifty thousand pounds a year. When
Sir Thomas Smith wrote that what a commonwealth desired most was "peace, liberty, quietness, little taking of
their money, few parliaments", he unconsciously linked

two crucial elements – taxation and representation. There could be neither few nor obedient parliaments so long as there was much taking of money.

Towards the close of her long reign, a new voice was being whispered in parliamentary committees, in the Commons' chamber and in country mansions. Slowly, hesitantly and inarticulately, the landed classes, speaking through the House of Commons and using the weapons of finance to add weight to their demand, were urging a partnership in state in which Crown and Parliament would sing duet. So long as the Queen and her loyal Commons agreed on their concept of a divinely inspired and carefully regulated society and on what was best for the common sort, harmony prevailed. The moment, however, that Crown and Parliament parted company in their views, the harsh sounds of constitutional discord were heard with increasing frequency until they reached a climax in the civil war of 1642.

The structure and pattern of Elizabethan government were deceptively simple. The ordered ranks, that tidy hierarchy of Queen, Privy Council, regional governments, treasury, law courts, Parliament and local administration, concealed a vital aspect of Tudor government: its sensitivity to the shifting nuances of public sentiment. The greatness of Elizabeth's accomplishment lay in the sixth sense that led her to demand of her subjects only what they wished to give, in the talent of bestowing upon the socially prominent elements of society the fruits of office while depriving them of the power of government, and in the artistry by which she enveloped all functions of state in a magic veil of pomp and circumstance in which "mere English" Elizabeth Tudor was elevated to a Goddess-Queen and her beardless boys at court became Olympian heroes in worshipful attendance.

All Elizabethans knew that "in pompous circumstance a secret of government doth much consist". Government was always on display and the imagination of the multitude was captivated by gorgeous dress, robes of state, gold brocade, and majestic processions. The symbols of state and authority were human and anthropomorphic, and as heroism was unimaginable without a flesh-and-blood hero, so authority was dull and unimpressive without the clash of cannon, the glitter of gold and the sound of horses' hoofs. The Goddess-Queen had to be decked in silver bodice, satin gown and silken farthingale, she had to live in gorgeous establishments and be surrounded by the trappings of endless wealth, for with ceremony put by, she was but another woman. Richmond Palace was "a splendid and magnificent house"; Hampton Court was "a noble and uniform pile" and all the walls shone "with gold and silver"; Whitehall, that most ancient of all royal establishments, possessed two thousand rooms; and Nonsuch, so called because there was none like it, was so adorned with precious metals that Elizabeth thought it afire when she saw it sparkling in the light of the setting sun.

If the fairyland quality surrounding kings was intended to captivate the eye, royal generosity was designed to win men's hearts and loyalty. Robert Cecil spoke from a lifetime of experience when he said that "bounty is an essential virtue of the king". The key to Tudor politics rested upon the control of this generosity, for influence and patronage made the political world go round. Although the stakes were not as high as they had been under Elizabeth's father, when subjects held it to be a grisly mark of a gentleman to have at least one relative hanged and quartered for treason, political morality under the Queen remained almost as predatory and just as susceptible to corruption as in the past. Lord Burghley planted a spy on Drake's ship in order to sabotage his venture; Mr. Secretary Walsingham had his paid eyes to tap the Queen's correspondence with her Lord Treasurer; and all men expected tips to ensure prompt service.

No Elizabethan official ever received an adequate salary; the Lord Keeper of the Great Seal earned a stipend of nine hundred and nineteen pounds a year; the Lord Admiral two hundred pounds, and the Principal Secretary one hundred pounds, but in 1601 all three posts were valued at approximately three thousand pounds per annum. Fees, tips, gratuities, and gifts for promoting a friend, urging a favour, giving information, and above all for tapping and directing the bounty of the Queen made up the difference between official salary and actual income. They were held as the legitimate perquisites of office in an age which regarded governmental posts as both public trusts and private sinecures.

At the sovereign's disposal were pensions, annuities, leases, monopolies, titles, and honours, or about twelve hundred places ranging in importance and profit from the great dignitaries of state, through the exclusive gentlemen pensioners of the court, down to the gunners of the Tower and the stewards and bailiffs of the crown lands. Between the sovereign and this swarm of suitors, anxious to partake of royal bounty, there existed an inner core of counsellors and favourites, who attracted to themselves the admiration and the wealth of lesser men desirous of protection or advancement in society. When old Lord Burghley died, a forsaken patron-seeker wrote to his son, Robert Cecil, saying that it was his desire "to be protected ... under the shadow of your wings", which he rightly judged to be as extensive as his father's. As the medieval baron had held men loyal to him by ties of lordship, so the sixteenth-century aristocrat based his political power upon the exercise of influence and built up personal followings held together by ties of patronage. "My good Lord," wrote one Elizabethan wise to the realities of political life, "advancement in all worlds be obtained by mediation and remembrance of noble friends." Remembrance was always made easier by the presentation of a well-timed gift. The amount was expected to be commensurate with the favour demanded, and the Countess of Warwick, when she was offered a hundred pounds to influence the Queen in a law case in Chancery, judged the amount to be too small. The essence of Elizabethan politics was clearly perceived by Lord Burghley in the simple formula for success which he offered his son. "Be sure," he said, "to keep some great man thy friend but trouble him not for trifles."

That a political system, based on patronage, gratuities, influence, factionalism, ceremony and queen-worship, did not deteriorate into simple jobbery, fawning corruption and senseless ritualism was one of the marvels of the Elizabethan age. Elsewhere in Europe, and particularly in France, personal hatreds, party factions and human avarice palsied the hand of royal government, but in England Gloriana succeeded in ruling by factions and parties, which she herself "made, upheld, and weakened, as her own great judgment advised". On the continent, men placed loyalty to God, to overlord and to estate higher than their duty to the sovereign, but during the "calm and quiet season" of Elizabeth's reign, subjects agreed with Lord Burghley when he said that he had "no affection to be of a party, but for the Queen's Majesty". The ruling classes of England were tied to Elizabeth by links of air which were yet as strong as iron, for the Queen made appeal to their self-interest and their love, and when she accounted it "the glory of my crown that I have reigned with your loves", she spoke no more than the truth.

Elizabethan England was exposed to all the disrupting forces of the century, feudal privileges, Renaissance pride, religious idealism and commercial cupidity; but instead of destroying the kingdom they gave new vitality and dynamism to the medieval ideal of balance, order and degree. In Spain respect for class descended to pride in caste, the harmonious commonwealth stiffened into rigid bureaucracy ruled by a pettifogging and pedantic monarch, and tranquillity and concord deteriorated into an orthodoxy of thought so rigid that Spaniards preferred to be illiterate rather than risk the charge of heresy. In France another woman of the age, Catherine de Medici, endeavoured to do for her adopted land what Elizabeth had done for England, to preserve "the reverence wherewith a king is girt about from God" and to cast the mantle of her feminism over all factions. But across the channel the Queen-Regent's magic was no more than clever legerdemain, her aspirations mere family and dynastic aggrandizement, her policy subtle intrigue; and though her methods were no more devious than Elizabeth's, the results were discord, bloodshed and monstrous civil war.

Five

Rage in Heaven

THE years preceding the birth of Elizabeth had been heavy with foreboding. In 1531 the heavens broke out into astronomic display, and "an ominous comet", bright with fire and with a giant yellow tail, lit up the western sky. The same year two flying standards were seen moving across the sky, and in Germany it was reliably reported that the air was filled with soldiers, headed God knew where but certainly sent to do the Lord's bidding. Everywhere there were signs of frantic battle, mysterious claps of thunder, fire-balls, strange and terrifying lights, and flaming crosses in the sky. Rage in heaven had commenced, and all the omens pointed to great and terrible events on earth. God and Satan were once again in mortal conflict, and, as never before, men's souls stood in jeopardy. On both sides the ranks were closing, and men were called upon to stand up and be counted, to declare themselves, and to give their lives in defence of the truth.

Two events of those years passed without notice, obscured by all the divine and atmospheric commotion. In 1531 three college students at the University of Paris – Pierre Le Fèvre, Francis Xavier, and Ignatius Loyola – tacked a picture of Jesus on the door of the room they shared, and in contempt other students dubbed the inmates the "Societas Jesu". Such was the quiet beginning of those militant shock-troops of the Church, the Jesuits. Two years later another scholar at the University made similar history: John Calvin suddenly, inexplicably but overwhelmingly knew himself to have become the chosen vessel of the Lord. A great light broke upon him and he began to realize "in what a quagmire of errors" he had wallowed and with "what filth and shame" he had covered himself.

Two students – Calvin and Loyola – both men of iron will and inflexible conviction, began the reordering of the religious ranks, the recasting of Christendom into two armed and militant Churches, and the reforging of the metal of which martyrs and heroes are made. The spiritual drive and religious energy marshalled by the two leaders represented a far greater break with the past than had the New Learning of Erasmus or the new religion of Martin Luther, for in both the Protestant and the Catholic camps the medieval atmosphere continued to predominate until well into the 1530s. Luther was a medieval man, closer to Wycliffe and Huss than to John Calvin or John Knox. The German monk's words brought fear to his enemies, his voice struck down the walls of Satan, and his faith moved mountains, but his appeal was to the heart, not the mind. He began as an academic reformer of abuses; and even when he was driven into open revolution, he was unhappy about the logical consequences of his protest, the abandonment of ancient ceremonies simply because they had been misused by evil men. Always, if foolishly, the hope of religious reconciliation remained, the expectation that Christian men of good faith could somehow settle their differences and live in brotherhood and peace. Even in open defiance, Luther continued to be a cherubic-faced monk with more of the publican than the fanatic about him. He hurled ink-pots at the devil in an understandable fashion, and, for all his reasoned logic about *The Bondage of the Will*, he wondered whether it was "not against reason that all mankind should be subject to toil, sickness and death just because one man took a bite out of an apple". If Luther's spiritual despair and shocked conscience at the sight of clerical corruption drove him into revolt, the medieval background from which he emerged – his German peasant blood, his monastic experiences, and his scholastic education – prevented him from crossing the threshold into the modern world. It remained for the second generation, for John Calvin, to dress the Reformation in modern garb and fit out Lutheranism in the armour of military discipline and doctrinal orthodoxy.

The first generation of the Catholic Counter-Reformation experienced the same change. The humanistic Christianity of Erasmus at Basle and the mysticism of Lefèvre d'Étaples in France represented the two last flowerings of the medieval world, a unique mixture of medieval learning, laughter and piety. Early sixteenth-century Catholic reform within the Church was tolerant, humane and individualistic. It was filled with men who, in their innocence, expected that good will, good scholarship and good fellowship would free the Church of corruption, heal the wound of schism, and cure the heart of error. In the end, however, the old Church died in the fury of the Protestant heresy. The long war of words fought in council and conclave led inevitably to blows and bloodshed. In defeat and humiliation the Catholic Church found new strength and new spiritual resources with which to roll back the armies of the devil, but the means were those of a new generation, the tempered and flexible will of Ignatius Loyola and his Society of Jesus, and not the soft compromise and idle words of humanistic scholars and mystics.

Of the two men who divided the Christian medieval world into warring camps, Calvin began as a French scholar and lawyer of *petit bourgeois* extraction who eventually overcame pathological shyness and grinding ill health to do the Lord's bidding, and Loyola was an untutored Spanish soldier and court reprobate of impoverished noble descent who willed himself to become a saint. The Frenchman was a theologian who had the strength to live by the terrifying conclusions of his own logic, the Spaniard was a sixteenth-century psychiatrist and catcher of men's souls who by the sheer strength of his will turned imagination into reality; but both men fought to conquer the world of the spirit and to fashion a disciplined and ordered army dedicated to God's service. Calvin and Loyola stood at opposite poles and in irreconcilable conflict, yet the French lawyer-theologian would not permit a stone to mark his grave (it was too inconsequential), and the Spanish soldier-saint would not sit for his portrait

(there was never time). Never were two men so different
in their background and approach but so similar in their
purpose and achievement. Each became the spiritual model
towards which his devoted followers aspired and each
branded his movement with the force of his own personality. By 1558 when Elizabeth succeeded to the throne,
Protestantism was no longer Lutheran and German but
Calvinistic and international; Catholicism was no longer
humanistic and Roman but militant and Jesuitical.

John Calvin was born on July 10th, 1509 to Gérald
Cauvin, the registrar of the town of Noyon in France.
For two generations the community had been divided into
furiously hostile camps over the bones of St. Eloy. Who
possessed the authentic remains and who the fake? The
canons of the Cathedral or the monks of the Abbey? Later
in life, Calvin commented on the confusion and profusion
of relics throughout France, and he calculated that the
wood guaranteed to come from the cross amounted to "a
good ship-load", the nails of the cross numbered fourteen,
while the worshippers of sacred relics ran "the risk of
reverencing the bones of some thief or robber, or of an ass,
a dog, or a horse".

Calvin was brought up to be a cleric. He was made a
chaplain of the Cathedral of Noyon at the age of eleven; at
fourteen he was sent as a scholar to the University of Paris,
where he studied the great schoolmen of the medieval past
– Aquinas, Bonaventure, Scotus and Gerson. Shy, intro-
spective and hypersensitive to the feelings of others, the
university scholar was intellectually precocious, morally
priggish, and so unyielding in his opposition to vice and
weakness that legend records that he was called "the ac-
cusative case" for his didactic and argumentative spirit.
At Paris, Calvin was swept up by the warm breath of
Renaissance humanism. His first published work of 1532
was a gloss upon Seneca's *De Clementia*. It was written in
impeccable Latin, bristled with classical learning and
exuded high ethical principles. At his father's sudden demand in 1528, Calvin added training in the law to classical
learning and medieval scholarship, and by 1533 the vessel
of his education was complete and ready to receive the
spirit of God. He had made himself into a jurist, theologian,

dialectician, and Latinist. Yet for all his intellectual feats he remained deeply dissatisfied, and found that "the more closely I examined myself the more was my conscience tormented by sharp stings so that there were no solace or comfort left to me save that of deluding myself by oblivion."

Oblivion was not John Calvin's fate, for in 1533 the Lord spoke. His servant was "immediately inflamed with so intense a desire to progress" that he renounced his ecclesiastical offices and spoke out against the evils of the Church of his birth. He fled to Basle and in 1535 commenced that true, perfect and final pronouncement on God's Word – *The Institutes of the Christian Religion*. First published in abbreviated form in 1536, *The Institutes* was brief by theological standards, only five hundred and sixteen pages, and within nine months every copy had been sold to men desperate to be told the truth. Calvin did for Protestant knowledge what Thomas Aquinas had done for medieval, and he did for his Church what the Council of Trent would shortly do for sixteenth-century Catholicism. He summarized and systematized the creed and disciplined and ordered the ranks of the true believers, so that the truth could be defended against the spawn of new heresies from within the Protestant faith as well as against the papal anti-Christ and the Romanish court of darkness. *The Institutes* was the quintessence of Protestant thought as formulated by Luther, Zwingli, Erasmus and Melanchthon. It was a faultlessly rational and convincing statement of the ultimate logic of the Protestant Reformation, which Jonathan Edwards called "a delightful doctrine, exceeding bright, pleasant and sweet".

The central tenet around which all others revolved was the existence of an inscrutable God who was bound neither by compassion nor by the laws of science but was "the Arbiter and Governor of all things", a sovereign and capricious force who "by His own power, executes what He has decreed". The inescapable corollaries to such a thesis were the doctrines of predestination and election. For Calvin it was impossible for a leaf to fall or a decision to be formed without the expressed command of the deity, and the gates of the kingdom of heaven were open only to those chosen

few who were the elect of God. Man, according to the
Calvinistic creed, was the product of sin and disobedience,
and in justice God found it unworthy of His omnipotence
to save any man, yet He selected for salvation certain men,
irrespective of their deserts, in order to reveal to the world
the full capriciousness and total freedom of His authority.
Calvin's God could not even be bound by His own sense
of justice. That Adam disobeyed God and brought upon
posterity the wrath of heaven by divine command, and
that the mouth that tasted of the apple was moved by
God's will, were historic facts which might seem unjust to
man's faulty reason, but in the divine scheme of things
they were in no way illogical, for God was "above logic;
indeed, God made logic just as He made the apple".

The Institutes was a call to arms, to labour, to do battle,
to die, and above all to witness God's glory and spread His
Word abroad. To Calvin, the whole world was "the theatre
of God's glory". The divine doctrine could never be victorious without commotion and suffering, for only Satan's
creed was ever accepted by all without contention. By
definition, Calvinists were poor security risks because no
earthly authority could claim their obedience. They were
the soldiers of the Lord, and true believers, said John Knox,
could never be expected to "frame their religion according
to the appetite of their princes". In Calvinism, Protestant
minorities found the strength to resist and the justification
to disobey established authority. Puritans in England, Pres-
byterians in Scotland and Huguenots in France were the
chosen instruments of sublime grace, and in abandonnig
themselves to the majesty of God's will, they felt themselves to be the equals of any earthly king. The structured
and hallowed hierarchy of social and political authority, so
dear to the hearts of the custodians of the well-ordered
commonwealth, was meaningless to men who hearkened
to the voice of inner conscience. The Word of God spoke
in their hearts and it was of greater import than the most
weighty instructions of pope, magistrate or king. Calvin
never argued the right of revolution, but the spirit of disobedience was implicit in his statement that "where the
glory of God is not made the end of the government, it
is not a legitimate sovereignty, but a usurpation". Peter

Wentworth summed up the Puritan position in England and elsewhere in Europe when, during a debate in Parliament, he presumptuously but positively told Archbishop Parker and the other lord bishops: "We will pass nothing before we understand what it is; for that were but to make you popes."

The vision of heaven on earth led John Calvin to make one of the grand experiments of all times – the founding of that "most perfect school of Christ that ever was on earth since the days of the apostles", the theocratic community of Geneva in Switzerland. In July 1536 he chanced to visit Geneva, where an impetuous, if irritating member of the elect, William Farel, was waging a furious battle against the forces of popery. Farel was as inflammatory as his brilliant red hair. Earlier in his tempestuous career, he had stood up while mass was being celebrated, walked up to the surprised priest, knocked the consecrated bread from his hand, and calmly announced to the incredulous audience that God was above in heaven and not in a piece of ritualistic trickery on earth. Just before Calvin arrived in Geneva, Farel had succeeded in getting the city council to proclaim its political independence from the House of Savoy and its spiritual liberation from Rome, and to vote "to live henceforth according to the Law of the Gospel and the Word of God, and to abolish all papal abuses". Such an ardent reformer could spearhead revolution but he could neither discipline himself nor his followers; he needed the iron will and organizational talents of Calvin to complete the transformation of the city of Geneva into the kingdom of God.

To the ordinary ordeal of living, Farel and Calvin added the ordeal of saintliness. Both men were victims of a beatific vision in which all God's errant peoples were arrayed in tidy and disciplined ranks within the fold. "It is certain," proclaimed Calvin, "that a Church cannot be called well ordered and governed," unless all members "submit themselves wholeheartedly to the Word of God in complete obedience." That the populace of Geneva contained many obstinate folk who preferred sinfulness to saintliness and sloth to serenity was a challenge which Calvin was ready to accept by instituting a government of God's elect who had a stake in paradise as well as in society.

In January 1537 the "perfect school of Christ" was out-
lined in a series of articles establishing a system of Church-
State government which, from the start, smacked more of
the schoolhouse than the house of God. Church and State
were fused into a theocracy in which the two swords of
Christ – the civil and the ecclesiastical – lived together in
perfect harmony: the Council of Two Hundred ruling the
city and the "Venerable Company" of clergymen inspecting civil morality and governing the Church. The Council
retained the power to legislate and punish, but the "Vener-
al Company" was expected to scrutinize the life of every
citizen and report any moral lapses, and to inspire the
secular government to acts of devotion and godly legislation. Discipline and her handmaid, inspection, were the
hall-marks of the new Geneva, for if the Church consisted
of all the believers and not merely the clergy, then it was
essential that every member be wholesome of heart and
pure in mind. "To accomplish this," Calvin wrote, "we
have decided ... to appoint and choose certain persons
of upright life and good reputation among all the faithful"
who shall have "an eye to the life and conduct of each
one." For the good citizens of Geneva there were not only
to be windows into their souls but also great doors into
their domestic, business and social affairs. The grand experiment in applied theology had begun, and henceforth
the life of every man was to be held up to the standards
of scriptural purity.

Attendance at church and morning prayers was strictly
enforced. Popery was exterminated root and branch, and
even the celebration of Christmas was prohibited under
pain of imprisonment, as a devil's mass and Bacchanalian
brawl. The theatre was denounced, especially the introduction of the new and degenerate Italian custom of allowing
women on the stage instead of the older and safer use of
boys to play female roles. The women who appeared in
theatrical productions, according to Calvinistic argument,
had no purpose in mind other than "to expose their bodies,
clothes, and ornaments to excite the impure desires of the
spectators", all of which was utterly "contrary to the
modesty of women who ought to be shamefaced and shy".

The initials IHS were monogrammed on all public buildings, coins and city flags; the number of bowling-greens was reduced to five; and in every respect Geneva became a Protestant Sparta.

It is far too easy to caricature Calvin's Geneva into a dreadful concatenation of a reformatory for juvenile delinquents, a Christian revival meeting and a school for saints, a veritable "dictatorship of the praying classes", in which neither common sense nor common happiness prevailed. Calvinism, however, was never "the haunting fear that someone somewhere may be happy", for Calvinistic Genevans, Puritan English and Huguenot French were not devoid of laughter and fun. Puritans danced, wined and made merry in the privacy of their homes. The problem was one of purpose: gaiety for man's sake was to be avoided, good fellowship which was the fruit of godliness was to be welcomed. The trouble with God's elect in the eyes of more politic men was their determination to thunder against the evils of this world and their conviction that it was the minister's duty to God to speak as "a dying man to dying men". Calvinist preachers were rarely known for their tact and moderation, for John Calvin never regarded the clerical office as so limited that "when the sermon is delivered we may rest as if our task were done". The preacher had to take care that souls were not lost as a consequence of slothfulness and lack of vigilance. The need to bring the Lord's way to all men made the elect of God a busybody, and nothing was too obscure, nothing too inconsequential to be considered by the Church elders. The Consistory, a body of the clergy sitting in company with twelve lay elders who were elected by the city council, decided cases involving fortune-telling, the singing of obscene songs, over-indulgence, blasphemy, adultery, witchcraft and heresy. Matters of apparel, women's hair styles, and two cases of adultery involving Calvin's own sister-in-law and his stepdaughter were brought to the Consistory's attention. The names given to children at baptism by too eager and too old-fashioned parents were carefully culled, and if found objectionable were prohibited. Such Catholic names as Claude and Martin were barred as indicating a secret and idolatrous reverence for saints, while such

questionable designations as Sepulchre, Sunday and Jesus
were outlawed as being in poor taste. Calvin, however, did
not have to struggle with the English Puritan habit of bestowing such godly and imaginative names as Renewed,
Fearnot, Accepted (an English Archbishop carried that
name), Be-Thankful, Faint-not, Love-God, Live-well, and
the mouth-filling Fight-the-godd-fight-of-faith. In 1546 the
inns of the city were reorganized as "abbeys" and placed
under strict government supervision, and a precise code for
guests and hosts was laid down which included among
other items the following:

If any one blasphemes the name of God or says:
"By the body, 'sblood, zounds", or anything like, or
gives himself to the devil or uses similar execrable im-
precations, he shall be punished ...

Item the host shall not allow any person, of whatever quality he be, to drink or eat anything in his
house without first having asked a blessing and afterwards said grace.

Item the host shall be obliged to keep in a public
place a French Bible, in which any one who wishes
may read ...

Item the host shall not allow any dissoluteness like
dancing, dice or cards, nor shall he receive any one
suspected of being a débauché or ruffian.

Item he shall only allow people to play honest games
without swearing or blasphemy, and without wasting
more time than that allowed for a meal ...

Item nobody shall be allowed to sit up after nine
o'clock at night except spies.

Calvin demanded that the city of Geneva should become the armed citadel of God, and that absolute discipline of behaviour and orthodoxy of thought should be
maintained as an example to all Europe. The self-appointed
pope of the Protestant world was more than a pastor, he
was a general; his followers were soldiers in the Lord's service, and it was essential to success that God's army should
be built upon obedience to the divine Word as revealed

in Scripture and interpreted by Calvin. One of the first to clash with Geneva's warden of morality was Pierre Ameaux, whose ancestral livelihood – the manufacture of playing-cards – had been endangered by the new discipline. In 1546, at a supper party given in his own house, Ameaux indulged in the ill-advised luxury of calling Calvin a preacher of false doctrines and prophesied that the government would soon be in the hands of fanatical French religious exiles who were flocking by the hundreds to the city. Ameaux's confidences were reported to the Consistory by one of his own guests. His attack was viewed as no mere personal affront to one of God's ministers, but as an insult to "the honour of Christ" whose servant Calvin knew himself to be. The Council of Two Hundred ordered Ameaux to appear before it and on bended knee to seek humble pardon of Calvin. That outraged defender of the Lord would have no such mildness shown to a man who had insulted the "name of God", and he prevailed upon the Council to reconsider its verdict and change the punishment to a more suitable one: Ameaux, clad only in a shirt, was forced to walk the streets of the city and on his knees beg the mercy of God and the city magistrates for his ill-advised words.

Ameaux's defiance was largely the result of economic grievance; the case of Michael Servetus was far more dangerous, since Satan's hand was clearly present in the heresy that denied the Trinity and the doctrine of original sin. Michael Servetus was a Spanish physician whom history has treated as a hero, but whom contemporaries, both Protestant and Catholic, viewed as the most dangerous of criminals. He was seen as a murderer of the soul, and his death by slow fire in 1553 was greeted with applause by the entire Christian world. Calvin had known of Servetus in their university days in Paris, and he had been horrified even then by the Spaniard's pseudo-Unitarian arguments. Servetus represented a pernicious threat from within the Protestant ranks, for he embodied the tendency of the Protestant faith to explode into a warring spectrum of religious sects ranging in alphabetical frenzy from Adventists, Behmenists, Bidellians and Christadelphians to Salmonists, Traskites and Tyronists.

Servetus lived in France for a decade but finally fled to Vienna and in 1553 published the *Restitution of Christianity*, a work that brought him to the immediate attention of the Catholic authorities. He escaped from prison a month before being condemned to the fire, and for reasons bordering on lunacy he sought safety in the city of the man who had denounced him in his university days, who had been writing vicious denunciations against his views, and who, in fact, may have betrayed his identity to the Catholic Inquisition in Vienna. The moment Servetus set foot in Geneva, he was recognized, arrested, tried and found guilty of heresy and sentenced to death by slow burning. Still possessed of Satan, he died on October 26th, 1553, at the hands of those who accounted the agony of the stake as slight compared to hell's fire. To Calvin, the ranks had to be preserved and heresy stamped out, for his Geneva was more than a Protestant stronghold and *The Institutes* more than a statement of righteousness. His city was the Tabernacle of the Lord and a model for all believers, and his book was the tablet of God's Word.

For all the portraits of the man and the intimate details recorded by his flock, John Calvin remains strangely inhuman. The slender scholar of university days slowly burned away, leaving an emaciated body and a face dominated by an uncompromising nose, tight and unsmiling lips, and eyes that looked with sorrow upon a world filled with ignorance and evil. Calvin the man was replaced by Calvin the elect of God. His anger was monumental, his will uncompromising, his logic irrefutable, and his task Herculean. He was never beset by doubt, only by ill health and exhaustion, both of which he willed away. He was not merely neat and orderly in his habits, but fastidious to the point of madness, for he could not endure even a speck of dust to mar the blackness of his gown. No detail was too trifling, no task done in the Lord's name too inconsequential. John Calvin must be numbered among the saints, if only because the intensity of his emotions, the strength of his convictions and even the adjectives required to describe him are all beyond human scale. Like the saints he is of interest to humanity, but he lies outside its power of compassion or comprehension, for, as he said himself, his strength was not his own but belonged to the Lord.

> I'm here a pillar in thy temple
>   Strong as a rock.
> A guide, a buckler, an example,
>   To a' thy flock.

On May 27th, 1564, five and a half years after Queen
Elizabeth ascended the throne, John Calvin died, but his
soul went marching on. Calvin's reputation rests not simply
on his record as master of that "perfect school of Christ"
but even more on his achievement in building a rival to
Catholicism, a tightly organized, self-sufficient and international church dedicated to bringing the standards of
heaven to earth. To Roman Catholics, Calvin's Geneva had
become the cesspool of an international and diabolical
conspiracy to overthrow all established order and to sub-
vert the true faith; to Protestants, the city was a source of
inspired preachers and organizers who went forth in God's
name to every country in Europe. Calvin himself was tire-
less in his efforts to organize the faithful on an international scale. His correspondence was voluminous, his
advice endless, and his encouragement to stand firm in the
knowledge of the Lord a source of strength throughout
Europe. He was in touch with Queen Elizabeth and the
King of Lithuania. He advised Thomas Cranmer in England, John Knox in Scotland, John á Lasco in Poland and
Admiral Coligny in France; and in each case his militant
message was the same: "If He pleases to make use of
you even to death in His battle, He will uphold you by His
mighty hand to fight firmly, and will not suffer a single
drop of your blood to remain useless." In May 1559 Calvin founded his Academy, the spawning-ground for religious revolutionists, and in the first year thirty-two ministers were dispatched to strengthen the army of the Lord
in its struggle against Catholicism. At the same time Geneva
attracted the faithful from all over Europe. Each year the
flood of exiles pouring into the city mounted: eighty-one
in 1549, one hundred and forty-five in 1550, five hundred and
eighty-seven in 1557 and over sixteen hundred in 1559. The
great majority came from France but several hundred flocked in from Italy, fifty or so from England, a scattering from

Greece and Tunis, and even a small colony from Spain.

Geneva under the firm leadership of Calvin had become the haven and oracle for militant Protestantism. It was the source of endless propaganda which poured from the city's new printing-presses and from the sharp pens of avid reformers, eager to instruct the elect of other lands on how to build their churches in the face of persecution and bitter official opposition. In France an entire state within a state was organized illegally by the establishment of interconnected religious cells or consistories, each of which was equipped with a pastor, elders and deacons, and was modelled on Geneva. The first of these was organized in Paris in 1555, and four years later Calvinist Presbyterian congregations had sprung up in seventy-two French urban communities. The spirit that directed the new Church and the ministers who guided God's flock came from Geneva. In 1559, thirty-two preachers went forth to labour among the Lord's followers in France; in 1560 twelve more followed; and by the following year the total number had risen to ninety-one. By the outbreak of the French Civil War in 1562, a religious organization had been fashioned that rigidly disciplined and controlled the faith and personal lives of possibly a million and a half persons in a country of sixteen million. The Consistory, which exercised inquisitorial powers over the beliefs and the daily activities of its congregation, was the basic ecclesiastical unit. Above the Consistory rose a tightly disciplined hierarchy, extending from the regional and provincial colloquies to the National Synod, a governing body of ministers and elders who trained Calvinist preachers and passed final judgment on God's Word and the actions of the faithful. The structure was as authoritarian and paternalistic as anything found in Geneva. Pastors were chastised for being too dull or too flippant; husbands were ordered to keep their household staffs in better discipline or not to beat their wives; and entire congregations were admonished to attend church more regularly.

Militant, disciplined, élite and elected, the French Calvinists, called Huguenots or "Night Spectres" for the quiet and stealthy way in which they slipped to church meetings in the dark of the night, felt themselves to be separate from the corrupt society surrounding them. It was natural that they should have organized themselves as an exclusive society of God's saints on earth, and throughout the 1560s cells were founded to spread the Word of God, to defend His faith and transform the realm into a kingdom of heaven. Under their impact the religious spectrum was polarized, and pacifistic Lutheranism and the doctrine of quiet submission to authority slowly gave way to Calvinism and a granite determination to resist. To men of iron will who viewed life as a spiritual drama, the claims of religion dwarfed any sense of loyalty either to dynasty or to state. The Huguenot felt closer to his Dutch, Scottish and English brethren than he did to his fellow Frenchmen, who were overwhelmingly Catholic. France in 1560 stood on the brink of ideological and civil war, when it could be written that "at one time friends and enemies were distinguished by the frontiers of provinces and kingdoms, and were called Italians, Germans, French, Spaniards, English, and the like; now we must say Catholics and heretics, and a Catholic prince must consider all Catholics of all countries as his friends, just as the heretics consider all heretics as friends and subjects whether they are their own vassals or not".

Whether civil war would have actually erupted in France without the numerically small but persistent voice of those "precise folk", who would "offer their goods and bodies to prison rather than they should relent", is a matter of guesswork. Forces were operating in sixteenth-century France that had little to do with religion, but they happened fatally to coincide in time with the gathering spiritual storm. Mounting feudal and provincial resistance to the royal bureaucracy, plus the growing irresponsibility of an aristocracy confronted by economic ruin, contributed heavily to the disaster of civil war that broke out in 1562. Add the elements of degenerate monarchy and incompetent governmental leadership and the witch's brew of discontent was complete. The language of sedition, however, remained religious; discontent, whether it was bourgeois or feudal, sought support from the one really organized and disciplined body within the state, the Calvinistic Presbyterian Church.

In England, the story was similar but the conclusion different. Calvinists hot out of Geneva had been frustrated in their original efforts to capture the Elizabethan religious settlement of 1559–60, but within a decade they launched a new campaign to seize the Church from within and to legislate the new Jerusalem into existence by means of parliamentary statute. Everywhere during the 1570s Puritan cells, similar to those in France and the Netherlands, were organized. In the universities, in the mansions of the aristocracy, in the houses of great financiers, and above all in Parliament, the "unspotted Lambs of the Lord" forged a party dedicated to the work of God's will in which the voice of the divinity spoke more clearly than the dictates of political belly-wisdom. In the eyes of fervent reformers, the Church of England remained a putrefied old oak in desperate need of purification and redemption. It lacked a pope and a mass but otherwise it retained the lavish trappings of the Whore of Rome. Worse yet, the Church was the child of worldly necessity and not of God. In the words of John Field, it had been "framed out of man's own brain and fantasy" and was even worse than popery. The campaign against the Church commenced in 1570, when both press and pulpit were utilized to re-educate the Queen and her people. Led by a defrocked Cambridge don, named Thomas Cartwright, the Puritans spoke out against the ignorance and inefficiency of the Established Church; they branded cathedrals as "dens of lazy, loitering lubbards", and the Prayer Book as a thing "picked out of that popish dunghill, the Mass-book, full of abominations".

The crisis, however, did not come until 1587, when the Puritan party tried to reform the Anglican Church by Act of Parliament. In doing so, they openly and blatantly defied the Queen's prerogative, incurred her wrath and usurped a constitutional function which Elizabeth firmly believed belonged to the Crown. Cope's Bill and Book, as the two Puritan statutes were called, demanded the abolition of the Anglican episcopate and Prayer Book and their replacement by a Presbyterian Kirk and Puritan creed. The Bill and Book had short shrift with the Queen, who ordered both to be withdrawn from the Commons.

Puritanism from the start was faced with a dilemma as old as man himself – the conflict of double loyalties. In a clash between man's law and God's decree the faithful had no choice but to follow the command of the higher authority. There was no doubt of their loyalty to Elizabeth, and when one good evangelist had his hand struck off for writing against the Queen's proposed marriage to a French and Catholic prince, he raised his hat with his remaining hand and shouted: "God save the Queen". Yet Elizabeth was adamant in her opposition to Puritanism in whatever form it happened to appear, for she sensed from the start a fundamental truth about the sect – Puritan creed and organization were totally incompatible with the theory of Tudor paternalism and the doctrine of the organic state. More specifically, she perceived that a community of saints deriving spiritual authority from God was not only contrary to the theory of episcopacy but also to the very existence of a monarchy which exercised historical and extensive prerogatives and claimed divinity from God. As early as 1573 the Established Church had acknowledged the threat, and the Dean of York pointed out the dialectic of Puritanism when he wrote: "At the beginning it was but a cap, a surplice, and a tippet [over which these preachers complained]; now, it is grown to bishops, archbishops, and cathedral churches, to the overthrow of the established order, and to the Queen's authority in causes ecclesiastical." If the divinity of bishops were denied, could the divinity of monarchs be far behind? Elizabeth's reaction was to growl that these Puritans "did not wish to recognize either God or the king", but she dared not destroy her loyal Puritans despite their provoking ardour and arrogant defiance, for at the other end of the religious scale there was beginning to appear an even more dangerous gentleman – the Jesuit.

Ignatius Loyola first made his appearance in the annals of recorded history as a "bold and defiant" court delinquent, "armed with sword and pistol", who came to the attention of the authorities for brawling in the streets and molesting women during the carnival season of 1515. In the words of his indictment he was "perfidious, brutal, vindictive",

Loyola himself described the depravity of his youth in somewhat less harsh but nevertheless sufficiently damning terms. "Up to my twenty-sixth year, I was entirely given up to the vanities of the world and felt a keen and empty craving to excel." Ignatius was born in 1491, the product of a Spanish aristocratic and chivalric tradition that had already degenerated into pride of caste, licence to brawl, and an excuse for idleness. The one unique quality that this empty-headed young man possessed was insatiable ambition, a driving desire to excel as a bravado, a warrior and a leader of men. He had been placed through family influence as a page at the royal palace at Arevalo, where tournaments were the routine of aristocratic life. Gorgeously arrayed youths thrust and hacked at one another with blunted swords and lances, and gaily attired damsels cheered on their gallants. Suddenly Ignatius found himself the victim of a palace upheaval in which his patron at court fell from royal favour. His career as a court parasite in jeopardy, he became a soldier stationed on the barren and mountainous frontier between Spain and France.

As a palace page, Loyola had perceived a basic truth about worldly power: success in society depended on influence and on the ability to control men and women in high office. In the frontier province of Navarre, he learned another lesson: grinding discipline and unthinking obedience were essential to any military organization. Realization of the facts of sixteenth-century life did not, however, lead to disillusionment. Ambition still remained, and the courtier-soldier yearned to achieve chivalric renown and splash the name of Loyola across the length and breadth of Europe. His chance came in May 1521 when war broke out between the Emperor Charles V and Francis I of France. What followed was a nightmare: instead of glory and honour came defeat and horror. The young knight was destroyed by the engines of modern war: his leg was smashed by a cannon-ball. Knightly heroism proved itself to be no match for modern science, and Ignatius found himself a prisoner to the sick-room and his military career as shattered as his injured leg. A knight with a limp was out of the question, for chivalric heroes could not be allowed to hobble. He endured a living hell to overcome what war had malformed; his leg was re-broken and reset, part of the bone was sawn off, and he lived for weeks upon a rack in order to stretch the shrunken limb back into shape. No matter the cost, he felt he had to avoid deformity, and he set his mind and soul to willing himself whole again.

From the torture of the orthopaedic rack and the surgeon's saw, he moved into the deadly tedium of convalescence. He daydreamed for hours, trying to capture in imagination the sight of flashing armour, the scent of perfumed ladies and the sound of clashing swords. He became so bored that he was even reduced to reading, and he called for the *Amadis de Gaula*, the book of courtly love, to help his imagination. Unfortunately the castle of Loyola possessed but two books – Ludolphus of Saxony's *Life of Christ* and a collection of legends about the lives of the saints. With intense distaste he read about saintly suffering and degrading humility, while he longed for tales of heroism and romance. In his desperation he tried to think of saints as knights of God, and suddenly a new world opened: the deeds of saints were equal to the grandest feats of knightly arms, and he pictured himself as a valiant knight in the service of Christ. As he lay in bed dreaming about the feats of St. Francis and St. Dominic, Ignatius yearned to cast aside sword and armour and don cowl and girdle so that he could do battle for Christ. The enemy was no longer a French invader or a rival knight dressed in black, but Satan himself and his host of demons, and courtly love and fair damsels seemed pale in contrast to the Queen of Heaven for whom Loyola longed to do heroic deeds.

Ignatius had become in his imagination a crusader in the old medieval tradition. If he were too deformed and crippled to fight for fair princesses and feudal lords, he could at least slay satanic dragons in honour of God. He was determined to make the name of Loyola ring through the halls of time as the champion of the heavenly kingdom. The moment he could walk, he donned beggar's garb and went to Manresa, a tiny village in Catalonia, where he lived in a cave and practised the art of sainthood so vividly depicted in Christian literature. He knelt in prayer for seven hours a day and whipped and mortified his body. He wore a girdle made of wire and a shirt woven with iron barbs, and he slept on the floor of the cave at night and fasted during the day. When he came down from his fastness to beg in the village even the beggars in the street called him "Father Sack", so thin and filthy had he become.

In the midst of his suffering, Ignatius made a dreadful and terrifying discovery: the strength that sustained him and the will that endured months of self-inflicted torture came not from God but from his own satanic pride. Loyola knew that he sought martyrdom on earth to be great in heaven and desired to excel at saintliness in order to achieve the recognition of God and man. The miracle of his conversion, the final consequence of those endless nights of torture in which he came to see the truth within himself and in the universe, was the purgation of his pride and dedication of his will-power to the service of God. He became the drill-sergeant of his own soul. His will, once it had been purged of pride, became master of his reason, of his emotions, and above all of his imagination. Loyola discovered that imagination, disciplined by a will of steel, could change darkness into light, could move mountains and endure even the fury of eternal fire.

When Loyola emerged from his ordeal, he was as much an instrument of the Lord as was John Calvin, but with a vital difference. Ignatius was no empty vessel filled with God's grace; he was a mortal man who by the sheer magnitude of his will had set out to be a saint and meet God halfway. He had drilled his imagination, analysed his conscience, scrutinized and inspected his soul, and regimented his body. The novice was now ready to join the ranks and do battle for the kingdom of heaven. Only the problem of finding, training, and organizing his spiritual recruits remained, and Ignatius set about writing the greatest of all books of instruction, his *Spiritual Exercises*, in which the initiate was told, step by step, how to exercise his will. The *Exercises* were one of the most powerful and perceptive ventures into psycho-analysis ever written. All the senses were harnessed and disciplined in order to sharpen the imagination to the point where fantasy and reality became one. The *Exercises* were divided into four steps or "weeks", during which the recruit moved from a general examination of his conscience to an intense meditation upon sin and its punishment in hell, and upon the miracle of Christ's life. The method was neither rational nor intellectual; instead it was physical. By an act of will the novice imagined himself to hang in agony upon the cross, to taste the bread and the fish that Jesus delivered to the people, to converse with the Disciples at the Last Supper, and to visualize Christ as the King of Heaven enthroned in His majesty and directing His armies against Satan. Throughout the *Exercises*, Loyola insisted that every sense be controlled by the imagination. "It will be necessary," he explained, "to see in imagination the length, breadth and depth of hell ... To beg for a deep sense of the pain which the lost suffer ... To see the vast fires and the souls enclosed, as it were, in bodies of fire. To hear the wailing, the howling, cries and blasphemies against Christ our Lord ... With the sense of smell to perceive the smoke, the sulphur, the filth and corruption. To taste the bitterness of tears, sadness and remorse of conscience. With the sense of touch to feel the flames which envelop and burn the souls."

The *Exercises* were not written to be read as literature, but to be studied as a manual of instruction in preparation for action in the battlefield, and from the start Ignatius's methods met with violent opposition from the very Church he sought to serve. Ecclesiastical authorities were alarmed by the hint of hysteria evident in his system of spiritual analysis. His converts suffered convulsions and fainting spells; they endured moments of suicidal depression and raptures bordering on madness. More serious, the doctrine of absolute free will rested as uncomfortably upon the shoulders of Catholic theology as Luther's thesis of the bondage of the human will and the sovereign power of divine grace. The Church remained darkly suspicious of Ignatius's assertion that he could discover God whenever he wished and that, "as the body can be exercised by going, walking and running, so the will of man can be trained by exercises to find the will of God."

The leader and his method stood ready, but where were the disciples who could conquer the world and roll back the forces of heresy and schism? At the age of thirty-three, Ignatius was forced to conclude that, if he were to lead anything more than a rabble of repentant prostitutes and idle and disappointed wives of the rich, he would have to return to school in order to meet and catch the men who had the strength to wield the sword of Christ. He started at the beginnng, joining children in memorizing his lists of Latin words and learning basic grammar. Each step in his education led him to perceive the need for further learning, and in 1527, in his thirty-seventh year, he left Spain for the University of Paris.

Loyola shared a room with two other university students – the gentle and scholarly Pierre Le Fèvre and the handsome and athletic Francis Xavier. Both men were at least fifteen years Ignatius's junior and both were ideally suited as recruits and lieutenants in the army of Christ if only Loyola could stimulate their interest and inveigle them into reading the *Exercises*. With Le Fèvre the conquest was easy. By careful and quiet scrutiny, Ignatius discerned that behind the mind of this young Aristotelian philosopher there lingered the heart of a superstitious Savoyard cowherd. Le Fèvre started out teaching his elderly and untutored room-mate the secrets of scholastic logic and ended a convert to the *Spiritual Exercises*.

With Francis Xavier the problem was more difficult, for the quarry was more wary. Moreover the 'swordplaying, dice-throwing Xavier had nothing but distaste for his Bible-praying and limping room-mate. Ignatius, however, won the younger man's respect by his learning and gained his love by his generosity, and in the end Francis Xavier was induced to partake of the *Spiritual Exercises*. By 1531 the leader had two converts and together they posted upon the door of their bedroom the picture of Jesus. By 1534, six disciples had been trapped by a saint who possessed the cunning of a soldier and the tact of a courtier. One he caught "the morning after", another he captured by the force of his words, and still another he led into a friendly game of dice, the loser pledging to take the *Exercises*. From the start Ignatius formulated the two most famous and controversial principles of the Society: the end justifies the means; and be all things to all men.

Armies of seven are rarely more than bands of fanatics or idealists. Yet in the case of Loyola and his followers, quality somehow made up for quantity, for these seven were men of steel. They left Paris and dedicated their spiritual swords to the service of the Pope and the Catholic Church. Somewhat hesitantly the Holy Father accepted these naive but magnificently trained and enthusiastic champions, and on September 27th, 1540, he blessed the foundation of the Order of the Society of Jesus. The aim of the new organization was clear – to restore the medieval Church to the position of uncontested spiritual and political power that it had enjoyed in the thirteenth century. If the aim was medieval, the means were modern. The Jesuits were no medieval monastic order, serving God by renouncing this world and retreating into a monastery. They were a military company in which every facet of life and every intellectual premise was subordinated to efficiency. The Jesuit ideal was the creation of a military corps in perfect fighting trim, a force in which every man would be ready to believe if necessary that "what seems black is white if the hierarchical Church so teaches". Every recruit was "like a corpse which can be turned this way or that, or a rod that follows every impulse, or a ball of wax that might be moulded in any form". Jesuits wore no special habit but dressed to suit the needs of the occasion. They did not spend their days in contemplation and prayer, but trained their minds and steeled their hearts so as to meet and defeat all men on their own terms. Jesuits were expected to talk finance to the Fuggers, scholarship to the intellectual, politics to the minister of state, and military tactics to the general. They were ordered not to shun the world of riches and power politics, but to join battle with Satan by becoming the confessors of the great and powerful. Ignatius knew from early experience that power over the souls of the influential few was more useful than the support of the masses in the war against evil. Deliberately, and with calculated results, Jesuits set out to control the confessional of kings, the education of princes, and the minds of the men and women who counted.

At the same time that Ignatius sought to place his disciples in the councils of the monarchs of Europe, he turned his attention to the organization of social welfare on a scale unheard of in the medieval past. He sought to stamp out pauperism, prostitution, unemployment and famine. In every major city of Europe, Loyola established an office to co-ordinate begging, find jobs for the unemployed, and urge the local community to build homes for the old and infirm. For the first time human suffering was being attacked on a rational and organized scale.

The institution that slowly evolved during the 1540s and 1550s was carefully designed to fight social evil, to counter the monster of heresy, to reconquer central Europe for the Roman fold and to win new converts throughout the globe. It was uniquely the creation of a soldier and a born administrator. Ignatius Loyola became the first General of the Order and demanded of his followers absolute obedience. The growth of the Order was spectacular; in four years Italy, Spain, Portugal, France, Germany and the Netherlands had Jesuit cells, and by the time of Ignatius's death in 1556 the Society had grown from seven members to an élite and highly trained following of fifteen hundred, organized in twelve provinces and sixty-five residences in most of the major cities of Europe. In every case, recruits were selected for their effectiveness as soldiers of God, and Ignatius once told his secretary that in those who offered themselves he looked "less to purely natural goodness than to firmness of character and ability for business", for he was of the opinion that "those who were not fit for public business were not adapted for filling offices in the Society".

By 1556 the Order had become a world power: Jesuits heard confession in the most august courts of Europe, sat upon the privy councils of kings, and maintained their representatives at the Imperial Diet in Germany. They held distinguished positions in the universities of the continent, where they exercised control over the shaping of young minds. They whispered advice to Philip of Spain and Catherine de Medici of France, and they were feared and detested by Protestants who viewed them as Satan's most pernicious instrument. By the time of Elizabeth's succession in 1558 the tide of Protestant victory had begun to ebb. Shortly central Europe was made safe for Catholicism and the Protestant heresy contained and limited to a northern arc extending from Prussia and Sweden through the Netherlands to England. By 1585 the war had been taken into the enemy camp; Antwerp had fallen, Holland was under attack, and England herself exposed to Catholic invasion and conversion. In each case the Jesuit leadership stood behind Catholic resurgence.

Outside Europe, Jesuit missionaries were on the move, bringing Christianity to the Far East, America and Africa. Only two years after the Society was founded, Ignatius sent his most trusted lieutenant, Francis Xavier, to India. In May 1542 he arrived in Goa, the rich trading-centre of the Portuguese East Indian empire. He was made vicar of all the lands washed by the Indian Ocean, a potential flock of millions upon millions of souls who might yet be saved for God. Arabs, Hindus, Gujarats, Persians, all speaking a host of different languages and dialects and worshipping graven images, awaited the coming of God's Word, if only it could be translated into a language and a meaning comprehensible to their heathen ears and minds. Xavier began the task of learning the babble of Eastern tongues, of explaining the message of Christ, of meeting every kind and manner of man, and of urging them to come to him with their troubles and accept him as their confessor. From Goa, with its Kaffir slaves and Portuguese Hidalgos, he moved to the pearl fisheries of Kerala, where simple folk who worshipped fire demons and serpents were struck by his black gown and monk's cowl and listened to his clanging bell and the few words of Tamil that he had mastered. The entire East lay before him, and Francis Xavier was never one to tarry when the hordes of China and Japan had yet to hear his message of good news. Thousands of Japanese received his blessings but he never reached China, for as he prepared to sail to Canton he was struck down with fever and died, a single soldier who had given his life to the greater glory of God: *ad majorem Dei gloriam*.

"To the greater glory of God" was the secret of Jesuit power. It was the grossest kind of blasphemy to the Calvinist, for the doctrine presumed that man's efforts could add to or detract from God's glory, but it was the source of the vitality that led Francis Xavier ever farther eastwards and Ignatius to shoulder the administrative labours

of a Hercules. Loyola's headquarters consisted of three
cells in a Roman slum. He worked twenty hours a day on
a wooden trestle table and slept on a portable cot. He kept
alive on chestnuts, bread and water, and he never found
the leisure to sit down to eat. All day he read reports, answered letters, and issued precise military communiqués.
Each lieutenant reported to him in writing upon every
particular of his life and upon the lives of those under
him, while subordinates were expected to comment upon
the success and quality of their superiors. Ignatius became an administrative machine in absolute control of
himself and of his army of spiritual soldiers. There was no
time for contemplation, for friendship, or for humanity,
for he had willed himself to become a saint and in doing
so he ceased to be human. The ranks of the sanctified, it
has been aptly said, had been joined by a "saint of will".

Ignatius Loyola was born Spanish and he stamped his
creation with his Iberian personality. In turn the Society
of Jesus branded the entire Catholic Counter-Reformation
with its proselytizing zeal, its efficiency, its insistence on
quick action, and its creed that, in the name of God, the
end justifies the means. The Jesuits with their versatile
dress, their military discipline and their theological semina-
ries were the hard core of the Catholic reaction to heresy.
Their energy was symptomatic of the new vigour that was
becoming manifest throughout Catholicism. A steeling
of the soul, a formulation of fundamental doctrine, and a
sharpening of the weapons to cut out diversity of thought
and faith were evident in every phase of the Catholic revival. The medieval Inquisition, that sharp-eyed shepherd
against the wolf of heresy, was revived and re-established
in Spain in 1480, in the Netherlands in 1523 and in Italy
in 1542. The quality of the new leadership and the spirit
of the Inquisition were summed up in the words of the
Inquisitor who coldly stated: "It is no great matter
whether they that die on account of religion be guilty or
innocent, provided we terrify the people by such
examples."

In 1545 Catholicism met in religious council to reform
the Church and clarify the creed. The labours of the Council of Trent lasted off and on for eighteen years. Controlled

by papal interests and later guided by Jesuit and Spanish leadership, the final pronouncement was a clear and unified statement of what the believer must profess in order to be numbered among the Catholic fold. Justification by good works and faith, combined with the ancient seven sacraments, were asserted to be the sole road to man's salvation. The Council further announced that only the Catholic Church held the keys to the kingdom of heaven and that the priesthood possessed supernatural powers transmitted directly from Christ. Latin was named the language of prayer and worship; the Church was made the interpreter and arbiter of the Bible; celibacy of the clergy was insisted upon; monasticism was pronounced to be the high road to salvation and the highest attainment of mankind; and the celestial hierarchy of saints and angels was restated. In a word, for the first time a test of faith was presented to the Catholic world, and a yardstick was created with which to measure heresy and root it out. As a final measure of defence an Index of prohibited books was established, so as to protect the minds of future generations against the poison of heresy and unorthodoxy.

On both sides extremism was triumphant, the faith was prescribed and the faint of heart proscribed. In England, Catholics were now told that religion stood higher than duty to the Queen, and Joseph Cresswell voiced the spirit of rejuvenated Catholicism when he said: "If I heard that the entire destruction of England was for the greater glory of God and the welfare of Christianity, I should be glad of it being done." In 1568 William Allen established an English college in Flanders in order to train Catholic missionaries for the dangerous work of re-Catholicizing England and giving hope and renewed strength to those true believers who still clung to their faith. Six years later the first three missionaries arrived; by 1578 their number had risen to fifty and by 1580 there were over a hundred. The Catholic revival in England received still further impetus by the arrival of the Jesuits under Edmund Campion and Robert Parsons. Their goal and charge was "to preach the gospel, to minister the sacraments, to instruct the simple, to reform sinners, [and] to confute errors".

Whether the Jesuits, who were smuggled into the realm,

were in fact traitors – fifth columnists sent to destroy the
Protestant Jezebel and to incite regicide – is difficult to
judge. Officially the Order preached obedience even to
heretical sovereigns, but as revolution was implicit in the
militant creed of John Calvin, so sedition was inherent in
the Jesuit judgment that matters of faith stood higher than
the concerns of daily life, and that the spiritual end justified the material means. Edmund Campion, when he was
caught and dismembered in the name of state security and
political orthodoxy, died blessing Elizabeth – "your queen
and mine" – but Robert Parsons was a professional re-
volutionist, and almost every plot to overthrow Elizabeth
betrayed his fine organizational talents.

Throughout Europe, Calvinist and Jesuit were setting
the pace. Each represented a supra-national creed enforced by militant and international organizations that
called upon loyalties transcending national boundaries and
personal ties. Both were politically and socially dangerous
movements, for neither recognized the limitations of common sense or common decency, and each was a haven for
men, some deeply pious, others viciously evil, who enjoyed
the extravagance of extreme action, whether it be in raping
nuns in the name of religion, torturing men's bodies with
rack and fire for the sake of their souls, or disregarding
even the most elementary laws of hospitality because of a
higher principle. The Puritan and the Jesuit were strangely
alike. Father Gerard was a Jesuit missionary in England.
He was an outlawed and hunted man, and when, in search
of a hiding place, he came to the country house of an English Catholic, he was only a few hours ahead of the law.
At great risk, his host offered Gerard sanctuary, and as he
led him up the stairs to a place of concealment, the hunted
priest saw on the landing a stained-glass window in which
was depicted a naked Venus. In outraged righteousness,
Gerard put his fist through the window and shouted that
the sight of such nudity was blasphemous to God. The
normal dictates of hospitality were not sufficient to restrain
the man possessed of Truth.

Ignatius Jurdain was a Puritan member of the Jacobean
House of Commons and a merchant from Exeter. He was
returning to his city in company with another member who

invited him to lodge the night at his manor house. Jurdain's host was a country gentleman addicted to profanity, and the godly Puritan accepted the invitation only on condition that the squire, his wife and servants should refrain from using bad language in Jurdain's presence, and that there should be a godly sermon both at the parish church in the morning and at the manor house in the afternoon. Again the limits of hospitality were being strained by a man eaten up by the zeal of his faith. The similarity between the two extremes did not go unnoticed in the sixteenth century, and it was that "wisest fool in Christendom" and coiner of bon mots, James of Scotland, who noted that "one Puritan presbyter equals one papist priest". Both Elizabeth of England and Catherine de Medici of France would have fervently agreed, though Philip of Spain would undoubtedly have missed the point.

Six

Catherine de Medici and the
Ordeal of France

A SPLINTER of wood from a shattered lance did for France what all the Emperor's armed men had been unable to accomplish during forty years of Habsburg–Valois rivalry: it destroyed the kingdom as an international power. On July 1st, 1559 a tiny wooden sliver from the broken lance of his jousting partner entered the eye and pierced the brain of Henry II. Within ten days the King was dead. Four years later France was torn by the first of nine monstrous civil and religious wars, during which the kingdom was scourged by foreign and private armies which burned, maimed and tortured in the name of divine justice. For thirty years France was to bleed, until humanity so sickened at the sight of human butchery that "peace without God" seemed preferable to "war for Him". During the coming ordeal, religious paranoia and the actions of desperate men strained to the breaking-point the bonds of political stability, but Valois France was destroyed not so much by the spectre of anarchy common to all Europe as by the rot that was eating away the heart of the French monarchy. In 1533, as a result of diplomatic caprice, two thoroughly worn-out houses were united with fatal consequences. The union produced the three ailing and degenerate sons of Henry Valois and Catherine de Medici.

Catherine de Medici was born in 1519, the year Charles of Spain was elected Emperor of Germany. An orphan at five days and from birth a pawn in the diplomatic designs of her Medici cousin Pope Clement VII, Catherine was raised in the spirit of the Italian Renaissance where patience and calculation were the qualities most likely to ensure survival. At eight, she was swept up in the Florentine revolution of 1527 and her fate was openly debated by the city fathers, some of whom suggested that she be chained naked to the city walls and raped by the Republican soldiers. Catherine survived the revolution with her virginity intact and her matrimonial usefulness to the Pope unmarred, and in 1533 Francis I of France was lured into accepting Clement's fourteen-year-old ward as the bride of the King's second son, Henry Duke of Orleans. Within months of the marriage, it became painfully apparent that papal promises were as meaningless as pontifical blessings and that the Holy Father had no intention of risking war with the Emperor to win Milan, Parma and Urbino for France. The French monarch had bought an Italian pig-in-a-poke, and Francis caustically remarked that he had acquired a daughter as naked as a new-born babe. Without Milan, Parma and Urbino, Catherine had nothing to her credit, not even noble blood, and from the start the marriage was regarded as a misalliance and the Princess as a Florentine shopkeeper's granddaughter. When her husband became heir-apparent in 1536, Catherine's position at court worsened. Henry became infatuated with the lovely Diana of Poitiers, and the Queen continued to fail in the one quality that might have compensated for her bourgeois vulgarity – fecundity.

For ten years Catherine was tolerated, and for ten years she remained barren. Then, beginning in 1543, she became a mother seven times over, giving birth in rapid succession to Francis, Elizabeth, Claude, Charles, Henry, Margaret and Hercules (re-christened Francis). An extraordinary trinity evolved: the slow-witted and obstinate royal husband, his sorceress mistress who at fifty retained the looks of a Venus, and Catherine the Queen. Diana of Poitiers's domain was the King's bedchamber from whence she wielded immense political power; Catherine ran the household and had to be content with turning the court into "a veritable earthly paradise", where, exclaimed one ecstatic admirer, ladies shone like stars in the sky on a

fine night. Like most earthly paradises all was not as perfect as it might have been. Henry II was indecisive and
easily influenced, the treasury was empty, and the court
was torn by aristocratic factiousness that verged on feudal
anarchy and rebellion.

War had made a mockery of royal finances, and by
1559 both Valois France and Habsburg Spain were bankrupt. The peace between them, signed at Cateau-
Cambrésis, was diplomatic recognition of the fact that not
even the riches of the Spanish Indies nor the suffering of
French peasants could continue to finance wars that were
beginning to approach modern proportions. By the mid-
century, cannons, which once measured three to four feet,
had grown into ten- and twenty-foot monsters and had
to be drawn by teams of twenty horses. Armies had swollen
to sixty and eighty thousand men – insatiable hosts compared to the tiny company of eight thousand knights and
bowmen at the battle of Agincourt in 1415. At the battle
of St. Quentin in 1557, a Spanish force of sixty thousand
smashed a French army of equal size, leaving three thousand Frenchmen dead on the field and taking six thousand
prisoners. It was this defeat that induced France to sue for
peace and Spain to accept the offer in 1559, for neither
country could continue financing wars that were costing
three hundred thousand livres a month. When Henry II of
France died, his treasury was faltering under a war debt
of forty million livres. The Crown's theoretical resources
stood at ten million livres but its actual income was probably only half that sum, and the interest on the royal
debt, which varied between twelve and sixteen per cent,
consumed every available penny.

Monetary desperation led to administrative malfeasance
and proliferation. On the principle that the king of France
could tax as much as he wanted, the main French source
of revenues, the *taille*, rose steadily until peasants fled their
land or feigned poverty, and merchants and artisans saw
their profits eaten up by wars in which only the nobility
prospered. Even so, the sums collected did not suffice,
and the King turned to selling existing offices and creating new ones for future sale. Cash in hand staved off financial collapse, but it cost the Crown its control over the

administrative and judicial organs of state. Purchasers of offices could not be dismissed, and they regarded their posts as marketable commodities and private sinecures, not as public trusts. Courtiers sold influence, judges sold justice, bureaucrats sold favours. Rogues grew rich, upright men were disgusted, and almost everybody lost confidence in a government that was rapidly moving from inefficiency into blatant corruption. When the great magnates in alliance with religious fanatics rose up against the Crown, the French monarchy, unlike the English, discovered that its most important weapon against feudal irresponsibility and provincial prerogatives was blunted and worthless, for a bureaucratic system that could not be disciplined was virtually useless. Elizabeth's justices of the peace were unpaid but honest, and the social prestige attached to office-holding in England was so great that the Queen had only to whisper the word "dismissal" and local officials came to heel. In France, however, long before civil war actually broke out in 1562, financial shortsightedness was slowly paralysing effective government.

Economic Nemesis descended in 1557 when not even eighteen per cent interest rates could tempt international bankers to rescue the French Crown, and Henry had to break his most solemn and regal promise and declare himself bankrupt. In the wake of fiscal chaos came political crisis, for the class worst hit by the economic crash was that section of society traditionally most loyal to the Crown – the lesser nobility.

Throughout the century, wartime deficit-spending and the wealth of the New World had been producing an inflationary cycle causing the value of the livre to drop by half, while rents from land failed to keep abreast of the rising cost of living. Social pressure required lavish hospitality, expensive marriages and costly apparel, and men and women were known to wear entire estates upon their backs. In the past, war had provided a form of outdoor relief for the aristocracy but with the advent of peace in 1559, the nobility were overwhelmed by the clamour of their creditors. In desperation they turned away from a bankrupt monarchy and sought the aid of the great feudal magnates.

The most dangerous of all social partnerships was taking shape: the great lords, already restless under the Crown and bristling with family vanity, were being joined by lesser folk who looked to them for protection and in return were willing to man their private armies, wear their livery and support their feudal brawling. The age of liveried retainers and baronial warlords had returned to France. The Duke of Montmorency, Constable of France, arrived at court in 1560 with eight hundred horsemen, and in an emergency he could have mustered twice that number. The Duke of Guise was recognized as an uncrowned king, so great was his feudal and political following; and the strength of the House of Navarre was derived from a host of vassals who still owed military service and homage. Even the King's own army, which was maintained at a paper strength of twelve thousand cavalry and sixteen thousand infantry, was little more than a conglomeration of hired bands of feudal retainers, paid for by royal taxes but wearing the uniform of various commanders who regarded their troops as personal henchmen. In the final analysis, the Valois, like the Tudors, relied upon their most powerful subjects for support. This was unfortunate, for the ducal and princely houses of France were showing dangerous signs of increasing perversity and conceit.

High society and the political configurations at court were dominated by three private dynasties – Guise, Bourbon and Montmorency. The insatiable pride of the Guises was accepted as becoming their exalted position in baronial society, and their irresponsibility was excused on the grounds that they were descended from St. Louis and Charlemagne. They were possessed of immense feudal holdings, scattered gleanings from the great days of the Dukes of Burgundy, situated along the borders of France, the Low Countries and the Empire. The family included two cardinals, a Queen Regent of Scotland, a Grand Prior of France, and the most distinguished soldier of the day. Fear of the great lords at home had led the French Crown to favour the partly foreign and princely dynasty of Guise, and Duke Francis and his brother Charles, Cardinal of Lorraine, were dominant figures at the court of Henry II. Charles was termed the "tiger of France", the proudest prelate and the richest ecclesiastic to wear a Cardinal's hat. Cultured, devious and dangerous, Charles of Lorraine aspired to a papal tiara while his brother, the Duke, grasped at the throne of France. Duke Francis was the soldier of the clan, the darling of the war party, a magnificent warrior, and a man who exercised a profound influence over the prosaic and methodical mind of a sovereign who vastly admired the Duke's passion for direct action and discipline.

Equally dangerous but less brilliant than the Guises were the Bourbons, heirs to the Valois throne in the unlikely eventuality that all four of Henry's sons should die without issue. The titular chief of the clan was "Weathercock Anthony", a man possessed of little except his royal blood and an aggressively Calvinistic wife whose dearest wish was to convert her husband. The hot-headed leader of the family was Anthony's younger brother, Louis Prince of Condé, a hunchbacked, belligerent and penurious young man who had nothing to lose and everything to gain from conspiracy and rebellion. Hatred of the Guises, not conviction, drove Condé into the Calvinist camp, and his conversion to the new faith signalled the dangerous union of baronial gangsterism and spiritual discontent.

The Montmorencys were government aristocrats – servants of the Crown. The entire family held high office: Anne, Duke of Montmorency, was Constable of France; his son Francis was Marshal of the Kingdom, Governor of Paris and Lieutenant-General of the Ile-de-France; another son, Henry Damville, became Governor and uncrowned king of Languedoc, and Gaspard de Coligny, his nephew, was Admiral of France. Estates, dignities and even a bastard daughter of Henry II were presented to the family as rewards for service to the Crown. Their house was divided religiously: the Constable remained a devout Catholic; his nephew, the Admiral, became an equally staunch Huguenot. Coligny was a rough, masterful, Bible-quoting and tactless man, the hero of Protestant hagiography and the villain of nationalistic histories, for he sold the city of Le Havre to the English for six thousand men, one hundred thousand crowns and the hope of God's victory.

The entire realm was divided among the three families,

and scarcely a gentleman of France was not in some way beholden to one of the rival clans for a pension, a sinecure at court, a suit favourably settled at law, or a marriage with a fat dowry. At Paris, that "sun and moon of France", the baronial chieftains met in the glitter of Catherine de Medici's court, where the Constable advised peace with Spain, the Duke of Guise counselled war, and the Bourbons fluttered aimlessly, urging nothing but their distinguished rank and princely blood. The contrast between the English and French courts was basic: Elizabeth was able to raise her authority above party and politics; Henry II became the instrument of aristocratic ambitions, and royal policy fluctuated unpredictably, depending on whether Guise of Montmorency held the upper hand. As the years passed, it became apparent that the Guises were winning. Mary Stuart, that delightful child-Queen of Scotland, was a niece of the Guise brothers, and her marriage to the Dauphin and heir-apparent of France was a major victory for their house. Duke Francis, alone of the great barons of the court, escaped defeat during the war with Spain and England, and he emerged in 1559 as the liberator of Calais from three centuries of English tyranny. Unexpectedly the peace of Cateau-Cambrésis brought the Guises to the zenith of their power, for it was during a tournament held in honour of the peace and wedding of the King's daughter to Philip of Spain that Henry II received the fatal splinter.

For a year the Guises ruled through Mary of Scots, who was now Queen of France, and her fifteen-year-old husband, who was declared to be of legal age but in fact did what his uncles dictated. The Dowager Queen, Catherine de Medici, was even more in eclipse than before, and the Bourbon and Montmorency factions were eased out of the good things of court and political life. The Cardinal was a consummate diplomat and politician, and the Duke a splendid soldier, but neither was a statesman capable of rising above family and factional concerns. Their position in France was similar to that of the Duke of Somerset in England during the minority of Edward VI: they inherited an empty treasury, a corrupt and swollen administration, and a realm floundering in economic inflation and torn by religious passions. What had been permissible under even a weak and obstinate monarch was considered the most rapacious tyranny under princely uncles-in-law, who were regarded by the Bourbons as foreigners and usurpers and by the Huguenots as the diabolical instrument of Satan.

Francis and Charles of Guise did little to alleviate their unpopularity, and they rapidly became the scapegoats for all the evils besetting the realm. Worse yet, they drove the Huguenot minority to desperation, for the Duke, if not his brother, clamoured for the blood of the heretics and the absolute triumph of the Catholic Church. If necessary, he said, he was quite ready to sacrifice his life for that purpose. Guise's words were prophetic: thirty years of bloodshed were necessary to assure the victory of Catholicism, and in 1563 the Duke was struck down by a Protestant assassin.

By 1560 Calvinism in France had reached dangerous proportions. It had become the focal point for every variety of discontent – feudal, economic, personal and provincial. Overtaxed merchants, underpaid bureaucrats, bankrupt noblemen, and disgruntled princes of the blood, all found outlets for their disenchantment in the Huguenot faith. In the midst of government crippled by dissension, ruinous inflation, furious persecution and mounting violence, provincial feudalism began to merge with the hierarchical organization of the Huguenot church. The new faith was organized into some two thousand five hundred churches, each with its spiritual pastor and baronial protector. Each consistory had its feudal patron who acted as captain and defender of the flock, each colloquy or presbytery had its great noblemen and colonel, and each provincial synod had its *chef-général*. As one Protestant minister wrote to Calvin: "The fire has been lit in all parts of the realm and all the water in the sea would not suffice to put it out." The Venetian ambassador summed up the situation when he reported that the grandees of the kingdom had adopted Calvinism for reasons of ambition, the lesser nobility because of their greed to acquire church property, the "lower classes for paradise", and the last element furnished the contributions on which the other two lived. On all sides –

at court, in the country, and in the hearts of men – there was a steadily growing willingness to risk civil war and revolution. That war did not in fact break out in 1560 was the result of accident, for just when the Guise-Bourbon and Catholic-Huguenot controversies were spilling over into armed action, the young king, Francis II, died of an abscessed ear and the government was taken over by Catherine de Medici as Regent for her nine-year-old son, Charles IX. Patience, cunning and the sickness of her Valois offspring had finally given the Queen what her bourgeois heart coveted above all else: political power.

It was the painter Vasari who best described the new Queen Regent. "Her charm," he said, "cannot be painted or I would have preserved its memory with my brushes." Catherine de Medici was no beauty. She inherited most of the least enviable characteristics of her family: bulging eyes, heavy lips, greasy skin, sharp and sloping nose, spreading hips, a ravenous appetite, and a passion for intrigue. "A lady of masculine proportions", a contemporary called her. Yet there were great charm and zest. She doted on court gossip, she had a passion for grand receptions and bustling activity, and she built exquisite palaces and filled them with all the sumptuous gaiety that only regal rank and mercantile private means could afford. She ate prodigiously and suffered from gout and indigestion, but "she exercised enough for two", loved to dance, shoot, and hunt, and was the first lady to ride side-saddle with a leg hooked round the pommel instead of sitting sacklike with both feet on a plank against the horse's flank. She rode far and fast, and surrounded herself with forty to fifty maids-of-honour, her notorious flying squadron of court beauties who excelled in equestrian style as well as in the gorgeousness of their apparel. Their hats, it was reported, were "adorned with plumes which floated in the air, as if demanding either love or war". Catherine knew well how to use sex to her advantage, and her *escadron volant* of lovely but approachable goddesses was one of her most effective political weapons.

Catherine de Medici, as her enemies took pleasure in pointing out, owed her wealth to trade and her birth to Italy. The rumoured cabinet of deadly poisons and love potions never existed, but in England and France Catherine's birthplace remained by reputation the land of Machiavellian devilry; what Thomas Nashe described as "the Academie of man-slaughter, the sporting place of murther, the Apothecary-shop of poyson for all Nations". The new Regent was undoubtedly an admirer of Machiavellian diplomacy, but her deviousness was always mitigated and often negated by her motherly approach to politics. She delighted in power, but loved gossip even more; she endeavoured to preserve the integrity of France, but doted upon her children above all other interests. She was what the Venetian ambassador described as "a clear and intelligent business woman", but she could always be enticed by the promise of a crown or a kingdom for one of her many offspring; she invariably confused principles of state with palace politics; and she ruled by a policy of calculated indiscretions mixed with the artless flutterings of a mother hen.

Catherine was a consummate manipulator of the political and diplomatic pack, but even with the cards stacked in her favour she rarely won, for she never understood the quality of her opponents. She brilliantly arranged to grasp the regency on the death of her eldest son and manoeuvred both Guise and Bourbon into accepting her control over the government of Charles IX, but her idea of ruling France was to move her couch into the King's bedchamber. What could not be solved by a bedside chat, a midnight supper, the suggestion of perfume, or the hint of marriage was beyond her intelligence. Her religion was a comfortable and orthodox variety of superstition filled with prophecies and amulets, and she regularly corresponded with the greatest of all fortune-tellers, Nostradamus. Her statesmanship tended to be little more than cloying maternalism, her boundless energy was no substitute for real ability, and her methods, though rational, were invariably shortsighted.

In December 1560, however, it appeared for a moment as if Catherine might indeed be the saviour of the kingdom and do for France what Elizabeth was doing for England – persuade court factions and rival religions to live in concord and peace. Catherine was more experienced than her regal sister across the channel but she was a dowdy forty-one compared to Elizabeth's vital twenty-six; she was a foreigner and a plebeian; and, most important of all, she never possessed the magic that could melt the chilly heart of treason, charm Catholics and Protestants into content-ment, and envelop every action in the mantle of greatness. Considering that she was "a foreign woman without friends, weighed down under the general terror", she accomplished a miracle: she persuaded Anthony of Bourbon to re-nounce his claim as the ranking prince of the blood and forgo the regency; she argued the Duke of Guise into re-maining at court and accepting a policy of pity towards the Calvinists; and she brought Huguenots and Catholics together in a national conference to establish a doctrinal solution acceptable to both faiths. Even Henry of Navarre, whose success was so closely dependent upon the frustra-tion of her dynastic dreams and who ultimately replaced her three Valois sons upon the throne of France, wondered what the poor woman could "have done with her husband dead and five small children upon her hands, and two families, our own and the Guises, who were scheming to seize the throne". Navarre and most later observers were agreed that Catherine de Medici might indeed have done worse.

The Queen's purpose was to pour balm upon troubled consciences and smooth the ruffled pride of courtiers. Un-fortunately, she lacked the authority and the magnetism to rule her quarrelling court, and her "policy of pity" was little more than a clever stop-gap, devoid of principle and reflecting only political necessity. Calvinists and Catholics throughout Europe maintained without reservation the creed: "one doctrine, one discipline, one religion". They merely quarrelled over the content of such a monolithic faith. The Queen Regent's willingness to compromise on points of faith had all the disadvantages of a policy of appeasement. The Huguenots did not want concessions; they demanded total victory, and they viewed the end of persecution and the Crown's effort to achieve a broad theo-logical solution as a sign of weakness and an invitation to make further demands.

Undeterred and probably unaware of the emotional and

psychological obstacles in her path, the Queen Mother made her plans as if she were doing an exercise in a handbook on Machiavellian diplomacy. Guise was more powerful than Bourbon, and a rather obscure point about the nature of the Eucharist seemed to be producing lunacy among Frenchmen; therefore it behoved the Crown to seek the support of the Protestants by ending persecution and in the name of sweet reason to bring priest and pastor together to setle their religious differences.

Admiral Coligny and the Prince of Condé were both graciously received at court, the heresy hunt was lifted, and government officials ignored the flaunting of illegal Calvinist services. Theodore Beza, Calvin's right-hand man and eventual successor at Geneva, was given a warm welcome at the French court, and one disgruntled Catholic protested that it was more cordial than "the Pope would have received if he had come". In August 1561 twelve Protestant ministers sat down with the bishops of the French church; unfortunately they met thirty years too late. Calvin and the Council of Trent had done their work, and the meeting served only to reveal the depth of the Queen's misunderstanding of religious feelings, and to indicate that quarrels of faith could not be settled by a mediator who was herself devoid of religious conviction and moral principles.

The results of the religious meeting were disastrous, for the Huguenots claimed victory for themselves and promptly increased their demands. They had discussed theology on equal terms with bishops and they now demanded the right to worship on equal terms with Catholics. In every bailiwick and town of France the Huguenot church moved into the open, proving itself to be just as bigoted as the intolerance against which it was rebelling. At Castres in 1560 Calvinists had been a tiny, persecuted and imprisoned minority, holding their services in secret and enduring the fury of the populace. In February 1561, by government order, all Protestants were liberated from jail; by April they were holding services in public before audiences of six hundred; by the end of the month, Academy students from Geneva were flocking into the town; on June 5th, Protestants for the first time dared to ignore the order to decorate their houses in honour of Corpus Christi day; in August the first Huguenot funeral took place; in September, elections gave them control over the city government; and in October, both Catholic and Protestant services were being held in all the town churches.

The crisis at Castres came in December and January. Friar Claude d'Oraison was preaching when a fervent Protestant shouted from the audience that he was a liar. The Catholic congregation promptly ejected the Calvinist, but that same evening the Huguenots of the town took up arms, seized the Friar, and expelled him from the district. On January 1st 1562, Catholicism was formally abolished, and in the following month, when a Trinitarian monk was discovered celebrating mass in secret, he was seized, dressed in his sacerdotal robes, placed backwards on a donkey, and paraded through the streets of Castres. The monk was then sat in a chair, shaved, presented with a consecrated wafer and asked whether he was ready to die for his idolatry. The poor man was not, and only his robes were consumed in the flames. Throughout France a Huguenot dialectic was forming, and within five years the young King, Charles IX, would have occasion to complain to Coligny: "Not so very long ago you were content with being tolerated by the Catholics, but now you demand equality! Soon you will want the power for yourselves alone, and will wish to drive us out of the country!" Except for the implied disloyalty to the person of the sovereign, most Huguenots in their secret hearts could not have denied the King's accusation.

If Catherine's moderation gave encouragement to the Protestants, it drove the Catholics to fury. For every Huguenot aggression, Catholics answered in kind. In Paris, when Calvinists pillaged the church of Saint-Médard, enraged Catholics burned the Protestant meeting-house. At court, Protestantism was so much in the ascendant that Catholics feared the Queen Mother and the King himself might be won to the devil's cause. Mounting religious frenzy began to seize men's minds, destroying the anodyne of custom, loosening the bonds of habitual obedience, and elevating the monsters of human cruelty and selfishness into instruments of God's purpose. Conscience was proving to be thicker than blood, and ties of religion were growing so strong that one government official sadly confessed that "an Englishman and a Frenchman of the same faith loved each other better than two Frenchmen of the same blood but of different religions".

Exactly what Catherine had worked hardest to prevent was taking place: France was being polarized into two armed and hostile religious camps. In April 1561 Catholic factions buried their family hatchets, and Constable Montmorency and Duke Francis of Guise joined forces in an effort to stem the Huguenot tide and save the French government from John Calvin. By October, each party – Huguenot and Catholic – was secretly making ready its weapons, and in March the inevitable occurred: one of the series of appalling atrocities committed by both religions during the winter and spring of 1562 exploded into civil war. On March 1st, two hundred horsemen under the command of the Duke of Guise discovered, in a barn near Vassy in the Duke's domain, a band of some five hundred Protestants at worship. Soldiers and churchgoers exchanged impassioned words; insults led to blows, blows to bloodshed, and Guise was hit on the nose by a rock. At that moment the Duke's soldiers unsheathed their swords and the Massacre of Vassy began. Reports vary, but possibly one hundred and twenty-five Huguenots died and over one hundred were wounded. When word of the slaughter reached Paris, the hot-headed Prince of Condé sent out the call to arms and war began.

The first civil war was the culmination of the steady drift towards violence. It broke out at that moment when it was easier to act than to think, to kill than to negotiate. In the provinces anarchy went unchecked. Protestants were busy pillaging and profaning Catholic churches, and putting idolatry to the sword. Catholics were equally brutal in their campaign against the poison of heresy and Satan. Blaise de Montluc, Governor of Guyenne, hanged every Huguenot who came his way and announced it to be his opinion that "one man hanged is a better example than a hundred killed". Montluc typified the leaders on both sides – men who preferred to begin with the execution and argue the case afterwards.

As early as 1559 the English ambassador, Nicholas Throckmorton, wrote to Elizabeth: "Now is the time to spend money and it will never have been better spent." In 1562 the English decided that the time to act had arrived, and at the Treaty of Hampton Court Elizabeth was persuaded by Coligny and Condé to part with one hundred thousand crowns and to dispatch an army of six thousand to help the cause of Protestantism in return for the port of Le Havre and the promise of Calais. If the Huguenots were willing to sell the realm of France for the sake of the kingdom of God, and if the prince were right, Gloriana was delighted to participate in the partition of the ancient enemy.

The war, in fact, decided nothing except that France would never go Protestant and that Elizabeth had underestimated the cost of intervention. The first civil war came to an end when the leaders of both sides were either killed or captured. Guise fell to the assassin's blade; Anthony of Navarre was killed in battle; Condé and the Constable were captured; and Catherine, on the principle that captives are reasonable peacemakers, urged Condé and Montmorency to negotiate the peace signed in March 1563. The results satisfied no one except the Queen Mother. Limited liberty of worship was accorded the Huguenots, which infuriated the Catholics and failed to appease the Protestants; Calvinists were irritated by having their faith prohibited in the city of Paris; and the Guise family failed to get satisfaction for the death of Duke Francis. They did have the doubtful pleasure of seeing his assassin, a fanatical young Huguenot nobleman, pulled to pieces by four wild horses, but they continued to harbour a personal vendetta against Coligny whom they deemed morally responsible for the murder.

The only positive result of the settlement was a lesson to Elizabeth of England not to meddle in French affairs. The moment peace was signed, Catherine gathered an army of forty thousand men and forty cannons and moved on Le Havre. If Queen Elizabeth, she said, does not return the city "to us willingly, God will enable us to take it by force". Gloriana never returned anything willingly, but in this case the siege was short and the English defence inglorious.

Victorious over Elizabeth, and with all her French generals either dead or humiliated, Catherine emerged the sole victor of the war, but again her triumph proved hollow. The Queen's solution to the ills that beset France was to set out in January 1564 upon a triumphal progress. She travelled with her young son, who received the accolades of both Protestants and Catholics, and with her squadron of alluring goddesses, whose smiles, it was hoped, would banish the bitter memory of war. The full bankruptcy of Catherine's policy was revealed in the shallowness of her own words. "They all danced together," she told the Duchess of Guise, "Huguenots and Papists alike, and so happily" that she had great hopes of a permanent reconciliation. Though Catholics and Protestants might dance together they had in fact only one thing in common: the darkest suspicion of the Queen Mother. Hers was the fate of all inveterate schemers for, as one English observer said, "she had too much wit for a woman, and too little honesty for a Queen". Philip of Spain called her *Madame La Serpente* and wrote that he trusted "neither her leagues nor her marriages". Calumny and rumours, bred of distrust for an Italian queen, found ready audience in both religions. The Queen, it was said, preferred heretics to faithful and godly subjects; she might at any moment barter the safety of the Catholic Church for the sake of a golden crown for one of her many children. Equally reliably it was maintained that she planned to cut the throats of all Godfearing Huguenots and waited only to turn their guard with false words and empty promises.

Distrust led to the renewal of war during the summer of 1568. The path to paradise was soaked in blood, and the fury with which Frenchmen tore at Frenchmen was worse than in the dreadful days of the Hundred Years War. Protestants stormed a Catholic monastery and forced the monks to hang each other; cities that had been induced to open their gates by the offer of honourable surrender-terms were put to the sword; at Orleans Huguenot captives were burned en masse in prison by Catholic mobs; at Auxerre crowds pulled to bits one hundred and fifty Calvinists and threw the pieces into the sewer; at Foix Protestants slaughtered one hundred and twenty Papists, and Catholics retaliated by killing seven hundred Calvinists. The temper of the times was epitomized by the revenge of Duke Henry of Guise when the Prince of Condé fell in battle. In retaliation for his father's murder, he ordered the Prince's body exposed naked upon a donkey's back. On both sides men lived only for hatred, and so many unspeakable atrocities were committed that the Venetian ambassador wrote that he could not better describe the state of the kingdom "than by comparing it to a leg, an arm, or any other member attacked by gangrene; when the doctor, having cauterized a wound, thinks that his task is finished, he sees another one opening beside it".

Toleration was born in the horrors of war. For a few men, such as Montaigne, liberty of conscience became a principle and guide to life, but most Frenchmen adopted it from grim necessity. Slowly, in the face of barbarism and outrage, a small group of men determined that "a man does not cease to be a citizen for being excommunicated". A thousand times, Montaigne said, he had retired to bed expecting to be betrayed or murdered before morning, and had gambled that death, when it came, would be done without terror or lingering torture. Life was intolerable under such conditions, and merchants and nobles, peasants and artisans began to argue that secure homes were more important than quiet consciences and the repose of the kingdom more desirable than the salvation of their souls. The Politiques, as the disciples of such belly-wisdom were called, grew in number with every act of vengeance and mayhem. Eventually, when enough men on both sides had demanded the end of war, peace was concluded at St. Germain in August 1570. The Catholics had triumphed in all the battles but the Protestants won the peace. Liberty of conscience and freedom of worship were granted to all Huguenots throughout the realm except in Paris and its environs; Protestants were made eligible for all public offices; and they received as guarantee of the government's good faith the possession of four cities – La Rochelle, Montauban, Cognac, and La Charité. Catholics were horrified by the terms of the settlement, and Montluc complained that the enemy had everywhere been destroyed by force of arms but now had "triumphed by means of their diabolical writings".

Despite Catholic protests, Catherine was satisfied with the peace of St. Germain, for it allowed the Queen to pose as the leader of a new alliance of Catholic Politiques and moderate Huguenots. In typical Medici fashion she planned a series of marriages to win allies for her policies and crowns for her children. Her youngest son, the Duke of Alençon, an ardent if charming Catholic of nineteen, was to marry that ageing champion of Protestantism, the thirty-seven-year-old Elizabeth of England, while her daughter Margaret was designated as the bride of young Henry of Navarre, the titular head of the Huguenots and Bourbon heir to the throne.

The Queen's ambassadors failed to come home with the virgin bride, but they did achieve a major diplomatic triumph when England gave up more than three hundred years of cherished francophobia and joined France in a defensive alliance against Spain. The Treaty of Blois in 1572 was a token of a fundamental change in the structure and balance of European diplomacy. As the power of France and the dynastic ambitions of monarchs receded, the might of Spain and the affairs of God loomed larger. Once armies had crossed into Italy as conquerors with no other purpose than the glory of kings and the loot of the Italian Renaissance. Now they marched as liberators and instruments of God's glory. Elizabeth of England and Catherine of France were of the old school; they preferred to keep diplomacy the concern of men, not of angels, and they regarded with the deepest misgivings Philip of Spain's argument that when dealing with heresy "it was better to go and put out the fire in a neighbour's house than to wait for it to spread to one's own". Both Queens were in agreement that, at all costs, the affairs of their respective kingdoms must be solved without benefit of Spanish troops, and in both countries there were men who urged that the best defence against Spanish good intentions was to foster the revolt in the Netherlands, where Philip was confronted with social and religious revolution.

In September of 1571 Coligny was again called to court;

this time to help arrange the marriage of Navarre to Margaret Valois. Though the marriage negotiations moved smoothly, Catherine again miscalculated, for Coligny began to exercise an inordinate influence over the neurotic and impressionable Charles IX. In the eyes of the Queen Mother, he was committing the one crime that could neither be forgiven nor ignored: he was stealing the affections of a son who until that moment had listened to no one but his mother. "After God," Charles had said, "the Queen, my mother, is the one to whom I have the greatest number of obligations." As usual, Catherine's solution was tragically myopic if eminently practical. Coligny would have to go, and the obvious instrument of assassination was the Guise family's blood-feud with the Admiral.

The staging of murder was complicated by the approaching wedding of Protestant Navarre and Catholic Margaret, which had been set for August 18th, 1572, and by the decision of the Huguenot nobility to attend in force. On both sides tension mounted: Paris was stoutly Catholic and viewed the growing number of Protestant nobles and their henchmen with fear and hatred; Navarre and his young cousin, Henry of Condé, entered the city with eight hundred cavalry, and the roads to Paris were crowded with some five thousand Huguenots determined to view the wedding. The Queen Mother was worried lest Coligny and Condé were plotting to kidnap the King, and the Protestants were filled with anger at Catherine's refusal to intervene in the Netherlands. Under conditions guaranteed to explode at the slightest spark, the government went ahead with its plans to dispatch the Admiral. The results were catastrophic. On August 22nd, as Coligny was walking down a narrow alley, his assassin shot from behind a small window. What saved the Admiral's life was the accident of bending down to tie a shoelace. The bullet ripped open his arm and smashed his hand. Every Huguenot in the city was up in arms at this outrage to their leader. They crowded into Coligny's residence, shouting: "That arm shall cost thirty thousand other arms!", and the Admiral indignantly demanded an immediate audience with the King.

Charles IX was the one weak link in the Queen's design. He was unaware of his mother's plans and told Coligny that he was "determined to have justice done on such a scale that it shall be a warning to every man in my kingdom". If the King carried out his threat, his own mother would be implicated; and at this moment Catherine lost her head. In her frenzy she chose to accept at its face value the Huguenot threat to demand thirty thousand arms in vengeance for what Guise had done to Coligny, and she determined upon the wholesale murder of all the Huguenot leaders so conveniently assembled in Paris. It remained only to win over her son. After two hours she triumphed, and a beaten and furious Charles turned and cursed: "Well then, kill them all, that not a single man may be left to reproach me."

The signal for bloodshed was set for the early morning of August 24th, the feast of St. Bartholomew. It had been decided to spare the Huguenot princes of the blood, Navarre and Condé, but no other nobleman was to escape. If Catherine intended to limit death to the Calvinist leaders, her plans tragically miscarried, for the moment the bells tolled, all Paris rose up and shouted "The Huguenots! The Huguenots! Death to the Huguenots!" Some were stabbed, some were hanged, some were drowned, some were thrown from windows and rooftops, and Henry of Guise personally supervised the death of Admiral Coligny. Private vendettas as well as religious hatred culminated in vandalism, barbarism and murder so that Paris, said one shocked observer, "was like a conquered city", and the Seine ran red with blood. Killing and butchery spilled over into the provinces, bringing the grisly total of deaths to ten thousand: one thousand at Orleans, eight hundred at Lyons and possibly four thousand in Paris.

Despite the torrent of blood, St. Bartholomew's Day achieved little except to divide further a kingdom that was literally falling apart. The Catholic world applauded. Philip of Spain announced that the deed "has given me one of the greatest joys of my life", and wrote to young King Charles that the extermination of the hateful heretic would be his greatest title to glory. The Pope had a medal issued commemorating the victory of God over Satan, and His Holiness ordered Rome to be illuminated for three nights in token of the triumph. If ardent Catholics viewed the

Massacre as a particularly holy act, Protestant Europe regarded it as one of unmitigated infamy. Elizabeth of England, dressed in the deepest mourning and accompanied by her full Council, listened in icy silence to the French ambassador's efforts to excuse and justify the slaughter. In Calvin's Switzerland, in the Netherlands and in Lutheran Germany, Protestants were aghast. Gruesome and generally inaccurate details were published: Charles IX was accused of having used Huguenots for target practice, shooting them down from his window in the Louvre, and William of Orange wrote that the French King would never be able to wash the red stain from his bloody hands. Even Ivan the Terrible of Russia, who was no stranger to savagery, wrote in protest.

After Catholic applause and Protestant shudders had died away and the bloody gutters of Paris had been swept clean, the Queen Mother was able to take stock. The inventory was far from satisfactory. From the blood of the aristocratic martyrs sprang the seed of an invigorated and republican Huguenot church, under new spiritual guidance and openly advocating regicide and war. In destroying the feudal leadership of Calvinism, Catherine had created a worse danger to the state, for the Huguenot party became a democratic theocracy which considered monarchy as well as Catholicism to be incompatible with godliness. In the south, where the Huguenots remained strong, feudal provincialism, sustained and encouraged by religious hatred, achieved its ultimate purpose: independence. After St. Bartholomew's Day, France was broken in two. Languedoc, the area south of the river Loire, went republican, establishing a council of state, an assembly of deputies, provincial councils, its own laws and fiscal machinery, and levying its own taxes upon Catholics and Protestants alike.

The governor and virtual king of Languedoc was Henry Damville, second son of the old Constable, and his support of the Huguenots represented still another result of the feast of St. Bartholomew, for Damville was a member of the Politique party and a cousin of the murdered Coligny. Though a papist, the slaughter represented everything he and his party had wished to avoid. Moderate Catholics were outraged, and the Politiques wondered when their own turn might come. Moreover, the Montmorency family regarded the death of the Admiral as another atrocity in their mounting blood feud with the house of Guise. St. Bartholomew's Day and the Queen's policy had driven the Politiques and the Huguenots into union, and Damville announced his recognition of the supremacy of young Henry of Condé, son of Prince Louis.

Final retribution, regarded by the Protestant world as divine in origin, came when Charles IX was stricken by a combination of remorse and congenital tuberculosis. After St. Bartholomew's Day he began to change, visibly to die. He constantly hung his head and dared look no man in the eye. At twenty-four, he looked sixty-four. His hand began to tremble; he was plagued with hideous nightmares; and in the end he was little more than a living skeleton. He died on May 30th, 1574, the worn-out scion of an exhausted house; and his final word was a suitable and tragic summation of his life: as he died he mumbled the single word "Mother". Catherine, in her efforts to save herself and her son's throne, had helped to destroy the one child who had been totally dependent on her, and into his place stepped Henry III, the child she feared and loved the most, and the Valois King who, in his determination to escape his mother's stifling affection, destroyed himself and everything the Queen had worked to protect.

The years between 1572 and 1576 were filled with fighting and political anarchy. Navarre reported to a friend that "we carry daggers and wear coats of mail and very often breastplates under our cloaks. I am only waiting for the opportunity to have a little fighting, for I am told that they are plotting to kill me and I want to steal a march on them". Everyone was waiting for the opportunity to kill, which they did unmercifully. The exchequer was empty, the kingdom in arms, justice dead, France divided, and the "only topic at the Court at the moment was that there was nothing for the King's dinner". Anything was preferable to continued war, but peace could only be purchased by total capitulation to the Huguenots and Politiques. In the end, Henry III and Catherine had no choice but to accept their terms, and the Peace of Monsieur was signed in May

1576. The government officially apologized for St. Bartholomew's Day; Protestants were granted complete liberty of worship throughout the kingdom; and four additional surety cities were placed under their control.

With a perversity born of bad luck and worse judgment, whatever steps the Queen took only created more pressing problems. From 1576 on, the Valois throne was crushed between two political-religious forces for which Catherine herself was in large measure responsible. From the start her aim had been to hold the balance between two equal parties and thus preserve the security of France and the throne of her sons. After 1576 the Crown, in the person of Henry III, was too weak to control its own creations. Possibly Catherine's consummate duplicity might have postponed the fate of the Valois dynasty, but the time for Machiavellian manoeuvring was past. Moreover, the gouty and ageing pilot had been dropped, for after the humiliation of the Peace of Monsieur, Henry cast off his mother's tutelage and set off alone to rule his kingdom.

Everything about the King, wrote the papal legate, "is contradictory". He was a sceptic, yet scourged and mortified his flesh. He could be every inch a monarch if he chose, but more often Henry of Valois elected to play the degenerate. He was avid for excitement yet constitutionally incapable of enduring it. He surrounded every thought with a coating of verbiage so thick that none knew whether the King spoke profound wisdom or merely gabbled without meaning. He sensed with unerring skill the truth about men and politics but was incapable of acting upon his own opinion, for, as he confessed, "nobody else would agree with me and I may possibly be wrong". Henry suffered from constant headaches, an infected ear and a maddening itch brought on by chronic eczema. Occasionally there were spells of frantic activity during which he drenched his body in perfume, decked it with ribbons and ear-rings, and painted his face with a mask of rouge and powder, from which peered sick and sunken eyes. He surrounded his royal person with effeminate young men who wore their hair in ruffles and spent their time in gaming, drinking and dancing. On one occasion he arranged a banquet served by the beauties of the court, dressed as men

and clad in green silk; another time he assumed feminine
attire and attended a ball with his bodice cut low and his
neck adorned with "a pearl necklace and three linen
collars". Long after he was mercifully dead, the Duke of
Sully remembered those days. "I shall never forget," he
said, "the fantastic and extravagant equipage and attitude
in which I found this prince in his cabinet: he had a sword
at his side, a Spanish hood hung down upon his shoulders,
a little cap, such as collegians wear, upon his head, and a
basket full of little dogs hung to a broad ribbon about his
neck." Such was the last Valois King of France.

While the crown faltered under the rule of a "Prince of
Sodom" and his "court of silk and blood", Catholics, under
the leadership of Henry of Guise, took matters into their
own hands. The Peace of Monsieur was regarded as a dis-
grace to France and an insult to God, and Catholics joined
together in a Holy League dedicated to the extermination
of heresy. The League openly sought military aid from
Spain and deliberately appealed to every variety of provincial and feudal greed. France again lay exposed to the
fury of two warring parties, and no matter which side won,
neither the kingdom nor the King had anything to gain.
Mercifully the war lasted less than a year, and by 1576
the Holy League had forced the Huguenots to accept a
more limited form of freedom to worship.

Though the Catholics again triumphed in war, whatever
hopes they may have had for the future vanished when the
King's younger brother died and Protestant Henry of
Navarre became heir to the throne. The youngest of Catherine's children had been christened Hercules and created
Duke of Alençon, but his name had been changed to Francis, and on Henry III's succession to the throne he became
Duke of Anjou. Anjou was one of those turbulent and
improbable characters who keep appearing in history. He
tried to win Elizabeth's hand in 1572 by a whirlwind court-
ship; he was consumed with pathological hatred for his
brothers; he openly conspired to snatch the succession from
Henry when Charles IX died in 1574; and he tried his hand
at treason by joining the Politique-Huguenot alliance in
open war against his mother and brother. Anjou was a
chronic pest, the master of five duchies, the possessor of

four hundred thousand crowns yearly, and a man obsessed
with a passion to wear a crown. In 1577, Henry III found
an opportunity to send his difficult and unstable brother to
make trouble for someone else. Unofficially Catherine
and Henry urged Francis to find himself a crown in the
Netherlands, where both the Catholic and Calvinist subjects
of Philip of Spain were in full-scale revolt. Unfortunately
Anjou was no more successful at war than he had been at
winning Elizabeth's hand in marriage (he had tried a
second time in 1580), and he was disastrously defeated in
battle by the very people he had come to protect, the
Netherlands themselves. Three years later in 1584, at the
age of thirty-one, he died of the Valois sickness, haemorrhage of the lungs.

His death upset the political and international apple-cart.
Throughout France primitive passions welled to the surface. No matter what the emotion – fear, greed, idealism –
Catholics were swept by the common determination that
France must be preserved from the horror of a heretic
king. The dynastic aspirations of Henry Duke of Guise,
the religious policy of the papacy, the absolute conviction
of the Jesuits, the international interests of Spain, and the
irrational fear of tens of thousands of Frenchmen who
disciplined their children and terrified themselves with
stories of sinister Huguenots rising up in the dead of night
to murder good Catholics in their beds – all these were in
accord: Henry of Navarre must never be King of France.

Anjou was dead scarcely three months when Catholic
demagogues whipped the Holy League into action. To
priest and friar, monk and prior, the League was an instrument of God's ultimate victory, and humble men joined its
ranks as if going on a crusade, but at least two men viewed
it from a more worldly perspective. There is little doubt
that Henry of Guise was dazzled by the prospect of the
throne of France once Henry of Valois was dead, and he
used the League to win a crown. Don Bernardino de
Mendoza, the resident Spanish ambassador at Paris and
undoubtedly the best informed man in France, was equally
sanguine. Mendoza was welcome in the innermost circles
of the Holy League. He was the valued friend and pay-
master of both the Duke and the Committee of Sixteen,

the secret revolutionary and frantic left wing of the League. As the man who controlled the League's purse-strings, Mendoza also called the tune which became increasingly Spanish in tempo. Spanish interests demanded that Henry of Navarre be barred the throne and that France be broken by civil war. The might of Spain had been ordained as the weapon to win all Europe back to the Catholic fold, and if heresy were to be exterminated in the Netherlands and England, Valois France must be kept pure in faith and helpless in diplomacy. In the Holy League Mendoza found the perfect instrument of Spanish policy, for each element – the feudal ambitions of the Guises, the religious hysteria of monks and priests, the social bitterness of the revolutionary left wing – looked to Philip of Spain for leadership and money.

In July 1585 the League demanded of a bankrupt and helpless Henry III that he revoke all edicts of toleration towards heretics and ban Protestants from the land. By September the Pope had proclaimed Henry of Navarre a relapsed heretic and incapable of lawfully succeeding to the throne, and in October, much to Mendoza's satisfaction, the bitterest and most extraordinary of all the French religious wars broke out. The War of the Three Henrys was fought by Navarre for survival, by Guise for a kingdom and by Valois because he had no other choice. By the winter of 1585–6 the League had three armies in the field, all heavily financed by Spain: one to destroy Henry of Navarre, one to handle the army of thirty-five thousand Germans who were marching to the aid of their Protestant brethren in France, and one to guard the King. As the conflict progressed, it became increasingly apparent that Henry III was not the master of his army, but its prisoner, and that Henry of Guise was king of Catholic France in all but name. With well deserved pride, Mendoza reported to Philip that "events here could hardly have gone more happily for Your Majesty's affairs".

By 1588 the war between the three Henrys had been reduced to a struggle between Henry of Guise, who sought to maintain his control over the kingdom and who coveted the crown of France, and Henry of Valois who possessed neither a son nor a realm, but who was determined to keep his crown and bequeath what little he possessed to his legal, if heretical heir, Henry of Navarre. The climax came in May on the Day of the Barricades. At the invitation of the revolutionary Committee of Sixteen who controlled the city's government, and in open defiance of the King's order, Henry of Guise entered Paris. Henry of Valois, in self-defence, mobilized the Swiss Guards. Rumours spread that he was planning a Catholic St. Bartholomew's Day and the murder of the Duke. The city instantly flew to arms, barricaded the streets, and pelted the King's troops with filth and debris. In panic the monarch fled, leaving the Duke "King of Paris" and virtual dictator of northern France. A month later Henry of Valois gave official recognition to political reality. He dismissed his ministers, surrendered the substance of power to the League, promised to change the succession, and in return was permitted the hollow satisfaction of calling himself King of France. In fact, however, Henry's capitulation was not complete. The Swiss Guards remained, and the servants he sent away had been more loyal to the Queen, his mother, than to him. It was symptomatic of the violence of the age that yet another murder was deemed necessary and acceptable to the solution of a political problem, and almost immediately the King began to arrange the carefully staged elimination of his rival.

The end came like the conclusion to a Shakespearean tragedy. On December 23rd, 1588, Henry Duke of Guise was murdered in the ante-room to the sovereign's bed-chamber while Henry King of France hid behind the curtains. The next day the Cardinal of Guise was struck down by assassins. The double murder produced the ultimate irony of thirty years of religious horror. Catholic fanaticism erupted, Paris revolted, the Holy League demanded vengeance and thundered regicide, and Henry III was forced into open alliance with his cousin of Navarre and the hated heretics in order to save his toppling throne. In the end the inevitable happened: on August 1st, 1589, the chain of murders was completed when a young Dominican monk, convinced that God had instructed him to deliver the Mother Church from such a monstrous monarch, set out to kill the King. He asked for audience, and as Henry stood before him, he drove a knife into the King's stomach. The monk was dead almost before Henry knew what had struck him, but murder had been done, and within hours the last of the Valois died. Protestant Henry of Navarre was now monarch of a realm swept by hatred, disintegrating into social revolution and overrun by foreign armies. His story and the miracle of his achievement belong to a later and final chapter, for Henry IV was a member of the generation that followed Elizabeth and is part of the epilogue to her age.

Catherine de Medici must bear her share of responsibility for the death of her son, even though she was already six months dead. She had taught her children the art of survival in an age of religious madness, and ultimately her own art destroyed everything that she held most dear – her offspring, her house, her adopted realm. As the Florentine ambassador said, she was always "prudent and very experienced in matters of this world", yet she never knew "what remedy to apply to so many present ills nor to the ills to come". Surely she had more than her share of ills, but just as surely she had the morals of an Italian pawnbroker and the instincts of a Machiavellian diplomat, neither of which mixed well with her destroying love for her children or had a place in a world where kings and commoners were willing to sacrifice men and kingdoms to religious conscience. When the Guise brothers were murdered at the command of her son, there is a legend that Cardinal Bourbon reproached her, saying: "Ah! Madam, this is your doing. It is you who are killing us all!" She did not deny the charge; instead she whimpered: "I can bear no more. I must go to bed." Less than a month later, in January 1589, she was dead, aged seventy-one and eight hundred thousand écus in debt. Even in death she failed to attain the grandeur that had so persistently eluded her in life. Her body was inadequately embalmed and had to be buried in haste in the shallow grave of a provincial church, and thereafter no one paid "more notice to her than a dead goat".

Seven

Philip of Spain and God's Obvious Design

"IF death", wrote the Spanish viceroy in Naples, "came from Spain, we should all very nearly live for ever." Like the mills of God, Philip of Spain ground slowly, and when death finally came to the King of Spain it was quietly told to wait while His Most Catholic Majesty discussed with his ministers and priests every particular of his impending funeral, ordered great bolts of black cloth to shroud his palace, and demanded that his coffin be brought to the bedside so that his putrid and withered body could be measured for the grave. As Philip the Prudent could not die without ensuring that his corpse would fit perfectly its final resting place, so for forty years he could not live without scrutinizing with agonizing care every detail of the government of his vast domain. When his father, the Emperor Charles, gouty and sick of heart, resigned the immense burden of his many kingdoms to Philip in 1555, not a king, but a prince of pedants, mounted the throne of Spain and shouldered the weight of the largest empire the world had ever seen.

The magnitude of Philip's failure, the martyrdom of an entire kingdom to the unselfish but gossamer vision of a Europe purged of heresy and united in the ample bosom of the Mother Church, has led scholars the world over to speculate on the character of a monarch who hid himself in a cell, twelve feet by twelve feet, as his empire grew ever

larger, who adorned himself in the severest black as the
gold of the Indies poured into his coffers, and who sought
the quiet of his study and the association of his ancestors as
Spanish arms won victories for God and Church on land
and sea. There is something terrifying about the words
used to describe the King. Solitary, reserved, dispassionate,
cold and imperturbable, are the adjectives most often em-
ployed by apologists and critics alike. The anecdotes about
his iron self-restraint are endless. One is told about a young
and nervous clerk who ruined an evening's work when he
inadvertently poured ink, not sand, on the King's letters.
With superhuman patience, Philip carefully explained:
"*This* is the sand, *that* is the ink." During his lifetime
Philip buried seventeen of his family, but he never showed
sorrow and ordered only thanks to God on the occasion of
each funeral. The most celebrated story told is untrue, but
it remains in character. When a frightened secretary
brought news of the disaster of the Armada, Philip barely
interrupted the motion of his pen to remark: "I give thanks
to God by whose hand I have been so endowed that I can
put to sea another fleet as great as this we have lost whenever I choose."

Even in his fanaticism Philip was without enthusiasm,
which made his words to Don Carlos de Seso more monstrous than if he had spoken in anger. The occasion was
the magnificent auto-da-fé of October 1559, staged by the
Inquisitor-General, to celebrate the King's happy return to
Spain and to demonstrate the royal determination never to
"live to be a king of heretics". The celebration was held
in the great square opposite the Cathedral of St. Francis in
Valladolid, and before an audience of two hundred thousand Philip took a mighty oath to defend the Holy Catholic
Faith with all the strength of his empire. Then, to the tolling of the bells, twenty-five condemned heretics received
final judgment. Thirteen escaped with imprisonment and
penance; ten were sentenced to burn alive but chose to die
as Catholics and were mercifully strangled before being
consumed in the fire; and two refused to recant and endured the agony of the stake. One of these was Don Carlos
de Seso, an Italian nobleman and godson of Charles V.
As he passed Philip on his way to execution, Don Carlos

accused the King of inhumanity and barbarism. Philip's flat
and epicene voice answered in words that held the hint
of terrible prophecy: "If my son were as evil as you
are, I myself would fetch the wood wherewith to burn
him."

Throughout his life Philip acted only after the most
painstaking deliberation, but once the decision had been
made, he moved with the inexorable conviction of a man at
peace with God. Philip's conscience was no servant to
ambition, and he always maintained that the divinity of his
royal office placed upon him a burden far greater than
on other men, for God expected more of kings than of
subjects. The entire structure of his government was designed to give Philip the time, the information and the
authority to decide for himself. His father, the Emperor,
had warned him to "depend on none but yourself", and
that advice became the rock upon which Philip built his
administrative system.

Spain and her dependencies were governed by an administrative pyramid with a royal council of state at its
peak and twelve regional and departmental councils at its
base. The lesser units, such as the councils of Castile, the
Indies, or the Inquisition, exercised immense authority, but
the council of state was little more than a debating forum
which the King kept divided into opposing factions and
used only as a source of information and as a means of
testing his ministers. Philip the Prudent never sought the
unanimous advice of his council for that would have
smacked of conciliar control. Instead, he confronted every
minister with his opposite number. If half the council
followed the lead of the Duke of Alva and espoused a
policy of strong medicine and direct action, Philip was at
pains to see that the other half was of the opinion of the
Prince of Eboli, who stood for mildness, diplomacy and
caution. The Venetian ambassador misunderstood the roles
of Alva and Eboli when he reported that they were the
"two columns which support the great machine: on their
advice depends the fate of half the world". Philip listened
with endless patience, but his ultimate purpose was to ensure that every policy urged by the one would be criticized
by the other. Information, not advice, was the King's ob-

session, and he read an ambassador's passing comment about English fleas as avidly as Mendoza's political analysis from Paris.

At heart King Philip was an antiquarian. His was a "little world made of cunning and elusive elements"; no detail was trifling enough to be delegated, no report long enough to warrant abridgment. "It is well to consider everything," Philip once said, and he set about following his own dictum. Government by annotation was the result. Mountains of papers arrived daily from Aragon and Naples, Milan and the Netherlands, Mexico and Peru, Africa and the Indies. Alva in Antwerp, Mendoza in London or Paris, Don Cristóbal de Maura in Lisbon, and Francisco de Toledo in Lima dutifully reported to their master, and he as faithfully read, corrected and annotated every word they wrote. With stultifying industry, Philip filled the margins with his illegible spidery hand, laboriously noting that a Latin scribe had spelled *quassi* with a single "s", commenting upon a detail of government, or curtly dismissing some opinion with which he disagreed.

The result was endless, infuriating delay; but patience was a virtue which Philip shared with Elizabeth of England. "Time and I are a match for any two" was more than a passing expression of Philip's faith that delay resolved all things; it was the essence of his life. Every petition, every memorandum from the council, every ambassador's report followed a carefully prescribed path and eventually added to the great heap of documents that weighted down the King's desk and consumed his waking hours. Everything the King handled had to be in precise and proper form, and Philip was loath to read any letter that did not address him simply as "Sir" and conclude with the words: "God guard the Catholic person of Your Majesty." Without time to deliberate, without the security of system, without every scrap of information by which to discover certainty, Philip was as helpless as a pedant without facts or a bureaucrat without organization. Only when every "i" had been dotted and every "t" received its cross, did the King finally make up his mind.

Philip's sombre palace outside Madrid stands as a monument to the man and the Golden Age of Spain. The

Escorial is a savage and sinister pile of grey stone cut from
a setting that only El Greco could have captured in paint.
Part monastery, part mausoleum, and part mansion for a
monarch possessed of a clerical turn of mind and consumed
by a Messianic mission, the Escorial is a perfect mirror of
the man who built it and the empire that sustained it. Long
before Philip returned to Spain, he had pictured to himself
just such a massive hiding place, safe in that "land of rocks
and saints". His father, when in Spain, had lived in the
exquisitely cool and arabesque rooms of the caliphs of
Granada and later had built himself a superbly impractical
palace in the best Renaissance style, but the son sought
not a home but a tomb, not the grandeur of Rome nor the
miracle of Muslim artistry but a Christian citadel and
hermitage.

In one task alone Philip would tolerate no delay; he
could not wait to see his dream translated into the granite
of the Sierra de Guadarrama. Massive, fortress-like walls,
six hundred and seventy-five feet long, five hundred and
thirty feet wide and almost a hundred feet high, split by
narrow and unfriendly windows, belied the luxury within
the Escorial. Every region of Philip's empire contributed to
the fulfilment of the royal vision: silver chalices and golden candelabra from Milan, tapestries from Antwerp and
Brussels, an infinite variety of woods from the New World,
marble from the Sierra Nevada, steel from Toledo, and the
works of Titian and Tintoretto imported from Venice. Even
in haste it took twenty years to construct and furnish a
palace exactly to the King's tastes. Philip gathered the
riches of his empire not for his personal satisfaction but
to honour God and St. Lawrence, whose grisly martyrdom
had inspired the architectural plan and after whom the
great church of the Escorial was named. St. Lawrence had
died on a gridiron and Philip's palace was laid out accord-
ingly. At the centre of the gridiron was placed the monastic
church, hidden, except for its great dome, by the towering
walls of monastic cells and royal apartments. In the vaults
beneath the church rested the family coffins filled with
Habsburg bodies; to one side was located Philip's inner
bedchamber, devoid of windows except for a shuttered
peephole looking out upon the Hieronymite monks in

Fan tracery in Henry VII's chapel

James IV

Henry VII

Margaret Tudor

Henry VIII

Elizabeth I

James V

Mary I

Mary Stuart

Edward VI

THE HOUSE OF TUDOR

John Calvin

Henry III

Henry IV

Henry VII of England

Philip II of Spain

The Execution of Mary Queen of Scots
in the great hall at Fotheringay

Sir Francis Drake

Sir Walter Raleigh

The Earl of Essex

Sir Richard Grenville

The opposing fleets in the Channel, showing the crescent formation of the Spanish ships

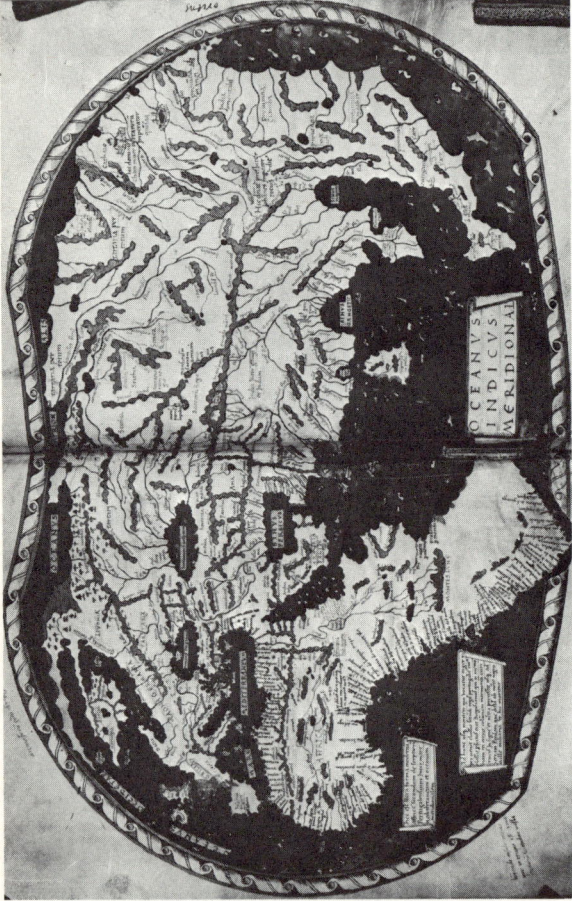

Map of the world by Henricus Martellus

prayer before the high altar of St. Lawrence. In lonely eminence, God's lieutenant on earth wrapped himself in the mantle of divinity and in solitary confinement meditated upon the heavy responsibilities of kings.

Philip allowed himself a single luxury: as monarch of twenty-seven kingdoms and an empire upon which the sun never set, he could indulge his collector's instinct, and even before the Escorial was half finished, the King had turned it into a vast library and reliquary. Books, manuscripts, relics, oddities and rarities poured in from agents all over the world. Philip had been educated in the tradition of Renaissance learning and his library with its four thousand volumes was no less precious to him than the endless shelves upon which were placed in rich settings the arm of St. Lawrence, the head of St. Undelina, two bones of the apostles Philip and James, and the remains of St. Justus and St. Pastor. Every facet of Philip's character found expression in the Escorial – his coldness, his pedantry, his magpie instinct, his austerity, his passion for privacy, and above all, his sense of divine mission. For all his golden locks, Habsburg chin and Germanic complexion, Philip was the perfect Spaniard. He was at home in the land of Ignatius Loyola and St. Teresa and her barefoot Carmelites, where every man's soul was his castle and the Lord walked "among the pots and pans".

Spain had been the product of a Christian vision come true; it had been won by blood and faith. Spanish soldiers had hurled back the onslaught of Islam and had carved out a kingdom for God. A handful of Spanish conquistadors, stout of heart and strong in the knowledge of God, had performed miracles and had toppled the empires of the New World. Philip belonged to such a Spain, for his image of himself as the instrument of God's glorious design was no more fantastic than Loyola's will to sainthood, St. Teresa's determination to reform the Church, Cortés's dream of empire, or Cervantes's romance of chivalry. In Spain, fantasies like those of the Escorial or of Don Quixote's windmills had a way of coming true, and in September 1559 Philip determined to return to his kingdom of miracles and accept his destiny as the chosen leader of the Counter-Reformation.

On October 25th 1555, the Emperor Charles, with tears in his eyes and supported by young William of Orange, announced his decision to abdicate and spend his remaining days in the Spanish monastery of Juste. Early the following year he resigned his Spanish dominions to Philip and later assigned his imperial crown to his brother Ferdinand. At fifty-three the "greatest emperor that the Christian world had ever seen", as his wife persisted in calling him, was white-haired and exhausted, his hand so arthritic that he could scarcely open a letter and the pain so terrible that he prayed for death. A constant diet of pickled partridges, eel pies, sardines, omelets, Rhenish wine and iced beer may have shortened his life, but Charles had grown old beyond his years in his constant efforts to discipline an empire as quarrelsome as a pack of wolves. Forty years of ceaseless peregrinations had taught him three things about his empire: heresy had to be recognized in Germany, fortune was a woman who loved not an old man, and his ramshackle dominions would be more orthodox in their faith and more manageable in their proportions if divested of the Lutheran and Catholic states of Germany and freed from imperial responsibility.

Even without the imperial dignity, Philip's titles were still impressive beyond measure. He was ruler of the three Kingdoms of Spain (Castile, Aragon and Navarre), lord of Burgundy and the Netherlands, archduke of Milan, sovereign of Naples and Sicily, monarch of the Indies, and king of England. More than any other, it was the English crown that symbolized the heavy burdens which the young prince had assumed. England had been regarded by his father as absolutely essential to the dynastic interests of the Habsburgs in their struggle against Valois France. The island kingdom completed the encirclement of France, secured the channel route between Spain and the Netherlands, and ensured a constant flow of unfinished wool cloth to the markets of Flanders. So important was the English alliance that in 1554 the Emperor Charles had bestowed his only legitimate son upon the ageing and ailing Mary Tudor. Philip had dutifully accepted the possessive caresses of his neurotic wife and had suffered exile in a land of heretics and barbarians who unmercifully insulted and cheated his entourage. As long as the Valois threat continued and there remained any real hope of an heir by Mary, Philip stayed close to England, but by 1557 it was apparent that his Queen's pregnancies were the fictions of a disordered mind and that France, after the defeat of St. Quentin, could easily be persuaded to sue for peace. By the time Mary died in November 1558, Philip was prepared to view the event as a blessed liberation which relieved him of the responsibility of rescuing Calais for the English, and freed him to sign the peace of Cateau-Cambrésis and marry Elizabeth Valois of France.

The French marriage brought unexpected blessings, for it was during the celebration of the wedding by proxy that Henry II received the fatal splinter in his eye. By default, Philip was translated into the unrivalled colossus of Europe: France was ruled by greedy uncles and a sickly boy-king; the Emperor Ferdinand was constantly watched by the Lutheran princes of Germany; and England was exposed to the doubtful charms and tender government of a Virgin Queen. Even the court astrologer, Nostradamus, deemed August 1559 a propitious moment for the King to return to Spain and transform the land of his birth into a "fortress, strength, treasure and sword" of God.

In Philip's estimation there was no time to waste. The soldiers of Satan, by their many triumphs among the Protestant princes of the Empire, had left his father a broken man and Germany a dying and divided realm. Scotland and England had both fallen to the devil's grasp, and in France the heretics waited impatiently to bathe the kingdom in blood. Everywhere heresy marched triumphant and unchecked, and Philip heard with alarm of the discovery of Protestant cells in Seville and Valladolid. The Inquisition had been alerted by chance to the growing peril: Calvinist propaganda intended for a heretic priest was delivered to another cleric of the same name. That worthy ecclesiastic read with shock about the worthlessness of good works and viewed with horror a picture of the Pope giving thanks to the devil. He immediately took the book to the Inquisition. A swift and thorough heresy hunt ensued, and an antidote to Protestantism in the form of a series of auto-da-fés was administered before the poison could infect disgruntled nobles and susceptible merchants.

Spaniards were shocked that even a few hundred disciples of evil had crept into a land "so Catholic, so firm and so true". In no other country in Europe was unity of faith and state so intimately and emotionally linked or the Inquisition held in such reverence. The *Suprema,* which governed the Inquisition, was God's special agency for preserving purity of creed and the King's effective instrument for maintaining royal authority over Church, aristocracy and citizenry. Each new auto-da-fé increased the prestige and power of the Inquisition, and no one was too insignificant or too lofty to escape its scrutiny. Even Archbishop Carranza of Toledo was quietly whisked away in the dead of night by order of the *Suprema* and vanished from human sight. The charge of heresy against him was grounded upon sentences torn out of context, and his secret trial endured for seventeen years. It is difficult to judge men who detected deviation of faith with the aid of red-hot pincers and stretched men upon the rack to force Satan to reveal his presence. Yet the twentieth century is no stranger to heresy hunts. Then as now, it was argued that all men must be formed from a single ideological mould, for only thus is it possible to be sure of your friends and recognize your enemies. Ideas, unless carefully expurgated, were considered dangerous, and deviation in thought, it was said, bred confusion and doubt, the inevitable harbingers of treason and ultimate defeat.

Had Protestantism been the sole consideration of the Spanish Inquisition, the office would have withered away for lack of work. What inspired the *Suprema* to unrelenting vigil and convinced good Spaniards that it was "guided by God for His praise and honour" was the constant fear in every Catholic heart of Moriscos and Marranos – Christian Moors and Christian Jews. As French Catholics saw Huguenots in their nightmares and English Puritans read with horrified fascination the atrocities committed by Jesuits and Inquisitors, so Spaniards were brought up upon grisly tales of Catholic children kidnapped and educated in the Jewish faith, of girls sold into Moorish slavery, and of

secret and Satanic practices high in the mountains surrounding Granada.

Fiction born of hysteria and reality grounded upon fact
are difficult to disentangle. Ever since the fall of Granada
in 1492 the Moors had been forced to choose between
Christianity and exile, but their conquerors eyed their conversion with the deepest suspicion and noted that they remained Moorish in dress, language and custom. The people
of Granada worked on feast days, observed Fridays more
carefully than Sundays, practised circumcision, and married their children according to the Islamic rites. The day
of reckoning had been postponed by Morisco money, which
persuaded the government not to enforce its own laws
against the use of Moorish dress and culture, but in 1567
Philip determined upon the total Christianization of such
doubtful subjects. His decision was typical, the result of
great deliberation by which he concluded that both conscience and national policy demanded strong action. Arabic
was outlawed, Moorish books, both innocent and pernicious, were destroyed, Islamic custom and dress were
forbidden, and during all marriage feasts, Fridays and
Church holy-days the doors of every Moorish family were
ordered to stand open so that all the world could inspect
the sincerity of their Catholicism. Faced with cultural annihilation, the Moriscos rebelled. Priests were butchered
and Christian families sold as slaves to the Barbary pirates
in exchange for arms. Moorish atrocities were countered
with Spanish reprisals and the entire province of Granada
was put to the sword.

War in the High Sierras was much more than a civil insurrection by an oppressed minority; it was another battle
in the great crusade that had wrested Spain from the infidel. Granada was regarded as the weak spot in the Christian armour through which Islam might again enter and
reconquer the peninsula. The Turkish threat was no fig-
ment of wild Spanish imagination. The Ottoman Empire
was at its apogee. In 1560 a Spanish fleet had been destroyed
at Los Gelves and the western Mediterranean opened up to
Turkish expansion; Suleiman the Magnificent had died in
1566 while hammering at the gates of Vienna; and the new
Sultan Selim II was currently being urged to send an army

of liberation to aid the Moriscos and reconquer Spain. Fortunately for Philip, Turkish attention was diverted towards Venice and the invasion of Cyprus, but even so the Moriscos received eight hundred trained soldiers from Algiers and a steady flow of arms and volunteers from their Moorish brethren in North Africa.

Treason and heresy in Granada and Muslim conquests in North Africa and the Mediterranean were equally dangerous, and Philip set about the total extermination of the one and the repulsion of the other. During 1570 Granada was overrun by Spanish troops and the Morisco menace destroyed once and for all. The entire Moorish population was transported to other parts of Spain and the province repopulated with Spaniards of untarnished blood and unimpeachable orthodoxy. Henceforth any adult male of Moorish descent found within ten leagues of Granada was executed, and any female sold into slavery. The price of victory had been heavy – sixty thousand Spaniards killed and an entire province turned into a desert – but purity of faith and security of the kingdom were worth the cost. Spain had to be made safe for Christianity at home before it could be used as a springboard against Islam abroad.

The union of Venice, the Papacy and Spain into a Holy League directed against the infidel was the necessary preliminary to achieve. The Venetians hated the Spanish demon of the south and deeply mistrusted the papacy, while the Pope feared Spanish hegemony only slightly less than he needed Spanish troops in the battle against heresy. It galled the Holy Father unspeakably when he discovered that his Spanish champion treated him more like a palace priest than as the supreme judge of Christendom. Fourteen years earlier Philip had been at open war with the ferocious and bitterly anti-Spanish Paul IV, and his troops had marched against banners consecrated by the Vatican. The King of Spain had regarded the Council of Trent as a conclave "in which the devil was working and plotting", and not until Spanish influence had triumphed over both French and Papal interests did he look favourably upon its decrees. Even a Henry VIII might have envied Philip his ecclesiastical arrogance, for that most Catholic Monarch taxed, disciplined and governed his Church without Papal interference, and at the same time interfered so much in the affairs of Rome that Pius IV, the gentlest of pontiffs, gibbered in rage that "if the King wants to be King in Spain, I want to be Pope in Rome". In the end, however, necessity prevailed over dissension, and a Spanish, Venetian and Papal fleet of six great galleasses bearing forty-four cannons each, two hundred and eight galleys, and one hundred transports carrying twenty-eight thousand soldiers sailed to the rescue of Cyprus in September 1571, a month after that island had been overrun by Turkish troops.

Once Philip had determined upon war he was willing to chance all in God's service, and the fleet was ordered to seek out the navy of the Sublime Porte and to destroy it no matter how great the risk. Christians met infidels in the Turkish waters of the gulf of Lepanto, where defeat would have meant annihilation and would have given the mastery of the entire Mediterranean to the Ottoman Empire. The battle was as much a clash of religions as of vessels. As the Turkish navy, in every way equal to the allied fleet, advanced, every Muslim sailor shouted his scorn and hatred of the enemies of Allah. When the moment came for Don Juan, Philip's illegitimate half-brother and commander of the Christian armada, to give the order to engage the Turks, a crucifix was raised aloft on every mast, and sailors and soldiers knelt in adoration.

The commanders of the two fleets met in the thick of battle where the pride of the Sultan's Janizaries clashed with the pick of the Spanish legions. Twice Don Juan's soldiers boarded Ali Pasha's flagship and twice they were repulsed by a torrent of arrows and bullets, but on the third attack the Turkish Admiral was struck down by a Spanish musket, and in triumph Don Juan ordered the head impaled upon a lance for both navies to behold. Christian cheers and Catholic crosses were raised high and the banners of Allah were pulled down on vessel after vessel. Of the Sultan's three hundred ships of war, a hundred and seventeen were captured, a hundred and thirty-three destroyed, and a bare fifty escaped to fight again. Eight thousand infidels were sent to their Muslim reward, eight thousand more were captured, and ten thousand Christian galley slaves were liberated. In the words of Cervantes the victory of Lepanto was indeed "the noblest occasion that past or present eyes have seen or future ones may hope to see", and a revelation to all nations who believed that the Turks were invincible upon the sea. Pope Pius danced with ecstasy at the news and showered Biblical thanks upon Don Juan, announcing: "There was a man sent from God, whose name was John." The great campanile of Venice sounded the fervent thanks of all Christendom, and the lofty arches of St. Mark echoed with *Te Deums*, but in the Escorial there was only quiet acceptance of God's will and the ceremonial presentation of the captured Sanjak, the great standard of the Sultan. The banner was bestowed upon the monks of the Escorial in solemn recognition of the Spanish contribution to victory and of God's manifest favour for His chosen champion.

Lepanto marked a turning point for Spain and her Messianic monarch. By 1571 the Philip of legend had begun to emerge – black, cheerless, already touched with necrophilia, and suffering in stoic silence the pains of asthma, kidney stones and gout. More and more his mind turned away from the infidel, whose continued existence for eight hundred years seemed to indicate a respectable role in God's ultimate design, to the more poisonous problem of heresy within the Christian flock. Spain had been made safe from Allah without and Satan within, but elsewhere the devil marched unopposed. If Philip were to be the good shepherd and to realize his dream of a Catholic and orthodox Europe, he would have to exterminate heresy in his own Dutch provinces and win England and Scotland back to the Roman fold.

In the years immediately preceding Lepanto, Philip had begun to change. His court had not always been devoid of pomp and circumstance. He had inherited from his father an enormous entourage of fifteen hundred persons, and his house was filled with life and laughter while his French wife and son lived. In 1568, however, death struck a double blow. In July, Don Carlos, heir to all of his father's possessions, died under circumstances that have been the theme of partisan novels and high romance ever since, and three months later Elizabeth Valois, who alone of Philip's wives had given him happiness, followed her stepson to the grave. The story of Don Carlos reveals Philip at his insensate best, but the tale is so wrapped in legend that fiction and truth are hopelessly mixed together and the picture of the King that emerges is so coldly stoic that it almost destroys any sympathy for the slow agony Philip must have suffered before accepting the fact that his son was mad.

Don Carlos was misshapen in mind and body. His back was hunched, his body dwarfed, and at eighteen he weighed only seventy-six pounds. He was a sadist and a paranoiac, roasting rabbits alive and torturing his horses to hear them scream. He found sexual satisfaction in whipping his steward's daughter, and it was while chasing that unfortunate girl that he fell down a flight of stairs and crushed his head. His life was saved by a painful and delicate operation, in which a circular hole was cut in his skull to relieve the pressure on his brain. For good measure, his father insisted on placing the withered corpse of the saintly cook of a Franciscan convent in bed with his son, and he always maintained that not surgery but the odour of sanctity had saved the Infante's life.

Despite the Franciscan cook, Don Carlos never totally recovered. From sadism he moved on to periods of homicidal mania during which he endeavoured to murder anyone who thwarted him. He grew to hate his father, to delight in giving away state secrets, and finally he attempted flight to Germany. Philip could not risk having his only son fall into the hands of his enemies. Don Carlos, even mad and deformed, was a potential tool in the dynastic schemes of the sovereigns of Europe. The King had no choice but to convert the Infante's apartment into a prison. In the early hours of January 19th, Philip entered his son's rooms and personally supervised the nailing up of doors and windows, and directed that no man should henceforth speak or write to his heir. Six months later Don Carlos was dead. Some said that it was suicide; some insisted that it was natural death brought on by the Prince's habit on hot nights of sleeping naked on a bed of ice; some whispered that it was murder ordered by a father who had detected the taint of heresy in the Infante, and who could never forgive his son's incestuous lust for his stepmother, Elizabeth Valois. Whatever the cause, Don Carlos's death, followed so closely by that of the Queen, filled Philip's life with anguish. Henceforth the King lived in mourning, increased the hours of his labour, and more and more turned his thoughts to the problem of exterminating heresy in the Netherlands.

The situation in the Netherlands had always been difficult. Even under Philip's father, fat Burgundian burghers and sly Flemish artisans had been jealous of their municipal liberties and suspicious of the Emperor's Spanish son. Heresy had found a fertile breeding place in this land of fleshy Rubenesque females and scrubbed and tidy Vermeer kitchens. At first the language of heresy had been limited to the quiet tones of Lutheranism, but by 1566 the streets of Antwerp, Brussels and Amsterdam were ringing with the strident voice of Calvinism. Charles had directed the most bloodthirsty edicts against his heretical subjects and had introduced the Inquisition to the Netherlands, but the Emperor had always preferred a live taxpayer to a dead Protestant and during his reign the Inquisition had remained inactive, though heretics had not.

Philip faced a serious decision: the choice between the orthodox realm or a prosperous people; and for the first eight years of his rule he had accepted his father's policy. The truth was that the Netherlands were the economic jewel of his empire. They consisted of seventeen provinces, half industrial, half commercial, part Dutch-speaking, part French, but all rich and held together in a loose union by their common allegiance to the Habsburg throne and by a States-General which was little more than an assembly of ambassadors who disliked Philip and his Spanish ways only slightly more than they loathed one another. Antwerp was a city of one hundred thousand people and boasted a bourse "for the use of all merchants of whatever land or language". It was the focal point of the European money market, the centre of the spice trade with the Indies, and the magnet which attracted the gold and silver of the New World. Louvain, next to Paris, was the leading university of northern Europe: the ports of Holland and Zeeland harboured five thousand sailing-vessels and were beginning to monopolize the oceanic trade; and Brussels was the source of the most prized tapestries in all Europe.

For centuries the Dutch and Flemish provinces of the Low Countries had been a source both of immense wealth and endless trouble to all who tried to govern them. Towns were jealous of their ancient rights, proud and impoverished nobles resented any encroachment upon their independence, merchants were reluctant to finance the dynastic wars of Habsburg princes, and clerics feared any rational reorganization of the ecclesiastical muddle of bishoprics and benefices. The Walloons of the south detested the Dutch-speaking north, the apprentices and journeymen of Ghent and Bruges could always be inflamed to violence, and nearly everyone, from Prince William of Orange to the weavers of Arras, feared the presence of the Inquisition and despised the Spanish soldiers who tramped the streets of Brussels and Antwerp.

In the spring and summer of 1566 social, religious and political discontent, which had been bubbling and seething for the past five years, erupted into violence and revolution. The lesser nobles bound themselves together to demand the abolition of the Inquisition and force Philip to promise that he would consult the States-General on all matters of religion. When Philip's regent submitted to these "Requests" and granted religious toleration, the Calvinist minority incited the masses to violence and spiritual hysteria. In August 1566, four hundred churches and monasteries were looted, tombs broken open, statues of saints smashed, and the gold pillaged from the high altar of Antwerp Cathedral. Monks and nuns were beaten and evicted; Catholic homes were sacked; and revolution and religious ecstasy engulfed town after town. At first Philip showed surprising restraint in the face of defiance and heresy, but if he were ever to fulfil his vow to the Pope to maintain the Catholic faith with all his strength and possessions, the King could not permit treason and godlessness to go unpunished. By the summer of 1567 Philip's "duty as a Christian prince" gave him no choice but to dispatch the Duke of Alva and ten thousand Spanish veterans to Brussels, where should it prove necessary, they were ordered to write God's will in blood.

Alva's soldiers were crusading Catholics who hated the

Dutch for their civilian habits, bourgeois greed and religious laxity. The Duke himself believed in immediate and terrible retribution and never doubted that his troops would swiftly settle a revolution led by common apprentices and heretic priests. "I have tamed men of iron," he boasted, "and shall I not be able to tame these men of butter?" Alva did in a year what all the prayers and sermons of the Calvinists had been unable to do: he united all elements and provinces in their hatred of Philip. A special court, the bloody Council of Tumults, enforced his law upon nobles and wealthy merchants as well as upon peasants and tradesmen. Aristocratic privileges, sacred rights and ancient laws were swept aside with a flick of the Duke's sword, and thousands were tried with military efficiency and executed without mercy. To judicial murder Alva added economic strangulation: he imposed a crushing tax of ten per cent on the sale of movable goods and five per cent on the transfer of land. The result was to drive merchants, tradesmen, manufacturers and aristocrats to risk civil insurrection. For four years the rebellion was limited to the northern provinces where privateers, the famous Dutch Sea Beggars, carried on an immensely profitable piratical war against Spanish shipping. At first they operated out of English ports, but in 1572 the Beggars seized the coastal city of Brille and won control of north-west Holland and Zeeland. Safe behind a morass of bogs, canals, estuaries and shallow broads, they were secure on land from Alva's Spanish legions and triumphant on the high seas, where the profits of piracy and commerce financed a war that lasted over thirty years and laid the foundations for Dutch naval and maritime supremacy.

The Dutch Sea Beggars found in William the Silent, Prince of Orange, possibly the only man in the Netherlands who had the vision, determination and reputation to keep the revolt alive. Why he earned the title of Silent is difficult to say. Certainly William was neither quiet nor taciturn, but he seems to have possessed the marvellous ability of keeping his thoughts to himself. He was a master at coating feudal ambitions with patriotic sentiments and associating his own dynastic designs with Dutch dislike of Philip's autocratic methods. The hero of the Netherlands may have had feet of doubtful quality, but he was a great leader of men and the successful champion of principles to which Dutchmen of every class and prejudice could adhere. Patient, practical and imperturbable, he discovered the formula that ultimately united the seven quarrelling provinces of the north into a nation. He called upon his countrymen "to restore the whole fatherland to its old liberty and prosperity out of the clutches of the Spanish vultures and wolves". It is little wonder that Philip placed a bounty on the Prince's head and offered a reward of twenty-five thousand écus to any man who could rid Europe of this "enemy of the human race".

In the winter of 1576 William the Silent almost succeeded in uniting the Netherlands when Catholics and Calvinists, Dutch and Walloons were shocked into a single community by the sight of Alva's troops putting Antwerp to the sword. November was bitterly cold and cheerless, and Spanish soldiers had been without pay for months. They rose in rebellion and turned upon the fat war profiteers, the rich merchants and the idle citizens of Antwerp in a mutinous effort to recoup their pay through plunder. During the "Spanish fury", the city was sacked, its women raped, and seven thousand of its inhabitants killed. Throughout the southern Netherlands, horrified Catholics put aside their fear of Calvinists and northern rebels and joined with Holland and Zeeland in the Pacification of Ghent to liberate the entire land from Spanish misrule.

Despite the "Spanish fury" at Antwerp, Philip managed to salvage a portion of his Flemish inheritance and to frustrate William of Orange's hope for total victory. Alva was replaced first by Don Juan and then in 1578 by the King's most able diplomat and warrior, Alexander Farnese, Duke of Parma, who won back the southern and Catholic provinces by combining brilliant military tactics with such diplomatic finesse that he soon had Catholics once again hating Calvinists more than Spaniards. Prince William met his match in this Spaniard, whose sense of military timing was without equal, and whose calculated moves and use of terrain made William's military efforts look amateurish and infantile. Parma was a pick-and-shovel general, spending more time digging ditches and diverting streams than drilling his men with pike and musket. Yet it was he who transformed Philip's undisciplined and cumbersome mercenary army, gleaned from every hamlet of Europe, into a professional and disciplined fighting machine that never lost a pitched battle for a hundred years.

This list of Spanish victories might never have been so impressive had not religious and linguistic dissension allowed Parma to drive a wedge between the north and the south. Protestants in the central and southern provinces looked with envy upon their brothers in God who had won dictatorial control in Holland, and they unwisely rushed to establish the kingdom of God's elect in the southern regions. In 1578 a Calvinist group d'état occurred in Ghent, and worried catholics began to ask themselves whether they had driven Spanish troops out of the front door only to let the soldiers of Satan in at the back. By 1579 religious discord had wrecked William of Orange's dream of unification, and each half of the Netherlands went its separate way – the south formed itself into the Catholic Union of Arras, the north into the Union of Utrecht. Divided, the Netherlanders could not resist, and step by step, village by village, canal by canal, the Spanish inched northwards. In desperation, in 1581, the seven northern provinces took the monumental step of renouncing their allegiance to Philip and proclaiming their independence, with William of Orange as their hereditary stadtholder.

Prince William never lived to see an independent Holland, for three years later, in July 1584, he was shot down by Balthazar Gérard, who murdered William not so much for the reward of twenty-five thousand écus as to prove to the world that a cabinetmaker's apprentice could kill a prince. Antwerp fell to Palma in the following year, and all well-informed sources in Europe assured Philip that his Dutch ulcer had almost been drained of its infection, and that the final phase of the war against Holland would be completed within the year. Diplomatic and military pundits reckoned, however, without the decision of Elizabeth of England.

The sixteenth century was no stranger to the fine distinction between hot and cold war. In fact, both Elizabeth and

Philip preferred intrigue, diplomatic assassinations, and the quiet fostering of domestic strife to open war. Such measures were safer and cheaper than armed conflict and could always be denied with diplomatic grace. Brinkmanship was an old and honoured art long before the great powers of the twentieth century gave it new meaning in an age of atomic holocaust. Ever since 1568 Elizabeth had been calmly and not very secretly offering aid and comfort to Philip's rebellious and heretical Dutch subjects. Of course, Philip was doing the same to Elizabeth, but that is the story of another chapter. Depending upon the vagaries of the diplomatic situation, Elizabeth had sanctioned the seizing of a Spanish treasure ship laden with bullion for Alva and his unpaid troops, had given haven to the Dutch Sea Beggars and allowed them to dispose of their loot through English commercial channels, and had permitted English volunteers and English capital to strike a blow for God in support of the Netherlands revolt.

Spanish military strategists in their frustration probably over-estimated the amount and effectiveness of Elizabeth's aid, but secret English help was a useful whipping-boy for Spanish failures, and as early as 1577 Philip's Regent in the Netherlands, Don Juan, had excused his inability to stem the revolt on the grounds "that the only remedy for the disorders of the Netherlands is that England should be ruled by someone devoted to Your Majesty. If the contrary case prevails it will mean the ruin of these countries and their loss to your Crown." When in 1585 Elizabeth committed the unpardonable diplomatic sin of bringing her unfriendly activities out into the open and sent a small army of five thousand foot and one thousand horse soldiers to the Low Countries, Philip reluctantly concluded that his half-brother had spoken the truth. The King of Spain knew England better than most of his advisers, and he feared war with that barbaric race "as a burned child dreads the fire". But Elizabeth gave her brother sovereign no choice, for the English heretical wolf, albeit ineptly, was devouring God's flock. If the good shepherd was worth his pay, if the dream of a lifetime were to be fulfilled, the Great Enterprise, in which the destruction of a heretical Queen of England was but the first step in the ultimate spiritual reunification of Europe, had to be set in motion.

Philip was never sanguine about the prospects of success. From the start he was alive to the terrible risks involved but content that God's will should be done. Actually, the vision of re-establishing a medieval Christian empire was not as fantastic as it may appear. Many Christians viewed the prospect as devoutly to be desired; Protestants and Catholics alike gave lip service to the ideal; and the chances of success after 1585 were probably greater than they had ever been since Luther posted his defiance on the doors of Wittenberg Church in 1517. Spain, that pillar of the Church and champion of Catholicism, stood at the apex of her military, moral and economic strength. The gold and riches of the Spanish Indies, which had been in 1503–05 a trickle of £213,400, had risen in 1580–85 to a golden flood of £16,890,000. No monarch commanded revenues equal to Philip's. The *alcabala* or ten per cent sales tax alone realized £585,000, while the kingdom of Castile regularly contributed over £1,400,000 a year to finance "God's obvious design". Spanish soldiers were the best in the world, toughened in a climate which was "nine months' winter and three months' hell", and so convinced of their own invincibility that it was said that in battle they postponed fear to another day. The reputation of Spanish arms was no myth: Parma and his iron legions had seen to that, and the fall of Antwerp encouraged even the cautious Philip to believe that Castilian pikemen and Aragon musketeers could perform miracles.

Spain was equally triumphant and invincible upon the high seas. Lepanto had been a combined Christian victory, but Spanish ports had supplied half the ships and three-quarters of the manpower, and in 1582 Spanish naval prowess was again confirmed when twenty-five Spanish men-of-war and two thousand troops, under the command of the Marquis of Santa Cruz, destroyed a French fleet of sixty great ships and seven thousand men. Impressed by such a feat Philip was inclined to listen to Santa Cruz's assurance that he could handle anything the English might send against him.

Diplomatically Spain stood on a pinnacle. From Malta

to Warsaw, from Buda to Antwerp, Catholicism was triumphant. The infidel was in obvious confusion under the dissolute and corrupt successors of Suleiman the Magnificent. France was impotent, held ransom to the wishes of Spain by the art of Mendoza and the greed of the Guise family. Anjou and the Prince of Orange were both dead and could no longer delay the ultimate return of the Netherlands to Spain; Antwerp was held by Parma, and his disciplined troops were ready to move northwards into Holland or westwards into England at a sign from the Escorial. Most important of all, Philip had inherited the treasures of the Portuguese empire and for the first time had the ports and facilities to outfit an Atlantic fleet to sail against that arsenal of heresy and haven of rebels, the British Isles.

Ironically, it was a Christian defeat at the hands of the infidel that gave Philip his chance to seize the impressive wealth and commerce of his Iberian neighbour and to complete the unification of the peninsula. In August 1578 at Alcazarquivir, King Sebastian of Portugal was killed and his troops massacred by the Emperor of Morocco. Immediately Philip pressed his claims to the Portuguese throne. Tact, diplomacy, bribery, the influence of the Jesuits, and a ceremonial invasion of the country won still another crown for the King of Spain. In July 1580 he entered his new kingdom at the head of a small army, which had such stringent orders not to pillage the land that the Duke of Alva ran short of ropes to hang the offenders. For the first time in nine hundred years the Iberian peninsula was united under a single monarch; for the first time in history a single empire encircled the earth. In America, Brazil joined New Spain and New Castile to bring all South and Central America under Spanish control. In Africa, Portuguese trading and supply stations gave Spain a claim to the entire continent and a route to the Far East. In Asia, Philip fell heir to the heavy Portuguese spice galleons plying their way between Lisbon and Goa, Malabar and Macao. Even more important to the destinies of Europe were the quiet coastal towns of Portugal with their docks and shipwrights, and the great port of Lisbon with its protected harbour where an entire Armada could safely anchor. Spain now had a vista to the west and the three thousand miles of rolling grey Atlantic, and Philip could seriously consider building a Catholic Armada that would cleanse the seas of Dutch Sea Beggars and English pirates and heretics, and open England to the brutal mercies of Parma's troops.

The King of Spain had more than men and money at his command. Philip's mission was not his own; it was shared by ten million Spaniards who had been brought up on the heroic exploits of conquistadors in America, crusaders in Granada, and the magnificent Spanish victories at Pavia, Lepanto and Antwerp. As Ignatius Loyola had willed himself to be a saint by the power of his imagination, so all Spain dreamed of a divine venture in which Castilian hidalgos, Catalonian priests and the peasants of Aragon would carry forward the banner of God. Spanish morale was sustained by a fairy tale which everyone from the Grand Inquisitor to the herdsmen of Navarre believed would some day come true. Miguel de Cervantes Saavedra was not alone in his Castilian conviction that faith and courage could transform romance into reality, fiction into truth; all Spain agreed with him. Cervantes knew all about the unembellished realities of life. He had accompanied his father on that impecunious and itinerant physician's travels; he had fought beside Spanish veterans in Italy and had been wounded at Lepanto; he had lived as a slave in Algiers and as a prisoner in a Spanish jail; yet Cervantes could still rejoice in Spain's Great Enterprise and cheer the Armada on its way. Don Quixote and all Spain somehow contrived never to look foolish even when mistaking windmills for dragons.

Ruinous inflation and indebtedness, an overtaxed and dying economy, a mortgaged empire, a population in which thirteen per cent of the families paid no taxes and did no work and another twenty-five per cent of the adult males wore clerical garb – all this was reality. But one can hardly blame Philip in his land of miracles if he saw himself as the chosen instrument of the Lord and if he agreed with Mendoza, writing from distant Paris: "I pray Your Majesty will hasten the Enterprise of England to the earliest possible date, for it would seem to be God's obvious design to bestow upon Your Majesty the crowns of these two kingdoms."

It is now time to shift the focus back to the England of Elizabeth. Had Philip and Mendoza been as successful in the tactics of cold war in London and Edinburgh as they were in Paris and Brussels, the contrast between Gloriana's successes and Catherine de Medici's failures might not have been so great, and the age might have belonged to Philip, not to Elizabeth.

Eight

Plot and Counterplot

SIXTEENTH-CENTURY diplomacy had most of the more in-
ane qualities of the Mad Hatter's tea-party. Periodically
everybody changed diplomatic seats, but the same old
dirty plates remained; ambassadors never meant what they
said, but somehow always said what they meant; the riddles
of diplomacy were as bewildering as any concocted by the
March Hare; and Elizabeth, Mary of Scotland and Catherine de Medici were as extraordinary in their diplomatic
tastes as any three sisters who lived in a treacle-well. For
all his shrewdness and secret sources of information,
Philip of Spain remained a baffled stranger to this Won-
derland of international politics. He could never fathom
the mercurial mind of Catherine if only because it was
so deceptively shallow. He regarded Mary as an emotional
and thoroughly unreliable female; and he agreed wholeheartedly with his ambassador who reported Elizabeth to
be a woman possessed of "a hundred thousand devils",
who fooled nobody by her idle chatter about becoming a
nun and passing her days in quiet prayer.

Dust had not yet settled on the thrones of kings, and
diplomats were as concerned with the pedigrees of monarchs as with terms of trade. Society took seriously Philip's
claims on behalf of his daughter, Isabella Eugenia, to the
thrones of England and France; Elizabeth thought it
worthy of diplomatic attention to protest against Mary
of Scotland's defiant display of the heraldic arms of Eng-

land on her escutcheon; and English ambassadors regarded it as an insult to be invited to eat with cutlery flaunting such armorial pretensions. Heraldry and the birthrights of kings were more than window-dressing left over from a bygone age. They were the only recognizable rules for living in a European family of adolescent states. The emerging nations, jealous of their sovereignty and fearful for their internal security, were endeavouring, in the only language they knew, to formalize their international relations. Diplomatic procedure remained in its infancy and the vocabulary had yet to be established; consequently, the language of heraldry and dynasty had to make do.

Ambassadors, as the accredited representatives of nation-states, successfully maintained the inviolability of their persons, but they were usually regarded and often behaved as if they were common spies. The principal interest of diplomats was not peace but information, and every resident ambassador throughout Europe had his carefully organized and well paid news service. The wealthier the kingdom he represented, the more secret his sources of information, for only the great powers could afford the sums necessary to glean the truth about monarchs, the plots of councillors and the secret plans of state. Don Guerau de Spes, the Spanish ambassador in London, had a spy on the Privy Council, and Mendoza, his successor, had an agent in the Principal Secretary's household. If the information concerned the sovereign no detail was too trivial to escape the watchful eyes of a diplomat, and the spy in the laundry took careful note of Elizabeth's menstrual periods.

Had ambassadors limited their efforts to collecting information and, like the Venetian resident at Rome, spent their energies in writing three hundred and ninety-four dispatches in three hundred and sixty-five days, the advice of Philip Commines might not have been taken so seriously. "Give them audience at once and be rid of them," he warned, "and for every one sent to you, do you in return send two." Despite scaffold and stake, the soft domestic underbellies of the new sovereign states of Europe were extremely vulnerable to attack. In an age which still judged loyalty to kin, to region and to God to be as commendable as allegiance to the Crown, ambassadors found a ready audience for their tempting proposals and a fertile ground in which to plant the seeds of treason and discord.

All men had their price though the purchase was not always reckoned in silver. Sir William Stanley could not be bought for gold – he had too much honour – but the prick of conscience and the hope of paradise led him to open the gates of the Dutch city of Deventer to Spanish soldiers. The Duke of Norfolk was above bribery – he was far too wealthy – but dynastic pride induced him to try his hand at treason. The great lords of the northern parts could not be won with cash – they were too proud – but they were captivated by the dream of a golden feudal past. Throughout Europe men sought a chance to strike a blow for their faith in themselves, in their class, and in their God. As a consequence, diplomatic residences in Antwerp, London, Paris and Amsterdam became the resorts of malcontents, and ambassadors became the *agents provocateurs* of treason. Mendoza in London or Paris, Parma's spies in every city of the Netherlands, and Sir Nicholas Throckmorton at the court of Catherine de Medici spun their webs of intrigue in the best cloak-and-dagger tradition. Secret messages were written in invisible ink which reappeared when the letter was immersed in water; dispatches were invariably in cipher; information was concealed in shoes with hollow heels and trick bottle-stoppers, or was tucked away in cod-pieces and in the lining of trunks; and couriers rode post-haste through the night disguised as dentists, priests and wine merchants.

In defence, monarchs occasionally jailed or evicted ambassadors, but such actions generally had unpleasant diplomatic repercussions. Usually it was safer to watch their activities, plant agents in their houses, supply them with erroneous information and bamboozle them with fake traitors and fabricated conspiracies. During the Ridolfi plot to murder Elizabeth in 1571, Sir John Hawkins, as a part of the government's web of counter-espionage, completely fooled the Spanish ambassador by his offer to betray the English navy to Spain. De Spes's assurance to his master that "I can discover nothing suspicious about it" is simply further confirmation that Philip was wise not to believe the opinions of his sanguine and gullible English ambassadors.

What gave European diplomacy a macabre and sinister flavour was the constant fear of the assassin's knife, and what drove Elizabeth's councillors to distraction was her total unconcern for even the most elementary precautions for her personal safety. Regicide was a tricky philosophical and moral problem, but the extremes of both faiths endorsed it on the grounds that good might come from evil and that the godless sovereign was an enemy to the human race. Moreover, political murder was quick and efficient. The Leviathan was still a weak and struggling infant, helpless without the support of strong and wilful monarchs. Remove the vigorous hand of kings, and "the state doth whole default, the realm is rent in twain in such a loss". The death of Henry II in France was grisly proof of this, and Europe abounded with men anxious to prove it in England as well. Lord Burghley was deeply aware that Elizabeth's crown was "not like to fall to the ground for want of heads that claim to wear it", and he prepared a careful report on "certain cautions for the Queen's apparel and diet", warning her to eat nothing that was not prepared and tasted by the royal cooks, to use no perfumes presented by strangers ,and to guard well her laundry and wardrobe.

For the first ten years of Elizabeth's rule, the "calm and quiet season" prevailed, and though the diplomatic configurations were as varied as a kaleidoscope, Spain remained safely in a quandary, France in the throes of civil discord, Scotland in the convulsions of Calvinistic revolution, and England in the hands of a benevolent deity who arranged that an embarrassed and unhappy Philip should continue as the Catholic champion of his heretical sister-in-law. The King of Spain's dilemma was England's greatest safeguard. Mary Queen of Scots was beyond a doubt Elizabeth's legal heir, and in the eyes of many Catholics she was the rightful ruler of England, but Mary was also a Guise, a member of that acquisitive and predatory clan that had so successfully merged its own destinies with those of France. Throughout crisis and reprisal, plot and counterplot, Philip could never convince himself that

he did not prefer heretical Elizabeth, free of French influence, to Catholic Mary, a slave to her French sympathies
and Guise uncles. For almost two decades Philip allowed his
artful sister-in-law to throw dust in his eyes, and believed
her ardent assurances that her heresy was nothing but political necessity. He turned the other cheek to the most
blatant provocations by English pirates; he read with cold
reserve the optimistic reports of ambassadors who urged
their intricate plots to rescue Mary and unseat Elizabeth;
and he refused to be stampeded into war with the country
that lay athwart his sea lanes to the Netherlands. It was
not until 1577, when the Guise family was brought into
the Spanish orbit, that Philip's awful perplexity was resolved. Only then could he begin seriously to consider
means to rid the Catholic world of the foul heretic and
unlawful Queen of England.

Ultimately every diplomatic move somehow involved
Mary of Scots, who bedevilled the international scene with
her charm, her intrigues, her idiocy and her claims to Elizabeth's throne. Like many storybook princesses, success did
not become the enchanting Dowager Queen of France.
Time and time again she proved herself to be petty, deceitful and self-centred, but Mary was magnificent in defeat,
and all her defects were invariably forgiven her. No gown
became her half so well as the cloak of adversity; no colour
could set off the golden-red hair, the great dark eyes with
their hint of tears or the heart-shaped lips as did the black
of mourning and the scarlet of martyrdom. By any normal
standard she was detestable; as a lady in distress, who could
offer her prince-valiant the crowns of Scotland and England, she was irresistible and exercised a fascination which
brought a host of men worthier than herself to their graves.
    From the moment of Francis II's death in 1560, mis-
fortunes beset his seventeen-year-old widow. Her Guise
uncles sought a new and brilliant marriage for their royal
niece and there was much talk of the nine-year-old Charles
IX and of the dwarfed and deranged fifteen-year-old Don
Carlos of Spain. Catherine de Medici, however, refused to
have Mary Stuart as her daughter-in-law for a second time.
Nor would she countenance the lordly Guises being linked

to Spain, and she threatened Philip with an English alliance if he married his son to Mary. Catherine made it clear that Mary's usefulness lay in her claim to the English throne and that her place was among the chilly lochs and cheerless hills of Scotland, where the Catholic faith was in grave peril and the French party had been destroyed by English arms and by John Knox's blasts upon his Calvinistic trumpet.

At one time French interests and culture had predominated at Edinburgh, and Scotland had viewed France as her "auld ally" in the age-long war against the English. James V, that ill-starred and melancholic sovereign, had died in 1542, shamed by his Scottish soldiers floundering in a bog in their panic to escape an English army. His widow, Mary of Guise, ruled as regent for the week-old Mary Stuart, and six years later the child Queen was whisked off to Paris, to be brought up French in anticipation of her marriage to the Dauphin of France.

The Scottish clans soon learned to dislike French foreign intervention as much as they had feared and detested English domination. Discontented nobles found in Calvinistic Protestantism a faith which sanctioned their distaste for French interference and provided a godly excuse for liberating Church lands from a government controlled by a foreign Catholic power. The new faith with its stark severity and rigid righteousness was peculiarly congenial to the black independence of their clannish souls and highland fastness. John Knox had been preaching against the enemies of "Christ Jesus and his holy evangel" in Scotland with varying results since 1545. He had been forcibly exiled to France and to nineteen months in the galleys, where the "grudging and murmuring complaints of the flesh" sharpened both his faith and his temper. After a sojourn at that "perfect school of Christ" in Geneva, the Moses of Scotland returned in 1559 to his homeland, where he began to preach a doctrine that found a congenial audience among lairds frustrated both by a French Regent and by a Church which was little more than a corrupt tool of the Crown and a source of patronage for those in political power.

Scottish nobles, steeped in the ways of feudal anarchy and independence and convinced by the hard logic of

Knox's sermons, were quick to act, and they banded together to protect the perfect faith and to oppose the Queen Regent and her French court and policy. In 1557 they covenanted to form the "Congregation of the Lord", a combined Church, army and parliament of the faithful and rebellious. By the summer of 1559 Protestant lairds were in full revolt against Mary of Guise and the French alliance, but it was gradually borne in upon ardent reformers and militant Scottish clans that victory would never be won by God's elect without English help.

Relations between Elizabeth and the Scottish rebels were complicated by her repugnance for John Knox, whom she had never forgiven for his tactless blasts against the monstrous regiment of women. Reluctantly Knox assured the Queen that his wrath had been directed towards her sister Mary Tudor and the Regent of Scotland, and that Elizabeth was obviously an exception to an otherwise perfectly valid rule. William Cecil and the English Council wisely determined to suppress such a grudging apology and warned the Scottish Protestants that if they wanted English arms and gold they had better muzzle Knox. As always Elizabeth was reluctant to commit herself or her troops to a course of action from which there was no retreat, but the lords of the Congregation gave her no choice. They were so consistently worsted in battle that Elizabeth was forced to send both her army and navy to Scotland. Ultimately, with British arms and the timely death of the Regent, the English and Protestant factions triumphed. By the Treaty of Edinburgh in 1560 French troops were withdrawn, and England and Scotland joined hands, for the first time in three hundred years, in a community of interests. Their strongest bond was a mutual fear of the new Queen, who arrived on a chill and misty day in August 1561 to rule a land of rebels and heretics.

Mary landed full of hope and determination to please, but if she thought that Gallic charm and Stuart guile could return her errant kingdom to the Catholic and French fold, she was tragically mistaken. Knox remained dour and unconvinced: "The very face of Heaven," he grumbled, "did manifestly speak what comfort was brought into this country with her – to wit, sorrow, dolour, darkness and all

impiety ... If there be not in her a proud mind, a crafty
wit, and an indurate heart against God and His truth, my
judgment faileth me." In the end, however, it was not religion but dynastic ambition that proved her undoing, for
Mary was anxious to exchange her bleak Scottish kingdom for the warmth and lustre of Elizabeth's throne. No
queen, possessed of the granite stubbornness of the Stuarts
and educated in the Renaissance brilliance of the French
court, would ever be satisfied with the crown of Scotland
if that of her "dear sister, so tender cousin and friend" lay
within her reach. She bombarded every capital of Europe
with matrimonial proposals, schemes to carry forward the
Catholic faith, and plans to inherit, by force if necessary,
the Tudor crown.

As far as Elizabeth was concerned, the only safe solution
was for Mary to remain a maiden queen, and relations between the two ladies became chillier with every new marriage scheme. Elizabeth not only endeavoured to frustrate
her cousin, she insulted her by the unbelievable suggestion
that Mary should marry that soiled hero of the English
court, Lord Robert Dudley, who was suspected of having
murdered his wife in the hope of marrying Elizabeth. Mary
was struck dumb at such a proposition; she sought a great
match, not the worn paramour of a rival queen.

Mary's ultimate choice of a husband was diplomatically
ill-considered and destroyed for ever any possibility of
happiness either as wife or queen. Henry Stuart, Lord
Darnley, was the "beardless and lady-faced" grandson by
a second marriage of Mary's own grandmother, Margaret
Tudor. He was three years the Queen's junior, stupid,
vicious and effeminate, but Mary could only perceive "the
lustiest and best-proportioned long man that she had [ever]
seen". On July 29th, 1565, Mary defied Elizabeth and married the one man guaranteed to antagonize the English
because of his Tudor connections, and the Scottish because
of his Stuart blood. "Woe worth the time," wrote the English ambassador, "that ever the Lord Darnley set foot in
this country." The time of woe descended with unexpected speed. It did not take Mary long to realize the truth
about the man she had married solely for his Tudor blood
and his closeness to Elizabeth's throne, and within a

year and a half double murder had been committed.

Mary of Scotland's marriage to a nobleman, even of Darnley's ancient lineage and royal blood, underscored the wisdom of Elizabeth's determination to remain single. Possibly Mary too often disregarded the medieval warning to wives – "Take care thou dost on no account say to him, 'my advice is better than thine' " – but the real trouble lay with Darnley himself. He proved to be a drunken, degenerate and vainglorious nobleman with the emotional stability of an adolescent and the moral fibre of an alcoholic. He coveted the crown matrimonial and the right to succeed Mary on the throne. When she wisely refused to grant his wish, he sulked and blamed the pernicious influence of the Queen's very private amanuensis and French secretary, David Riccio, a bass in the royal quartet and the object of Mary's affections. It was "Seigneur Davie" who dined alone with the Queen, read to her, played cards with her till two of a morning, and who shared not only her confidence, but, as gossip reported it, her bed as well. Darnley regarded himself as a cuckolded husband and an impotent sovereign, and he determined to have his revenge.

Lord Darnley set about organizing all who detested Riccio for his influence and lowly birth, or who sought to limit the Queen's authority. On a Saturday night in March 1567 Darnley's henchmen surrounded Holyrood House, and Darnley and Lord Ruthven broke into the Queen's chambers where Mary and her ladies were at supper. They demanded Riccio's presence outside in the ante-room, and when he hid behind the Queen's skirts and refused to move, they dragged him shrieking from the room and cut him to pieces with fifty-six thrusts of sword and dagger. Mary, seven months pregnant, was at her emotional best. To Darnley she demanded why such a wicked deed had been done, "considering that I took you from low estate, and made you my husband". To the rest of the company, she cried out: "I will think upon a revenge." She ordered Riccio's body to be buried in state in the Royal Chapel; she gave the dead secretary's office to his eighteen-year-old brother; with gold and fair promises she set about undermining the alliance of those who had hated Riccio; and she laid her plans for revenge upon her husband.

Had the Queen planned only the quiet murder of her spouse, she might have kept her throne, for Scotland abounded with men who loathed Darnley, but Mary Stuart mixed love and homicide in proportions fatal to her crown and reputation. From an infatuation for a weak and vicious Darnley, she fell headlong in love with James Hepburn, Earl of Bothwell, as bad-tempered, impetuous, oversexed and politically inept a hero as ever rescued a damsel in distress. It was the Earl who performed the murder, carried off the Queen in a carefully prearranged "rape", and finally married Mary Stuart by Protestant rites. The Queen's role as a murderess, if not as an adulteress, is open to debate, and her innocence has been passionately argued for the last four hundred years. Mary may not have known officially about the conspiracy to lure Darnley to his death, but she certainly must have guessed at the scheme, and she lent herself as bait to the trap. Her husband had been convalescing from an attack of smallpox, and Mary rushed off in a wifely fashion to nurse him and to bring him to Edinburgh, where he was lodged in a small house in Kirk o' Field, outside the city gates. On February 9th, 1567, the Queen conveniently remembered a promise to attend a wedding and failed to sleep that night in her husband's house. Early on the morning of the 10th, the city was rocked by an immense explosion; Darnley, his house and a part of Kirk o' Field had gone up in dust.

Public opinion was deeply shocked by the news, but Mary might yet have saved herself had she been willing to sacrifice her lover. Instead she ran away with Bothwell, announcing to the entire world that she would "go with him to the world's end in a white petticoat ere she [would] leave him". The sixteenth century could condone murder in a queen, but not impropriety. Mary was acting like a guttersnipe, and the streets of Edinburgh rang with cries of "Burn the whore!" In June she was imprisoned, forced to abdicate in favour of her fifteen-month-old son, and persuaded to acknowledge the regency of her half-brother, the Earl of Moray. Scotland, however, had not heard the last of their Stuart Queen, for a year later she managed an utterly romantic escape and within weeks had collected an army of six thousand enthusiastic supporters.

Enthusiasm, unfortunately, was no substitute for the discipline and training of Moray's troops. In forty-five minutes the battle was over and so was the Queen's career in Scotland. Three days later, on May 16th, 1567, Mary fled to England, arriving on Elizabeth's doorstep just in time to participate in the first determined effort to remove Gloriana from her throne.

The moment Mary crossed the border and became the embarrassing and difficult "guest" of her Tudor cousin, Elizabeth discovered, as her archbishop remarked, that she had "the wolf by the ears". She dared not send Mary home, where barbarian Scots might venture to execute their divine-right monarch; she feared equally to give her rival sanctuary in England, where Mary was certain to become the magnet for every species of malcontent. The "calm and quiet season" was over for Elizabeth, for the same social, economic and religious tensions that were tearing France apart were slowly loosening the ties of loyalty in England as well. English Catholics were hearkening to the quickened tempo of religious hysteria across the Channel, and Puritans were beginning to murmur that "no papist can be a good subject". Once again there were uneasy stirrings in the northern shires, where the word of a Percy, a Neville or a Darcy was dearer to conservative hearts than the most weighty command of a Tudor Queen. The days of private armies had passed, but local influence and patriotism remained strong, and the northern earls were restive in the uncomfortable harness of domesticated aristocrats. Mass was still celebrated despite Prayer Book and Articles, statutes and proclamations, and the parish clergy stubbornly resisted the best efforts of reforming bishops to purge them of their idolatrous ways. The return of the good old days, when men were true to their faith and to their overlord, and when they lived free from interfering bureaucrats and prying Protestants, was a dream for which men in the northern counties were still willing to risk the gallows.

More was doing in the north than old-fashioned feudal rebellion: traitors now looked to Rome and Madrid for aid in destroying the English Jezebel. Their cause was linked to the success of the entire Counter-Reformation, and their conspiracies coincided with the mounting rift between England and Spain. As early as 1566 Elizabeth and Philip had grievances against one another. Gloriana insulted her brother-in-law by sending as her resident ambassador to Madrid a married cleric who lacked both good breeding and good birth. When Philip indignantly ordered him home, Elizabeth in her turn was outraged by such arrogance. The same year English ports were opened to Dutch Sea Beggars – rebels, pirates and heretics, Philip called them – and English money and volunteers were sent to foster rebellion in the Spanish Netherlands. By 1568 the cold war was warming up. Elizabeth sanctioned unofficial piracy on Spanish ships in the Caribbean and the Channel, and when Philip retaliated in September 1568 by almost annihilating Sir John Hawkins's third trading and slaving incursion into the cherished Spanish monopoly of the New World, the two nations seemed on the brink of war.

In December 1568, Philip's patience all but broke. A Genoese merchantman, heavily laden with gold loaned to Spain in order to pay Alva's troops in the Netherlands, was confiscated when it put into an English port to escape Dutch pirates. Elizabeth promptly seized the bullion and impudently re-negotiated the loan with the Italian bankers. Outraged, Philip placed an embargo on English shipping to the Netherlands, and Elizabeth countered by freezing Spanish assets in England. At this propitious moment Mary Stuart wrote the Spanish ambassador "that if his master will help me, I shall be Queen of England in three months, and mass shall be said all over the country".

Mary, with her French ways and Highland wit, was proving to be a most unwelcome and tiresome guest in England. She stole every heart with a tear-stained smile for one, a diamond ring for another, and a well-phrased promise to anyone who dreamed of riches and high office. When the Queen had first set foot in Scotland, it had been said that "many simple men shall be carried away with vain hope, and brought abed with fair words". Six years later the warning still held true, for Mary could offer anyone what Elizabeth Tudor kept only for the crowned heads of Europe – the hope of matrimony and the vision of a throne. The man who was "brought abed" by such a dream was my Lord of Norfolk, Elizabeth's cousin and the first peer of the realm. Thomas Howard, fourth Duke of Norfolk, was a simple man whose intelligence was just enough to encourage caution but insufficient to perceive the folly of his actions. He should have known better. It was not accident that he was England's sole remaining duke, for the Tudors never looked kindly on too much princely blood or feudal independence, and the life expectancy of a member of the Norfolk house was not great. His great-grandfather, the Duke of Buckingham, had been executed for treason in 1521, his grandfather had been imprisoned and his father executed for the same offence in 1546, and his cousins, Anne Boleyn and Katherine Howard, had fared no better as the wives of Henry VIII. But Stuart smiles blinded him to Tudor scowls, and he allowed himself to be talked of as a proper husband for the woman who might yet unite the thrones of England and Scotland.

By the spring of 1569 the devil's brew had reached the boiling point. The Earls of Westmorland and Northumberland were armed and waiting in the north; Don Guzman de Silva, the Spanish ambassador in London, was busy plotting with Catholics and court factions; courtiers opposed to William Cecil were looking hopefully towards Mary and Norfolk; the papal anathema declaring Elizabeth to be a heretic and divesting her of her divinity was being prepared at Rome; Philip had written to Alva to ascertain the cost and effort required to unseat the Queen of heretics and restore the Queen of Scots to her rightful throne; and Mary was waiting expectantly at Tutbury to be rescued by an army of gallant heroes on white chargers. Had Philip been less cautious or less nagged by doubt, had Alva been willing to risk his disciplined troops in England, had the papal thunder been better timed, had the feudal relics in the north been slightly more powerful, had Norfolk been more courageous and de Silva's assassination plots better conceived, the Elizabethan age might have ended in civil and international war. As it was, the wheel of fortune still turned in Elizabeth's favour. The Queen lived and her enemies were once again confounded.

England and Spain approached war, then hurriedly retreated, for both Elizabeth and Philip were reluctant to commit their countries to the final ordeal of arms. The northern rising was crushed during the winter of 1569, and eight hundred feudal tenants paid with their lives for devotion to a dying way of life. The hum of the spinning wheel and the ring of the coal miner's pike were slowly drowning out the voice of the feudal magnate. Almost as an afterthought and as a lesson in ineptitude, Pius V issued in February 1570 the long-deferred bull of excommunication against Elizabeth. Ecclesiastical thunder fell on deaf ears; at home the Queen was closer to the hearts of her subjects than ever before; abroad Philip was too worried with rebellion in the Netherlands and Turkish penetration in the Mediterranean to put teeth into an otherwise harmless papal threat. The only consequence of the proclamation was to darken the lives and burden the hearts of good English Catholics who, until Elizabeth was anathematized, could at least remain loyal without violating their consciences.

Though triumphant, Elizabeth was still saddled with her Stuart cousin, who seemed to thrive on adversity and derived renewed hope from every defeat. Councillors advised the Queen that she had taken to her heart "the daughter of sedition, the mother of rebellion, the handmaid of iniquity, and the sister of unshamefastness". Yet Elizabeth persisted in viewing Mary as an anointed Queen, who must be treated with respect and if possible restored to the throne of Scotland. Unfortunately, Mary Stuart never learned from experience. She sat placidly among her ladies, her nimble fingers embroidering exquisite needlepoint and her fertile mind spinning endless clever conspiracies, the central theme of which was always Elizabeth's death. Even her own brother-in-law, Charles of France, was moved to exclaim: "Ah! the poor fool will never cease until she loses her head."

The same words might have been said about Norfolk, who had learned nothing about the dangerous consequences of treason when he escaped with a warning from the fiasco of the northern rebellion. Within a year, both the Duke and the exiled Queen were irresponsibly enmeshed in one of the more brainless conspiracies of the century, concocted by the ebullient and peripatetic Robert Ridolfi, a Florentine banker in London and a secret agent of the Pope. In its final form, the plot proposed that Alva should land at Portsmouth with ten thousand troops and march on London, where Norfolk would seize the Queen, rescue Mary Stuart and marry her, and restore the Catholic faith. Everyone except Alva was taken in by the polished and enthusiastic Italian, and even Philip put aside his Cassandra-like fears for dreams of success. Ridolfi's intrigues fared no better than the more realistic plans of the northern earls. Norfolk was arrested for a second time and finally executed in June 1572; the Spanish ambassador was unceremoniously shipped back to Spain; and Elizabeth gave up any pretence of dealing with Mary as a sister queen and blood cousin. Mary Stuart was imprisoned at the cost of fifty-two pounds a week at Sheffield Castle, but most Englishmen complained that she still was not treated for what she was – "a monstrous and huge dragon" of sedition.

There is no doubt that had Elizabeth listened to her Parliament, Mary of Scotland would have died in 1572. Loyal Englishmen were convinced that she was an immoral and dangerous female and were determined to "cut off her head and make no more ado about her", but Elizabeth could not bring herself to execute a divinely ordained sovereign. To do so was impolitic (it set a dangerous precedent) and immoral (Mary was one of God's lieutenants on earth). So Mary Stuart lived another fifteen years, surrounded by English spies but still possessed of a queen's household and always confident that some new plot might yet succeed.

For the next ten years there was relative quiet in Sheffield: just the usual letters to Philip, the Pope, the Duke of Guise and James of Scotland, all successfully smuggled out of the castle, and all urging her friends and relatives to strike a blow for God and the Stuart cause. Around 1580 the tempo of international intrigue began to increase as Mary gained renewed hope from abroad. The house of Guise had moved into the Spanish orbit and Philip was beginning to consider seriously the militant advice of his new ambassador in London, Bernardino de Mendoza, who inaccurately reported that England was in such a state that "if even so much as a cat moved the whole edifice would crumble down in three days". The Ambassador was not a man who let nature take its course, and in 1583 he plotted with a young English Catholic, Francis Throckmorton, to raise the Catholic gentry, rescue Mary and assassinate Elizabeth. When Throckmorton was arrested he did not long withstand interrogators who twisted the handle of the rack to give meaning to their questions. In the end, the tortured man could only whisper: "Faith broken, honour lost," and every detail of the conspiracy was known to Mr. Secretary Walsingham. Throckmorton died on the scaffold, Mary's mild imprisonment gave way to a closer watch and less friendly jailers, and Mendoza, to his lasting indignation, was ordered home as a common disturber of the peace. "Tell your mistress," he haughtily informed the English guard who saw him off at Dover, "that Bernardino de Mendoza was born not to disturb kingdoms but to conquer them!"

The Spanish Ambassador's defiance was in accord with the prevailing wind from the Escorial. England had to be conquered and punished. If the assassin's knife could not reach Elizabeth, then Parma's troops would have to assume the task so necessary to God's purpose. In the eyes of the Catholic world, the Queen of England was, like William of Orange, a menace to humanity. In London, the Queen's ministers were justifiably frightened. William of Orange had been murdered in his own house at Delft in June 1584. Six months later the Privy Council got wind of a Doctor William Parry, reformed burglar, ex-spy, and member of Parliament, who planned to assassinate Elizabeth with a bullet blessed by Rome. In August 1585 Parma's troops swept into Antwerp. It seemed inevitable that next they would either strike northwards against a demoralized and ill-led Dutch and English army or, if Philip gave the order, against that sink and source of all heresy and sedition, England itself.

As war grew steadily closer and the plots to murder the Queen grew more desperate, patriotic feeling in Parliament and the Privy Council exploded into a terrible anger against Mary Stuart. It seemed monstrous that the

cankered heart of treason should go unpunished, that an
avowed adulteress, murderess and arch-liar should continue to live. Years earlier, John Knox had warned that "if
ye strike not at the root, the branches that appear to be
broken will bud again". To angry Puritans, frightened
ministers and loyal Englishmen, it was clear that Mary of
Scotland was the root of all evil, but the problem was how
to make Elizabeth see her cousin for what she really was –
a common traitor. The mantle of her divinity had to be
torn aside, so that even Elizabeth would no longer believe
her cousin's regal and pious assurances of innocence. In
the end, Mary Stuart was destroyed by her own insatiable
passion for intrigue, and she was caught by her own cunning. First the trap had to be laid, then baited. Mary was
moved to Chartley House where all means of communica-
tion with the outside world were closed, save one. The
exception appealed to Mary's fondness for mystery. Her
letters were smuggled in and out of Chartley House in
waterproof packages slipped through the bungholes of beer
kegs. News from abroad arrived in the French ambassador's diplomatic pouch and was sent on to Mary, but before it was placed in the beer kegs it was deciphered, read
and copied by Elizabeth's Principal Secretary, Francis
Walsingham. The system satisfied everyone: Mary was
lulled into a false feeling of security and received secret
news from Europe for the first time for years; Walsingham
learned everything Mary read or wrote and waited
patiently for his victim to enmesh herself in still another
plot; and the astute brewer was handsomely paid by both
Mary and Walsingham, as well as receiving an inflated
price for his beer.

Walsingham did not have long to wait for the unsuspect-
ing flies to walk into his parlour. First a priest named
John Ballard entered. He assured Mary that sixty thousand
Spanish soldiers were waiting to rescue her, and informed
Philip that an equal number of Catholics would rush to
arms once Parma's troops landed. Then came Anthony
Babington, who gave his name to the plot; and finally John
Savage, who had taken a great oath to kill Elizabeth. When
communications with Mary had been established, and the
plotters had appeared on the scene, all that Walsingham

needed was written evidence that Mary Stuart was a party
to the secret. On July 17th, 1586, she fell into the trap and
wrote to Babington expressing her fervent approval of
what he and his colleagues proposed to do. Two weeks
later, Walsingham had all the evidence he required. The
assassins were promptly rounded up, Mary's two secretaries
were arrested, and Elizabeth was persuaded to permit the
trial of her cousin for attempted murder.

When Mary Stuart stood trial for her life before thirty-
six commissioners on October 11th, Puritans and Privy
Councillors had achieved their purpose: the legal deposing
of a divine-right sovereign and her condemnation as a
public menace to the Tudor Crown. As usual, however,
Mary of Scotland rose to the occasion and was at her infuriating and infectious best. She haughtily denied all
knowledge of the Babington plot: she passionately protested that queens could not be tried by any one except
God Himself; and when her enemies had done their worst,
she dismissed the damning evidence with a smile, saying:
"God forgive you lawyers, for you are so sore fellows.
God bless me and my cause from your laws, for it is a very
good matter that they cannot make seem bad."

The demand for Mary's life now reached a climax, and
the House of Commons, without a dissenting vote, peti-
tioned the Queen that Mary of Scotland be executed. Still
Elizabeth hesitated. She had lived with Mary for so long
that to put her hand to her cousin's death warrant was
like ordering the execution of a part of herself. Who knew
the terrible events that might descend from heaven in retribution for destroying an anointed queen? How would
James VI of Scotland react to the execution of his mother?
What would Henry III of France do to avenge the death
of his sister-in-law? And the greatest mystery of all, what
about that leaden colossus, the King of Spain? In vain
Elizabeth's councillors assured her that to James the hope
of succeeding to the crown of England was more important than his mother's life, that Henry III cared nothing
for his hysterical relative, and that Philip was no more
dangerous to England as Mary's avenger than he had been
as her rescuer. Still the Queen held back, and she dropped
broad hints that if Mary must die then let her be choked by

a pillow or silenced with poison. She ordered her secretary, the unfortunate Davison, to write to Mary's jailer to inquire whether he would perform the task, but Sir Amias Paulet's Puritan conscience would have none of it, and he wrote back refusing to "make so foul a shipwreck of my conscience as to shed blood without law or warrant". Elizabeth dared procrastinate no longer, and on February 1st she called for pen and ink and signed the death warrant, but even then she sidestepped the responsibility of sending it to Fotheringay where Mary was imprisoned. Once signed, she threw it to the floor, and when Secretary Davison asked her pleasure, she answered vaguely that the document should be taken to the Lord Chancellor to be sealed and recorded. The Privy Council knew well their Queen's ways, and Burghley, Walsingham, Leicester and others quietly dispatched the warrant to Fotheringay.

Execution was done on a cold Wednesday morning in February. The great hall at Fotheringay was cleared of its tables and chairs and turned into a death chamber. In the centre, opposite a blazing log fire, was placed a three-foot-high wooden platform, draped in black cloth, upon which stood a straightbacked chair and the block. Late, as usual, and dressed in black velvet with a lace kerchief at her throat and a white veil over her auburn-gold locks, Mary entered the hall, walked serenely to the scaffold and seated herself upon the chair to listen to the warrant signed by her royal cousin. "Stubborn and disobedient" were the words used. No one doubted the first, but many thousands, including Elizabeth herself, wondered whether a Queen could justly be called disobedient, and, if so, to whom.

Even at the eleventh hour, the Dean of Peterborough sought to win Mary from her faith and tactlessly urged her to repent, "for the hand of death", he said, "is over your head, and the axe is put to the root of the tree." The Queen calmly bade him be silent. "Peace, Master Dean, you have nothing to do with me, nor I with you." The supreme moment had arrived, and no one knew better than Mary Stuart how to play her part or how becoming was the red of martyrdom. The black velvet cloak fell from her, and she knelt ready for death in bodice and petticoat of scarlet silk. Twice the axe struck and Mary Stuart's

head tumbled to the wooden floor. The executioner
reached down to grasp the severed head by the hair and
hold it aloft, and as he swung his grisly burden high, he
shouted: "God save the Queen". Suddenly the romantic
legend of a lifetime was shattered and the truth was revealed for all to see: in his hand the executioner held not
a head, but a golden wig, and on the floor rolled the crop-
ped white-haired head of the Queen of Scotland.

Londoners went mad with joy at the news and came
close to burning the city to the ground in a frenzy of bon-
fires and merrymaking. The good citizens believed that a
new era had begun, in which all men would live without
fear now that the source of so much evil had been destroyed. Elizabeth knew otherwise, and she wept and raged
at her Council and vowed to have poor Davison's head
in revenge. How many of those tears were sincere, how
many politic, no one can say. Doubtless many were shed
for diplomatic reasons: Henry III had lost a sister, James
VI a mother, and it behoved Elizabeth to weep at a tragedy
committed without her knowledge and against her will.
She grieved that she had ever signed the warrant, and passionately assured the crowned heads of Europe that she
had had no intention of executing it. Still other tears were
directed in fury at counsellors who had failed to do away
with Mary Stuart in her sleep, and who had now confronted
the Queen with a public execution and an international
scandal. Finally, a few tears must have fallen for a sister
queen, a dead cousin and an old rival.

For all the charm which had incited Norfolk, Babington, Throckmorton and a host of others to treason, for
all her regal blood and royal titles, Mary Stuart remained
a pawn on the international chess-board, and her death
did not affect one whit the final conclusion of the game.
Long before Mary died, the King of Spain had made up
his mind that the retribution of heaven upon the heretical
and monstrous queen of England had been too long de-
ferred. He believed with Mendoza that his Great Enterprise was God's will, and that once he had won England,
the Netherlands would fall by default, for it was "God's
obvious design" that he should "lay down the law for the
whole world". Elizabeth also had come to recognize that

the paths of England and Spain must end in violence, and
in her heart she believed with navigator John Davis that
Englishmen were the saved people, predestined to "give
light to all the rest of the world". The odds had been taken,
the sides drawn, and Europe waited and speculated on
which of them, Elizabeth of England or Philip of Spain,
was the shining Messenger of the Lord.

Nine

The Great Enterprise

A GOLDEN glow envelops the story of the defeat of the Invincible Armada, distorting, dramatizing, and immortalizing one of the most unsatisfactory and untidy battles in naval history. A lgendary English fleet of only thirty sail, but captained by heroes of Olympian proportions, conquered the lumbering Titan of Catholic Spain and won for Gloriana the command of the seas. Freedom triumphed over the overwhelming weight of tyranny, mere human courage prevailed against the soulless Juggernaut, and a chosen few stood fast against a godless multitude. Alas, nothing is sacred to the scholar no matter how hallowed the myth, and the legend of those long August days and sleepless nights, when Philip's great ships swept up the Channel to visit the censure of God upon a middle-aged female, has been sadly profaned by historians in their quest for truth. "The elements against which valour and human daring are impotent because it is God who rules the seas" can no longer be held responsible for the Spanish defeat, for we know that the breezes blew Catholic as often as Protestant, and on two crucial occasions a shift in the wind saved the Armada from total destruction. The heroism of a handful of beardless boys must be set against the known fact that Elizabeth's captains were seasoned veterans with pugnacious beards, and sailed in vessels individually superior and collectively more numerous than those of the enemy.

It is true that on inspection fact and fiction bear little resemblance to one another; yet the actual events of the summer of 1588 are no less extraordinary for being true. The story of the Armada still abounds with courage and endurance, and reality has added a note rarely heard in mythology: the pathos of a venture upon which Spaniards sailed knowing full well that they had little chance of success unless God performed a miracle, and of an expedition which modern scholars now realize was doomed even from its conception.

From the start the Great Enterprise was grounded upon the extraordinary fallacy that Philip's great ships, laden with men and arms to reinforce Parma, could rendezvous with the Duke and escort his troops from Flanders to England. All the logistic and strategic thinking that had gone into the Armada – the orders not to engage the enemy, the decision to anchor off Calais, the proportions of cannon-balls to musket shot, of sailors to soldiers, of men to animals – all were based on an assumption that was false. Parma knew it and begged for time to seize a deep-water port before the fleet sailed. Dutch seamen, who navigated with ease through a maze of shoals, sand-bars, inlets and islands in their shallow-draught flyboats, knew it. Even Philip knew it, for Luis Cabrera de Córdoba, who reported Parma's warnings, bluntly informed the King that "it is going to be impossible for the Duke of Parma's ships ever to meet the Armada". Spanish ocean-going galleons were too deep to approach Dunkirk, he said, while Dutch coastal sloops, slight but deadly, could prevent Parma's barges from ever venturing out of the harbour. Echoing the Duke's own opinion, Cabrera asked the crucial question: "Why not give it up now and save much time and money?" Why not, indeed!

The answer lies deep within the mind of the man who secluded himself behind the granite walls of the Escorial. The Armada did not spring fully armed from the head of Philip the Prudent. It was the work of a mind incapable of great imaginative bounds, a brain which inched, never leaped, to a conclusion. The decision to invade England was made only after every other possibility had been thoroughly inspected and dismissed. The heretical poison that Elizabeth was spreading throughout Christendom could be stopped only by the invasion of an island protected by the rolling breakers of the Atlantic. Philip, better than anyone on his council, knew the risks entailed: the uncertainty of wind and current, the nonsense of assuming that devout English Catholics would rush to arms, the appalling odds against victory in a naval engagement fought five hundred miles from home and in waters every cove and eddy of which were familiar to the enemy. Philip had turned to the best advice available anywhere in Europe. Don Alvaro de Bezán, Marquis of Santa Cruz and Admiral of the Ocean Seas, had urged the King first to destroy English naval power in the Channel and then at his leisure to seize the island, but the cost of such an operation had proved too great, for the Admiral had demanded five hundred and ten sailing vessels, forty galleys, six galleasses, ninety-four thousand men and provisions for eight months. The King realized the economic absurdity of such a fleet and sought the opinion of the Duke of Parma, who suggested that possibly an army of thirty-four thousand infantry and cavalry might be ferried across from Flanders in a single night if complete surprise could be achieved. Even Philip regarded the element of surprise as hardly possible. So out of a half-dozen impossibilities, a theoretically feasible scheme was devised: a much smaller navy would be collected at Lisbon, large enough to terrify the English but designed primarily to convoy Parma's barges to the Thames estuary, not to engage an English fleet. This plan was to be the instrument of God's victory and the endeavour to which Philip and all Spain put their shoulders.

God's will never burst upon Philip like a beacon in the night, for the King did not presume to know God's purpose. Yet it seemed manifest that the Lord must desire the destruction of the English Jezebel. If the Armada was the only way of achieving a purpose so obviously in accord with the divine design, then God could be depended upon to sustain the faithful and give them victory. The mathematical odds meant nothing when fighting shoulder to shoulder with the Lord. Lepanto had been clear proof of that. When Philip had planned the fleet which destroyed Muslim sea power, he had had no clear notion of how victory could be achieved so far from Spain and so deep within Islamic waters. He had been content to labour quietly in the Lord's vineyard, and it had been sufficient that his Christian fleet was dedicated to a holy purpose. Philip the Prudent had been willing to risk all on a single engagement against the infidel at the battle of Lepanto, and now, seventeen years later, he was satisfied to leave the details of victory to God. Caught up in his sense of mission, the distinction between fact and fancy began to blur. It was enough that God's Armada should sail, while such matters as how Parma's barges and Sidonia's great galleons would meet and what wind would drive Justin of Nassau's flyboats back to Flushing were problems that could safely be left to Providence. Nor was Philip's confidence entirely misplaced. The age of miracles had not passed, and during the hair-raising moments when the Catholic Armada was within inches of running aground upon the sands of Dunkirk there were wonders a-plenty. The only trouble was that God failed to give Spanish sailors and soldiers something more than valour with which to defend ships technologically as outdated in relation to their English opponents as are bombers to intercontinental missiles.

The real tragedy rested in the fact that the Armada was the very best of its kind. Upon it had been lavished the riches of the Indies, the ceaseless labours of shipwrights, victuallers, ironmongers and carpenters, and the fervent prayers of an entire kingdom. From every province of Philip's empire, 123,790 cannon-balls for 2,431 heavy guns and long-muzzled culverins were transported to Lisbon. Unheard-of quantities of powder and shot for small arms were piled high on the wharves. Salt fish and hard biscuits were brought in from Andalusia, hemp and tar from the Baltic and oil from southern Italy. Almost every race and nationality – Castilian peasants, French adventurers, Moorish slaves, Italian mercenaries – were packed into ships which had been begged, borrowed, built and stolen from every corner of Europe. If pen and paper could have launched the Armada, it would indeed have been invincible. Philip, once he had determined that his fleet was God's sword "for the triumph of His cause", could not wait to see it forged, sharpened and ready to strike. Yet set-backs, delays, dishonesty and disasters impeded every step of the way. Pestilence, malnutrition and dysentery decimated mariners and landsmen while the Armada lay in harbour, fouling its own berth and consuming meat, fish and hardtack as fast as they could be brought in by ox-cart and barge. Ships that on paper were seaworthy fighters turned out to be hulks, their rigging rotten, their hulls sprung, and their crews peasant boys more accustomed to the plough than the topsail. In desperation Philip deluged his captains with instructions and wrote endless letters to the cannon foundries at Madrid, the naval arsenal at Lisbon, and the military warehouses at Barcelona, worrying them with a single theme – "Success depends mostly upon speed. Make haste!" Creaking and groaning in every joint, the Spanish military colossus made ready, while Philip buzzed, nagged and fretted like a well-intentioned but distracting gadfly.

Then on April 29th, 1587, a disaster struck the Armada that delayed its sailing for a year. Sir Francis Drake with twenty-six of the Queen's stoutest and fastest ships appeared among the moored galleys and merchantmen, the loaded freighters and refitting galleons of Cadiz harbour. Santa Cruz's own warship was in port, newly launched and tied up waiting for her armaments and stores; so were sixty-five other vessels, possibly half of which were being made ready for the great fleet gathering at Lisbon. Sir Francis had arrived with instructions "to impeach the purpose of the Spanish fleet", and once in the harbour the terrible Drake was like a fox in a chicken coop. Throughout the night he systematically scuttled or burned some thirty vessels, paying scant heed to the Spanish cannonade from the forts of Cadiz, and brushing off the ineffective darts and sorties of the swift but slightly-armed Spanish galleys. "The loss", said Philip, "was not very great, but the daring of the attempt was very great indeed." The loss was to be greater than the King imagined, for Drake's daring was not complete. From Cadiz he swept up the Spanish and Portuguese coasts, pillaging coastal shipping and plundering fishing villages. Mean and petty work it may have been, but when the Armada finally sailed the fish supply was meagre and inferior, the barrels leaked and the food spoiled. Sir Francis Drake had destroyed the Andalusian fishing industry, and he had burned the well-seasoned barrel staves and iron hoops prepared for the kegs of food and water that would keep men and animals alive on the long voyage from Lisbon to Calais.

By May 1588 the Armada was finally ready. Ships had been tarred, caulked and freshly painted, supplies had been stored away, galleons and merchantmen had been rebuilt to conform to the traditional Spanish idea of warships as floating castles at sea, crews had been assigned, soldiers taken aboard, and Medina Sidonia, the Captain-General of the fleet, was reasonably satisfied that everything humanly possible had been done to organize a naval host that spoke six different languages and consumed its supplies even faster than they rotted in damp holes and leaky barrels. At last the nineteen thousand two hundred and ninety Castilian and Portuguese soldiers, eight thousand three hundred and fifty sailors, one thousand gentlemen volunteers from every noble household in Spain, six hundred monks, priests and chaplains, innumerable servants, physicians, surgeons, ordnance experts, and over two thousand Turkish, Moorish and heretic slaves who laboured at the oars of the light galleys and the heavy galleasses were packed into a fleet that numbered one hundred and thirty sail and weighed less in total tonnage than the U.S. battleship, *Missouri*, manned by only two thousand five hundred sailors.

The fighting heart of the Armada was the twenty Portuguese and Castilian galleons, great lumbering fortresses carrying up to fifty-two guns, their main timbers four and five feet thick. They were built high in the stern and wide in the beam to give their musketeers an elevated platform from which to rake the enemy with gunshot and to cast grappling hooks to prevent escape. In addition to the clumsy galleons, which rolled and plunged and required a mild hurricane to move, there were four Italian galleasses, each mounting fifty guns and rowed by three hundred slaves. They were larger, heavier and more seaworthy than the light-oared Mediterranean galleys, yet could outmanoeuvre the galleons and match their firepower. The second line of the Armada consisted of forty merchant-men and carracks, some of them so large that "the ocean groaned under their weight" and all of them armed primarily to defend themselves from Barbary pirates and Muslim corsairs. The largest of the merchantmen, the Portuguese East Indiamen, were built like gigantic tubs, slow, seaworthy and practical. They had been refitted and re-armed and constituted a fighting force almost as formidable as the galleons. No fleet could do without its pinnaces, light, graceful and fast sloops, which were the eyes, ears and maids-of-all-work of the navy, and Medina Sidonia had managed to collect thirty-four of these useful vessels. Such was the fighting strength of the Armada. It was expected to escort some two dozen supply ships laden with men, horses and siege-guns for Parma's invading army, vessels which could not defend themselves in a fight but might contribute to the awful majesty accompanying a fleet so impressive that even the English Admiral considered it to be the greatest the world had ever seen.

The man who sailed in command of a fleet "wonderful great and strong" was peculiarly unfit for his position, not because he was a self-confessed land-lubber who easily caught cold, was always sick at sea and had begged Philip not to place him in command of so important an enterprise, but because Don Alonso Perez de Gusmán el Bueno, Duke of Medina Sidonia, was not a man who could call forth miracles. Efficiency, loyalty, calmness, affability and honour were qualities that the Duke possessed in abundance – he was, in fact, a splendid and soothing chief of staff – but the very virtues for which Philip selected him as the successor of that grizzled old seadog, Santa Cruz, ultimately destroyed him. Medina Sidonia was the product of generations of aristocratic breeding; his house had long since been squeezed dry of any vitality, and all that remained was dignity. The Duke was personally dedicated and hard-working, and invariably did the right thing. Throughout the disaster of the Armada, there is scarcely a decision that he made for which he can be condemned. As a Christian he was magnificent, as an admiral he was blame-less, but as a leader of men he was a total failure, for Medina Sidonia could not inspire in his subordinates that extra ounce of nerve, that wild belligerence, and that endurance which in the end wins battles and performs miracles.

In one quality alone, the new Captain-General of the Ocean Seas was suited to his command: he was a nobleman of deep and unfanatical devotion, and he was emphatic that the Armada should not be sustained by a mood of militant exaltation. His fleet was sailing upon a divine mission, and the men who worked the guns and climbed the rigging were embarking upon a crusade to restore the true faith to England and liberate the tens of thousands of faithful Catholics who had suffered privation and suppression at the hands of the heretics. The papal excommunication against Elizabeth had been reissued, and it was now the holy duty of the Armada to enforce that sentence against a Queen who was branded "an incestuous bastard, begotten and born in sin of an infamous courtesan, Anne Boleyn". The list of Elizabeth's sins was endlessly and disgustingly long. She was a profaner of the sacraments, persecutor of the faithful, suppressor of the old nobility, protector of profligates and licentious minions, prostituter of God's Word, torturer of innocent priests who were systematically torn upon the rack and dismembered in public, murderess of her cousin who was the lawful possessor of her crown, and finally a scourge of God and the shame of womanhood. The destruction of such a foul and monstrous dragon of heresy could not be accomplished in a spirit of revenge or conquest. It could only be achieved in humility and righteousness, and officers and men, sailors and soldiers were ordered to confess and hear mass before setting sail. Gambling and swearing were outlawed, prostitutes were forbidden on board, and no unclean thing or person was allowed to accompany so sublime a venture. Medina Sidonia himself, passing through lines of kneeling crusaders, bore to the Armada the holy standard of the fleet from the altar of the Cathedral of Lisbon.

Throughout the fleet, every seaman and soldier thrilled to a sense of moral superiority which more than compensated for the sour taste of military inferiority. It was not too much to count on God's help against barbarous, heretical people who made no account of soul or conscience, disobeyed God, disregarded the saints and thought nothing of the Pope. "We are sailing against England," said one Spanish sea captain, "in the confident hope of a miracle" which will send "some strange freak of weather" or will deprive "the English of their wits"; otherwise the heretics will knock the Armada "to pieces with their culverins". These words were not intended as a grim prophecy but as a straightforward statement of the consequences of not having God on one's side. When the fleet finally took to sea, Spanish confidence was just as firm as that of the enemy, but it was of a different brand. It was based on the inability of an entire realm to entertain seriously the possibility that a mission supported by the Church and the entire heavenly hierarchy could be defeated; English confidence was grounded on an equally sublime conviction that their cause was just, but also upon the knowledge that their ships, captains and tactics were superior to those of the enemy.

The English had good cause to be confident. It was no idle dream when Sir Francis Drake bragged to Walsingham that he doubted "not but ere it be long so to handle the matter with the Duke of Sidonia as he shall wish himself at St. Mary Port among his orange trees". The English had the best navy afloat and the most dreaded and celebrated captains in Europe, especially *El Draque*, Drake the Dragon, whose vanity was without equal but who spoke no more than the truth when he stated that he "knew what great fear his name inspired all along the coast of Spain". His reputation alone was worth the mightiest galleon in the Queen's navy.

When Elizabeth's subjects prayed to God to set a wall about England and evermore mightily defend it, they might more reasonably have raised their voices in thanks to the Queen's father, old King Henry. It was he who had built the dockyards from which Elizabeth's great ships slipped into the sea, and had reorganised the admiralty so that a navy existed, at least on paper, even in peace time. By 1588 England had eighteen heavy men-of-war, built according to the revolutionary and imaginative notions of Sir John Hawkins, the Treasurer of the Navy, and the shipwrights of Bristol, Portsmouth and Plymouth. Pumps had been improved, rigging modified, hawsers lengthened, but the most basic change was in the shape and proportions of the hulls. Reflecting a new approach to naval war and the function of the galleon in battle, the English did away with the towering superstructure of the traditional warship, and streamlined their vessels by increasing their length, cutting down on their width, and levelling off their deck lines. The lofty castles at bow and stern, that added so to a ship's weight and made them difficult to sail, were discarded; and the pit or centre, where reserve contingents of soldiers huddled, protected by the thick sides of the galleons, was boarded over to make two new decks for heavy ship-destroying guns. The new outline was the technological expression of a profound tactical revolution which no longer treated the sailing vessel as a means of conducting land war at sea, but as an instrument of destruction suited to the ocean. Sink the enemy, not board and capture him like some fortress to be scaled and sacked; this was the aim of English sea captains in their trim warships that could out-point, outmanoeuvre and outsail anything the Spanish had afloat.

Along with the new hull design came the introduction of lighter but more numerous and longer-range guns that could hurl a nine-pound shot half a mile. Spanish guns were heavier and could heave a thirty-pound ball with indifferent accuracy possibly a quarter of a mile if the nine-foot barrel did not happen to explode. On both sides gunnery was still in its infancy. The amount of powder, the strength of the barrel, and the timing of the charge in synchronization with the roll of the ship were matters largely of guesswork, and neither navy had any real idea of how many cannon-balls would be needed to sink a galleon or at what range a nine-pound shot hurled at high velocity or a thirty-pounder thrown less violently would penetrate the thick timber of a man-of-war. The Spanish regarded their massive cannons in terms of siege guns. They assumed that the real work would be done by small arms or mortars designed to destroy men, not ships, and they had brought with them what they imagined to be an overabundance of heavy ammunition – fifty rounds per gun. The English carried even fewer cannon-balls, and Drake was evidently willing to meet the enemy with only thirty rounds per gun despite the fact that English tactics called for staying well away from the Spanish ships with their deadly musketeers and grappling-hooks, and using their own greater mobility and longer-ranged culverins to fire broadside after broadside into the Armada. The English, however, were prepared to experiment with the new methods of war and could always replace their cannon shot; the Spanish could do nothing but haul off and invite the enemy to board. When instead they received salvos of iron they could answer only with guns that could never reach the enemy and ammunition that could never be replaced.

The fundamental problem for the English was not how to win the battle but how to maintain a fleet in readiness against an enemy whose exact time of arrival was unknown and whose plans were uncertain. On this point Elizabeth and her seadogs clashed. Drake's advice, sent from Cadiz in 1587, had been explicit: "Prepare in England strongly and most by sea!" Elizabeth was equally insistent: ships were financial monsters and she was too poor to feed them. Her army in Holland, that "sieve that spends as it receives to little purpose", was eating up one hundred and twenty-six thousand pounds a year; she had raised another fifty thousand pounds with which to pay a German army to invade France and destroy the Catholic Duke of Guise; and she had promised to scrape together still another subsidy for Henry of Navarre to keep him from total bankruptcy. It was costing the Queen at least twelve thousand pounds a month to feed, arm and pay a fully mobilized fleet, and all this had to be done on a normal peacetime income of two hundred and fifty thousand pounds per annum. Under the circumstances it is little wonder that Lord Burghley sourly lamented: "A man would wish, if peace cannot be had, that the enemy would not longer delay, but prove, as I trust, his evil fortune," or that Gloriana constantly maintained the fiction that she was not and had no intention of ever being at war with Spain, and that her greatest desire was to see Philip's rebellious Dutch subjects back in their true allegiance once again. Neither Philip nor the Queen's sea captains agreed with her or believed her, but at least such a pretence allowed

Elizabeth to keep her fleet in harbour and to spare her war chest. Except for full mobilization resulting from a false alarm in December 1587, the thrifty sovereign kept her fleet in dock, partly decommissioned and only half staffed, and saved herself over two thousand pounds a month. Even during the summer of '88, when she reluctantly permitted full mobilization of a fleet of about two hundred ships, she complained that the cost was bankrupting her.

The Queen's worries did not end with finding the fourteen shillings a month that it took to feed and pay a single seaman or with collecting the stores of food for a fleet that ate up most of its provisions before ever venturing out of harbour. Despite half measures and penny pinching, Elizabeth's naval arm remained strong; the greatest danger was from the unknown enemy lurking within the kingdom, the nightmare of a Catholic fifth column where hid "the secret treasons of mind and heart". Everyone was aware of the rottenness of the home defences: English cities were unwalled, ungarrisoned and defenceless; stout English yeomen had grown soft and fat during decades of peace, and possessed neither the strength nor the training to draw the long-bows that had given victory at Agincourt and Crécy; the magnates of the north still secretly nourished a fondness for medieval attitudes; and, most serious of all, no one knew how many silent allies of the Pope lurked in every English home. Possibly three hundred of Cardinal William Allen's seminary priests still crept from their priest holes and cellars to strengthen the faithful in their determination and to perform the miracle of the mass. Twenty thousand copies of the Cardinal's writings, urging, encouraging and assuring the flock that the day of liberation was near, were being read and circulated from one Catholic house to the next. How many sympathetic readers there were was the crucial question. Cardinal Allen hopefully estimated that two-thirds of the population were, in their secret hearts, loyal to the Holy Church, and English exiles in Europe lived on a roseate dream of a rich and prosperous land where sturdy Catholic peasants would rise up at a signal from Rome or Madrid and deliver "Catholic friends and brethren from the damnable and intolerable yoke of heresy". Two-thirds, one-half, one-third, the fractions meant little in an island sustained by boisterous xenophobia and darkly suspicious of anyone who did not admire all things English. If the small voice of conscience spoke louder than did loyalty to Crown and country, as it so often did in France, then, despite the government's efforts to round up leading Catholics and to root out with axe and rack the Jesuit spies and seminary priests, there was no real defence against the danger of religious hysteria. But Elizabeth thought otherwise. She was willing to take the gamble that her clownish subjects were more English than popish and that patriotism would prove more enduring than faith. She was right, but at the time no one could be certain, and the warriors who sailed to meet Philip's crusaders did so with the fear that their houses might at any time be burned down behind their backs.

The two fleets sighted one another for the first time off Dodman Point during the early evening of July 30th, the English sails sparkling in the red glare of the setting sun, and the Spanish galleons black silhouettes in the fading light. The long haul from Corunna, where the Armada had refitted after leaving Lisbon, had been made in just under ten days. The weather was abominable, as it had been all that summer, and five Spanish ships – four unseaworthy galleys designed for Mediterranean waters and a seven-hundred-and-sixty-eight-ton converted merchantman – had failed to reach the rendezvous off the Lizard. Though Medina Sidonia's fleet had already been reduced to one hundred and twenty-five sail, Charles Howard, the English Lord Admiral, had nowhere near that number in readiness. A cautious Queen, who did not trust her Dutch allies, had insisted that five galleons and thirty merchantmen and pinnaces under Lord Henry Seymour should patrol the approaches to Dunkirk and Nieuport, lest Parma make a sudden dash in his barges for the English coast. Fourteen great galleons and possibly fifty other vessels under Vice-Admiral Sir Francis Drake were stationed at Plymouth, but only fifty-four of these had been able to slip out against the wind to confront the Armada in open water; the rest of Howard's navy was victualling and arming in various Channel ports. Given time, the Lord Admiral could collect a grand fleet of some two hundred vessels, which he proudly described as "the best ships in the world": Hawkins's eighteen sleek galleons weighing between three hundred and seven hundred tons, seven smaller galleons, one hundred and fifty merchantmen of varying sizes, and possibly thirty pinnaces and light frigates. It was these figures that determined for both sides the nature of the running fight up the Channel. Sidonia had orders not to engage such a formidable enemy unless conditions were favourable or the English forced a fight; and Howard's design was to test his strength against the Spanish by a series of running broadsides and wait until he could marshal a numerically superior fleet. Until the crucial battle off Gravelines, when the Lord Admiral's ships had been joined by Seymour's five galleons, the action from Eddystone to Calais was a noisy gun-duel of swift English seadogs circling an infuriated Spanish bull.

The Armada was indeed a bull. It had rushed into the arena expecting to find matadors flourishing red capes and ceremonial swords, and toreadors on heavily padded horses, and had imagined that it would engage an ancient and worthy enemy who fought according to the rules. It had anticipated a relatively fair fight in which men were often killed and occasionally, almost by divine dispensation, the bull was granted its life. On such terms the Armada had been willing to fight and if need be to die. Instead, it encountered English galleons, armed with long-range guns, that refused to play the game and sought to kill without honour or mercy.

On the morning of July 31st, Medina Sidonia was alarmed to discover that the English, who had slipped out from Plymouth well to the lee of the Spaniards, had during the night, incredible as it seemed, gained the weather gauge. Naval historians often consider this feat to have been the decisive manoeuvre of the week-long engagement, for thereafter Howard never lost the advantage of position. Decisive the move may have been, but it was no great feat; it was merely portentous evidence that Hawkins's newly-designed vessels could tack well into the eye of the wind and achieve any position they chose. In answer to the English manoeuvre, the Duke ordered his fleet to battle stations

and placed his squadrons in a perfectly executed crescent
formation, his strongest galleons clustered at the point of
each horn, his troop-carriers and clumsier merchantmen
in the centre. Then he unfurled and hoisted high in the
morning breeze the sacred banner of the Armada. Stitched
on one side were the imperial arms of Spain and the figure
of the crucified Christ, on the other the image of the Madonna and the words, "Arise, O Lord, and vindicate Thy
cause". At a signal from the Admiral's flagship "every man
in the fleet knelt down and prayed our Lord to give us victory over the enemies of His faith". Howard countered
with a piece of chivalric nonsense, sending his sloop, the
Disdain, to deliver his personal challenge to the Duke.
There was a fundamental difference, however, between
the two gestures: for the Spanish it was the traditional
way of fighting, secure in the guardianship of heaven; for
the English it was mere heraldic posing before getting down
to the serious matter of sinking the enemy.

The Spanish, in their dangerously strong defensive crescent, handled expertly vessels most of which had been baptized after the celestial host – the *San Marcos, San Mateo,
San Felipe, San Juan, San Lorenzo, San Martin* and *Nues-
tra Señora del Rosario*. They waited with confidence for
the gaily coloured English fleet – the red-painted *White
Bear*, the black and white *Bonaventure,* the brown *Lion*,
the green and white *Revenge* – to commence the attack.
The enemy, however, had no intention of facing almost
certain death by sailing between the deadly prongs of the
crescent and engaging in a general mêlée of grappling and
boarding. Instead, they approached, wheeled off, and, fir-
ing four shots to the Spanish one, raked the Armada with
burst after burst of cannon shot. The entire encounter was
nothing more than an extensive gunnery practice, neither
side doing the other any harm, for Howard never came
close enough either to risk the timber-splitting Spanish
thirty-pounders or to permit his own nine-pounders to
penetrate the Spanish hulls.

Thoroughly frustrated, both sides gave up the fight, and
Medina Sidonia proceeded majestically up the Channel
with Admiral Howard worrying him from behind and add-
ing ship after ship as both fleets approached Calais. On

the evidence of the first few days of battle, the English were increasingly alarmed that after all the Armada might meet Parma, and there seemed to be nothing they could do to prevent it. The Spanish, plagued by bad luck and unable to come to grips with a swift and nimble enemy, were equally concerned. One great ship, the forty-six gun *Rosario,* carrying fifty-five thousand golden ducats and four hundred and eighteen sailors and soldiers, fouled her neighbour, broke her own bowsprit and lost her foremast. She was unable to keep up with the fleet and fell prey to Drake's waiting galleons. Another vessel, the *San Salvador,* suddenly exploded in full sight of the fleet, sending hundreds of sailors and soldiers into the sea. There is a legend that a Spanish captain caned a Dutch master gunner for insubordination, and the gunner, in a rage, thrust a flaming linstock into the stern powder magazine and himself leaped through a porthole into the ocean. The story made good copy in Holland and grew with every telling, but it is probably grounded on nothing more substantial than that the *San Salvador* did in fact blow up and like the *Rosario* fell into the hands of the English squadrons.

Between Eddystone and Calais the unsatisfactory and indecisive battle of July 31st was repeated three times over. Throughout the week Spanish discipline and morale remained as impressive as ever, even if their supply of cannon-balls was running desperately low and they had inflicted no damage upon the enemy. The English were still unable to stop the Armada and their cannonading continued to bounce harmlessly off the thick sides of the Spanish men-of-war. If the laurels of victory had been handed out on August 6th, the decision might have been given to Medina Sidonia, who had brought his fleet, as instructed, safely to anchor off the Calais Roads to wait for a chance to rendezvous with Parma, encamped thirty miles away at Dunkirk. Reports of Spanish successes were already spreading in every capital of Europe, forerunners of those marvellously embellished and brilliantly detailed stories of Drake being captured while trying to board the *San Martin,* and of the English fleet sunk or fleeing in panic for shelter. Mendoza, who could scarcely restrain his eagerness for news, was sufficiently convinced by the early rumours

to order kindling for a huge victory bonfire in the court-
yard of his Paris residence. Had he known the truth, however, as it was slowly being borne in upon Medina Sidonia,
he might have hesitated to spend his money, for it was on
the day that the Ambassador ordered wood for his fire that
the balance of war shifted decisively and disastrously
against the Spanish.

On Sunday morning, August 7th, Medina Sidonia was
told by couriers from Parma that the Great Enterprise
was hopeless and the fleet was doomed. Parma's troops
and barges were bottled up at Dunkirk where the harbour
was too shallow to receive the Duke's heavy galleons, and
the Armada, its stores spoiling, its ammunition expended
and its water barrels leaking, had passed the point of no
return. The wind and a superior English fleet prevented
any chance of retreat through the Channel, while ahead
lay the treacherous and uninviting waters of the North
Sea. Whether the thousands of doomed men on board realized the terrible truth is doubtful, for their courage remained high and they continued to have confidence in
divine intervention. Not even faith, however, could withstand the unnerving sight of eight blazing fireships driving
down on the fleet during the early hours of August 8th.

The possibility that the enemy might resort to fire to
dislodge the Armada from its anchorage was only to be
expected. Fire at sea was the gravest menace faced by men
and ships, and Medina Sidonia had ordered every galleon
to mark well its anchor and be ready to slip, but not to
cut, its cables, in order to side-step the fireships if they
should penetrate the ring of pinnaces stationed to intercept and tow them harmlessly to shore. What the Duke
was unable to guard against was hysteria in his own ranks.
To the dread of fire at sea was added a fearful rumour:
the English had hired Federigo Gianibelli, the Satanic
Italian inventor of the Hell-burner. These infernal monsters had floated down on Parma's bridges and waterworks
during the siege of Antwerp, had blown hundreds of men
and months of bloody labour to smithereens and had almost saved the city. What the Spanish fleet saw drifting
in on the early morning tide were not Gianibelli's floating
bombs but something just as awesome – eight small

frigates, their rigging and tarred decks on fire and their cannons spiked and loaded so that the white-hot guns would
explode and add molten metal and thunderous explosions
to the flaming inferno. The pinnaces were unable to intercept all of these deadly vessels "spurting fire and their
artillery shooting" and sounding like Gianibelli's Hell-
burners, and Spanish nerve, strained by sleepless nights
and exhausting days of inconclusive fighting, finally snap-
ped. Against orders, the captains cut their cables and ran
for it. The Armada was no longer a fighting machine but
a formless throng of ships headed for certain destruction
at the hands of the English or on the sandy shoals of the
Flemish coast. Next morning, only five ships remained in
position, having obeyed Medina Sidonia's orders to slip
cable and return to their anchorage. The rest were scattered up and down the coast, and one of the cumbersome
giant galleasses had fouled its rudder and run aground.
Like a monstrous tortoise on its back, it was lying helpless
on the sand-bar off Calais harbour.

The decision to panic the Spanish fleet from its berth
was a reflection of the swelling confidence within the English fleet. For a week, captains and seamen had been testing
their galleons and new naval tactics against an enemy that
remained medieval and Mediterranean in its military
thinking. What they had learned was both heartening and
alarming. Ship for ship, Howard's galleons were better
manned, better gunned and better constructed than the
Spanish, but it was also apparent that English nine-pound
culverins could do Medina Sidonia's heavy battleships no
real harm unless Howard was willing to close the range and
risk Spanish heavy artillery. This the Lord Admiral was
now prepared to do, for Seymour's squadron had joined
him the previous evening, and at last he had a decided
numerical superiority. At daybreak on August 8th, English trumpets called the Queen's fleet to action.

Somehow, despite the treacherous sands of the Dunkirk
bar and the English sea wolves at his heels, Medina Sidonia
got his fleet back into its familiar defensive crescent formation, but it was a sorry shadow of the Armada that had
sailed with such confidence from Corunna. Pinnaces,
freighters and a number of smaller merchantmen were

still scattered up and down the coast, but twenty-five of his most powerful galleons and galleasses had recovered from the panic of the night before and answered the Admiral's call to battle stations. The odds were not as desperate as they appeared, for the English had no more than twenty-five men-of-war capable of handling the hard fighting core of the Spanish fleet. All day the battle raged. Drake's ships swept in close but never quite close enough for the Spanish to grapple and board them. The English delivered terrible broadsides and then veered off, either to wheel about and thunder still another salvo or to move on to the next Spanish galleon. For the first time Medina Sidonia's warships ran red with blood and even from a distance the English could see the gore dripping from scuppers and cannon hatches. As the four-foot oaken walls were finally smashed and the lighter superstructures demolished, men died as often from flying splinters as they did from gun and musket shot. Spanish gallantry was magnificent, but as cannon after cannon was smashed or ran out of shot, there was little else left with which to fight. The *San Mateo*, with half her company dead and scarcely able to stay afloat, invited her tormentors to stand to and fight like men, and when an English officer, judging her condition to be hopeless, climbed the rigging of his own warship and offered terms of honourable surrender, he received a musket-ball for an answer. As the English galleon backed away, the Spanish crew jeered at the heretics for being cowardly hens who dared not board and fight man to man.

In every action of the battle the story was the same – a magnificent Spanish fleet that begged to be allowed at least to die honourably. Time and time again the crescent formation was broken only to be reformed, and when the last cannon was fired and the battle over, Howard was still unaware of how desperate was Medina Sidonia's plight. The enemy, he reported, "consisteth of mighty ships and great strength", and all he had been able to do was "pluck their feathers little and little". Howard was depressed; a sudden rainstorm and his own shortage of food and ammunition had allowed the enemy to escape. Actually, however, the Spanish fowl was mortally stricken, and Drake judged correctly that Parma and Medina Sidonia would never shake hands and that neither of them would "greatly rejoice at this day's service".

Indeed Medina Sidonia had no cause to rejoice, for his condition next morning was even worse than he had imagined. Not only had he been beaten in open battle off Gravelines and saved from total destruction only by a chance squall, but also, during the night, three of his finest warships had been lost, one having gone to the bottom and the others having run aground to save themselves from sinking. More serious than leaking hulls and broken rigging was the wind that was driving the entire fleet to certain destruction on the shallow sand-bars off Flushing. Then about noon the miracle for which thirty thousand men had so fervently prayed was delivered. As the leadsmen called out the depth and sailors could almost feel the sand under their ships' keels, the wind suddenly boxed the compass and steadied at a point which allowed the entire fleet to slip past the Dutch coast in safety and into the grey-green waters of the North Sea.

It might have been more merciful had God withheld His miracle and the stricken monster died swiftly and mercifully upon the sands of Zeeland and Flushing. At least sailors and soldiers would have been spared a slow and agonizing death from cold and starvation, or the futile hours spent manning pumps and climbing rigging which ended only in catastrophe on the cliffs of Scotland and the heavy surf of the Irish coast. There was no question of returning to fight again, though the Duke and all his captains vowed that they would stand and do battle if only the wind would shift. As it was, they had no choice but to be swept on into the North Sea with Howard at their heels, and to endure the two thousand five hundred-mile ordeal that would bring them back to Spain, a beaten and broken fleet, so sick and exhausted that one vessel, unable even to lower sail and drop anchor, went ashore as she reached safety in Santander harbour.

When Medina Sidonia was finally able to take stock, he discovered that the Armada was in greater peril of dying from thirst than of being destroyed by the English, who trailed behind at a respectful distance. The Duke did the best he could for his exhausted and demoralized men. Horses and mules were cast overboard to save water, and every officer and man, no matter what his rank or profession, was reduced to a pint of water and a half-pint of wine a day. In a desperate effort to restore discipline, twenty captains, who had disobeyed the Duke's orders during the disastrous battle off Gravelines, were court-martialled and sent to row in the remaining galleasses.

Howard gave up the chase on August 12th. Had he stayed on another two days he would have been better able to guess the ultimate fate of the enemy, for on the 14th three Italian merchantmen dropped behind and vanished into the cold expanse of the North Sea. Each day, as the fleet ran northwards before the wind to a point where it could turn west around the Shetland Islands, the Armada grew smaller as the slower and clumsier vessels dropped away into the fog. Each morning there was the sad ceremony of throwing the dead overboard, and by the 21st three thousand men were mortally ill. For two more weeks the battered galleons made no progress at all in their desperate efforts to tack against a perverse wind. Doggedly they tried to inch westwards, far enough to avoid being swept by giant Atlantic rollers on to the sheer cliffs and boiling shores of the Irish coast. Eight great ships, one of the galleasses, and two of the heavy freighters failed in the attempt. Vessel after vessel was flung upon rock and sand to be pounded to pieces by tides and waves. Their crews drowned, and at Sligo on a five-mile stretch of beach, Sir Geoffrey Fenton reported "eleven hundred dead bodies of men, which the sea had driven upon the shore".

So many lurid tales have been written about the savage doings on the Irish coast that it is impossible now to say what really happened. Maybe it was true that, as one of the immense Spanish galleons broke up on the rocks of the Blasket Islands, a maddened nobleman struck down the pilot, screaming that he had wrecked the ship by treason, and that of all the gentlemen and sailors on board only the pilot's son, who had lashed himself to a spar, survived. Possibly also, officers and noblemen, if they escaped drowning, were killed by Irish peasants for their finery, and the Prince of Ascoli, Philip's illegitimate son, was murdered for his silk stockings, satin doublet and gold lace. It would, however, be closer to the truth to say that both aristocrats and commoners were butchered by order of Sir William Fitzwilliam, Elizabeth's Lord Deputy of Ireland.

More ships survived the agony than could humanly have been expected, and perhaps a second miracle took place: the amazing strength that allowed Medina Sidonia and his bleeding crews to bring home a limping squadron of some sixty-six sail. It was a useless and tragic feat. Half the vessels never sailed again, and two-thirds of the men who were still alive when the Duke sighted Spain, arrived home only to die of disease, dysentery and hunger within the month. In all ten men-of-war had been lost as a consequence of war: two captured by accident, three stranded on the Flemish and Calais beaches, and five sunk by English guns. Another eleven, and possibly a dozen freighters, were demolished on the long flight home, partly because the winds and the immense surge of the Atlantic cast them on the jagged rocks of the Irish coast, but mostly because men dying of privation and exhaustion could not man their sodden and leaking ships. Twenty smaller vessels remain unaccounted for. Some authorities say they were "lost, fate unknown"; others claim that most of them eventually found their way back to Spain.

By the time the jubilant word of what had happened to Philip's proud vessels had made its way to England, the supreme moment of Elizabeth's reign had passed and the long recessional had begun. When the Armada first approached the Lizard on July 29th and Captain Thomas Fleming of the pinnace *Golden Hind* rushed to report the news, interrupting Drake's immortal game of bowls upon Plymouth Hoe, legend maintains that the old buccaneer dismissed him with the flamboyant statement: "We have time enough to finish the game and beat the Spaniards too!" Whatever Drake may have actually said or felt, most Englishmen were less insensate about the approaching ordeal. Certainly by the time the game of bowls was finished the chain of beacons had been lit, and within hours London and even distant York knew that the crisis was finally upon them.

No one could be sure that England's naval wall, however much it had been blessed by a Protestant deity, would be able to hold back the Catholic onslaught, and highly exaggerated reports were trickling in from the Netherlands that Parma's legions were only awaiting Medina Sidonia's galleons and a favourable tide to commence the invasion of the island. The Queen could not hope to muster an army to match Castilian pikemen and musketeers seasoned by years of hard fighting in and around Antwerp, but she could counter a mercenary Spanish army with the theory of a nation in arms. The responsibility of Elizabeth's subjects, from sixteen to sixty, to maintain themselves in fighting trim was built into English history, reaching even further back than Harold's ill-trained shire levies which broke and fled at the battle of Hastings. But an ancient and rusty obligation had now become a pressing patriotic duty. For centuries hired bands of semi-feudal retainers had been sent to fight on the continent, but for the first time for over three hundred years the realm faced a serious threat of invasion. A creaky and decayed feudal system still worked to some degree and members of the nobility rushed to offer their Queen troops raised from their own retainers and paid from their own purses. Lord Morley, though his estates were diminished, raised a company of one hundred and twenty horse and foot soldiers; Lord Dacre, despite his many creditors, did almost as well; and the wealthy Earl of Pembroke attended upon the sovereign with three hundred cavalry and five hundred infantrymen.

The backbone of the Queen's defences, however, was no longer an antiquated feudal machine but a system of national musters, whereby the Tudor government endeavoured to keep in military readiness a percentage of the kingdom's manpower. In March 1573 a royal commission had taken a muster of all the shires and had found them woefully unprepared. Derbyshire reported that it could muster four thousand men but could afford to train only five hundred in musketry and bowmanship. Other counties announced that they were too poor to organize any kind of militia. The same excuses, prevarications and incompetence were again found in 1577, and almost every shire begged that the three hundred and twenty pounds needed to train a company of four hundred men was too great a load for its taxpayers to carry. Fortunately by 1588 the Privy Council had whipped the muster into reasonable shape and the counties opened their pocketbooks as the emergency grew near. Essex reported a potential of thirteen thousand and sixty-two infantry and three hundred horsemen, and promised almost four thousand men fully armed with musket, shot and pike. In shire after shire, the gentry, bullied and encouraged by the Privy Council, had taken over local defence, and despite feuds, confusion and shortage of money, they had organized, at least on paper, an impressive national levy capable of putting into the field an army of a hundred thousand men. In actual fact, it was quite impossible to feed, arm and discipline such a force, and muster-masters grumbled that almost every man was "rawly furnished, some lacking a headpiece, some a sword", and what equipment was available was "evil, unfit or unbecoming". In July 1588 the best the Earl of Leicester, Captain-General of her Majesty's forces, could collect and feed at his camp at Tilbury was an army of twenty-three thousand, and in all probability the actual number was closer to ten thousand. He complained bitterly when four thousand men from Essex arrived without a barrel of beer or a loaf of bread among the lot, and he sourly announced that he was more "cook, caterer and huntsman" than a Captain-General.

Whatever their fighting deficiencies may have been, Leicester's brave lads made a magnificent audience for the most dramatic moment of Gloriana's reign. On August 18th, ten days after the Armada had fled northwards before Howard's fleet, the Queen determined to inspect her loyal troops gathered in full war regalia at Tilbury. She arrived with great white plumes in her hat and confidence in her heart, for the news from Howard, who had given up the chase near Scottish waters, was increasingly hopeful. It is true that Puritan Francis Walsingham complained about the "half-doing" that had bred "dishonour and leaves the disease uncured", but with the Armada running for home with its Catholic tail between its legs and not a single English ship lost, the disease for the moment did not seem very dreadful. The Queen was always satisfied with half-doings; in fact she preferred them, and she was now ready to receive the accolades of her jubilant subjects and stout defenders. She spoke to throngs who were still dazzled by the famous red hair (now a wig), the ruddy and healthy complexion (now liberally helped by rouge pot and rice powder), and the "princely resolution" (made more majestic by a white velvet gown and more resolute by a silver breastplate). Gloriana wore well her fifty-five years, and she could still marshal words and command emotions that not even the dead hand of history can deprive of their splendour:

My loving people,
We have been persuaded
By some that are careful of our safety,
To take heed
How we commit ourselves to armed multitudes,
For fear of treachery.
But I assure you,
I do not desire to live
To distrust my faithful and loving people.

Let tyrants fear.
I have always so behaved myself that, under God,
I have placed my chiefest strength and safeguard
In the loyal hearts and good will of my subjects;
And therefore I am come amongst you,
As you see, at this time,
Not for my recreation and disport,
But being resolved,
In the midst and heat of battle,
To live or die amongst you all,
To lay down for my God,
And for my kingdom,
And for my people,
My honour and my blood,
Even in the dust.
I know I have the body of a weak and feeble woman,
But I have the heart and stomach of a king,

And of a king of England too,
And think foul scorn that Parma or Spain,
Or any prince of Europe
Should dare to invade the borders of my realm;
To which, rather than any dishonour shall grow by me,
I myself will take up arms,
I myself will be your general,
Judge, and rewarder of every one of your virtues in the
    field.
I know, already for your forwardness
You have deserved rewards and crowns;
And we do assure you,
In the word of a prince,
They shall be duly paid you.

Though the Queen was as good as her word and paid her
soldiers to the last farthing, which is more than Philip did
for his crews when they crept home to Spain, her loving
people felt that somehow they had been deprived of their
full quota of deserved "rewards and crowns". The romance
of war had a sour ending, for the news of the Armada's
fate was delayed, mercifully for Philip, infuriatingly for
Elizabeth, who wanted above all else to decommission her
fleet, dismiss her soldiers and save her exchequer. Howard
returned home triumphant, but men talked of might-have-
beens, not of laurels won. They did not know that wind,
rock and water on the Irish coast were giving them a far
greater victory than English guns could ever have hoped
to achieve. The watch still had to be kept, for the war, so
gloriously begun, first with the rape of Cadiz and then with
the defeat of the Armada, did not end, but deteriorated
into a costly and endless struggle in Holland, France and
Ireland. On the high seas, Philip profited from defeat and
learned how to defend his ports and treasure fleets. In
Ireland, an English ulcer, fostered by Spanish gold, consumed the Queen's carefully hoarded revenues, loaded her
government with debt and destroyed a host of military
reputations. Elizabethans had every right to feel that the
Spanish beard had only been signed and that Philip's fighting strength and determination remained almost as great
as ever.

It was a full generation after the defeat of the invincible Armada that elderly Elizabethans, scornful of a Stuart king who feared his own shadow and manifested such unkingly habits as drivelling at the mouth, picking his nose, and closeting himself with pretty young men, began to look back upon the great days of '88 through a golden haze of nostalgia and to see an event of decisive and heroic proportions. Even today from the comfort of our armchairs, it is difficult to evaluate an enterprise that could have ended only as it did – in catastrophe. The boast that Elizabeth's seadogs, strong in their knowledge of a God who was aggressively English, saved northern Europe for Protestantism, guaranteed the independence of Holland, secured France for the Bourbon dynasty and made England safe for the great age of Elizabethan literature rings hollow. Shakespeare never made direct reference to the English triumph. From the start, Parma questioned whether the conquest of England was necessary to the destruction of Holland and Zeeland, and he argued that Philip's major effort should have been directed against Dutch deep-water ports and ocean shipping. Only then might Spain have chanced the invasion of an island protected by the largest and finest navy in the world. In France, it is difficult to imagine the course of history being very different had God wrought a miracle, and bemused English wits and destroyed Dutch flyboats, so that Parma and Medina Sidonia could have met and crossed the Channel to England. Even if Henry III had never dared to order the death of the Duke of Guise or had escaped the assassin's blade, Henry of Navarre still remained the rightful heir to the throne, and after thirty years of religious and feudal bloodshed the demand for peace, grounded firmly on history and legality, could not have been long denied.

Yet, after the analysts have finished their work, there remains something to be said for a victory that has become the touchstone of Protestant mythology, for the destruction of the Armada was an immensely significant event in the transition of Europe into the modern age. The medieval profile, with its longing for unity, orthodoxy and theology, was smashed beyond recognition by the nimble galleons and deadly culverins of Howard's fleet. In

England, love of that blessed isle allowed no place for loyalty to a European commonwealth, and as the Armada disappeared into the mist of the North Sea so also did the memory of the medieval and seamless cloak of Christendom. Even in the English Jesuit college at Rome it was reported that English students cheered at the destruction of an armada which had never lost its Spanish flavour, though it sought to represent all Christendom and defend a medieval dream.

On board the Armada, history had also been made. Of valour there was an abundance, but in the final reckoning even courage became the senseless, arrogant histrionics of men and admirals whom time and technology, and, it would seem, God as well, had passed by. Militarily and spiritually the Armada belonged to the feudal crusading past. King Philip's father had discovered that fortune was a woman who loved not old men, and now the son learned that she was no lover of old-fashioned ways.

As the capitals of Europe learned the full magnitude of the disaster, king, pope and general grieved, each according to his nature. In Rome, Sixtus V congratulated himself that he had not after all lent the King of Spain a million golden ducats. In Brussels, Parma went straight to the most tragic aspect of the calamity: "What adds," he said, "more than I can here express to my grief at this disaster is that it was humanly impossible to remedy it, or aid in any way." In Madrid, Philip wrapped himself in the mantle of his anguish and true to his character returned to work. "In God's actions," he said, "reputation is neither lost nor gained: it is best not to talk of it." Philip as usual was right in theory but wrong in fact, and even Sixtus V could not refrain from exclaiming upon the wonders of Elizabeth and the fearless Drake, who together had tweaked the nose of the Spanish colossus. In London the fanfare for Elizabeth was even less restrained, and heroic Englishmen "did nothing but talk of what a great Queen she was and how they would die for her".

By the year of the Armada the Queen had reached the autumn of her life and was content to sit by the fire and remember the soft fresh face of Leicester and the great deeds of her beardless boys, but her realm was in a more daring and jubilant frame of mind. The decade of heroes had begun, and men of more than mortal stature pranced and quarrelled around their goddess Queen. Gloriana was doubtless flattered that her Titans were willing to go anywhere and try anything for Queen and country, but she found them, as often as not, as mischievous and irresponsible as a pack of schoolboys. The Olympian posing of Raleigh, Essex and Drake may have added magnificence to her middle age and lustre to the achievements of her reign, but their juvenile antics drove Elizabeth to distraction and were better suited to poetry than to the serious business of war and politics.

Ten

A Decade of Heroes

Iᴛ is only proper to introduce a tale of heroes with the traditional words: "Once upon a time" there lived a generation of men so exaggerated in their behaviour and so flamboyant in their aspirations that not even the fearsome words of Faustus could describe the fiery zeal which consumed them.

> Philosophy is odious and obscure;
> Both law and physics are for petty wits;
> Divinity is basest of the three . . .
> 'Tis magic, magic, that hath ravished me.

Proud as Lucifer, they disdained to bargain with the devil or, like Faustus, sell their souls for four-and-twenty years of "all voluptuousness". The magic that ravished them lay within themselves: the exotic, petulant and boundless self-confidence that led Raleigh to assert that "style is the man", and George Peele to shout: "King of a molehill had I rather be than the richest subject of a monarchy." One and all – Raleigh, Essex, Frobisher, Drake, Leicester, Norris, Gilbert, Sidney, Grenville – were willing to "pay nature's debt with cheerful countenance", for they courted death and never feared it. Within their good Puritan souls there burned an awe-inspiring sense of election, but these chosen few were no empty vessels filled with the spirt of the Lord. The dynamism that urged them on was devoid

of heavenly reward or hellish punishment. They required
of God only that He grant them the chance to show their
true metal, forged in the fire of their egotism. The adventure of life, said Raleigh to his son, was "a troublesome
bark", and it was up to each man to make good his "station
in the upper deck; those that live under hatches are ordained to be drudges and slaves".

Whatever may be said against these heroes of Elizabethan England, they cannot be accused of dullness or
slavishness. They spoke proudly and persistently of their
duty to God and Queen, but Elizabeth knew that neither
the threat of prison nor the fear of hell could discipline
her warriors, and, in letter after letter, she was reduced to
impotent rage and helpless pleading. She was infuriated by
Leicester's expensive and footless prancing about Holland,
his peevish insistence on being styled Governor-General,
and she angrily announced that she was "utterly at squares
with this childish dealing". Before Drake set out on the
haphazard expedition of 1589, Elizabeth sought to prevent disobedience by warning him to beware lest vainglory
"obfuscate the eyes of your judgment". The advice fell
on deaf ears, for, as the Queen suspected, Sir Francis Drake
and Sir John Norris "went to places more for profit than
for service". They ignored their sovereign's orders to strike
at Spanish warships and naval installations at Corunna, and
instead went looking for honour and plunder in an abor-
tive attack on Lisbon. Elizabeth was particularly irritated
with the entire venture since her favourite young courtier,
the Earl of Essex, had rushed to join the fray, loudly announcing that "if I speed well, I will adventure to be rich;
if not, I will not live to see the end of my poverty".
Gloriana ordered her errant boy back to court, and she
grimly reminded Drake and Norris: "As we have authority
to rule, so we look to be obeyed." Elizabeth might have
spared herself the cost of the ink; she had endless
authority, but when glory and gold were concerned she
was rarely obeyed. To honour, her beardless boys were
willing slaves; to the standards of Tudor society and the
wishes of their Queen, they were lighthearted rebels. Duty
to themselves as a breed of men apart was the root and
branch of their faith, and almost in anguish Essex cried

out: "I am tied by my own reputation to use no tergiversation!"

Heroes, like saints, become grotesque caricatures or lifeless reflections when held up to the mirror of humanity. What is the normal man to think of the extraordinary behaviour of Sir Richard Grenville during the last encounter of the *Revenge*? The occasion was one of the least glorious of Elizabeth's efforts to finance naval warfare with the profits of piracy. A small English fleet of six vessels under Lord Thomas Howard, bent on plundering the Spanish treasure fleet, was caught in 1591 by twenty of Philip's "galleons of the Indian guard". Howard had been hovering off the Azores for months in fruitless expectation of the treasure *flota*, and had just begun filling his water kegs and resting his crew at Flores when a Spanish fleet of fifty-three sail swept in from the west and surprised the English at anchor. The Admiral ordered his ships to cut cable and run for it, and he managed to get five of his vessels away to safety. Sir Richard Grenville in the *Revenge*, however, preferred to take on the entire Spanish navy singlehanded and smash his way through to the open sea. It remains a mystery whether Grenville's action was sheer bravado touched with insanity, in which, like Drake, he regarded the war with Spain as a personal conflict between himself and Philip's empire, or was a suicidal endeavour to save his comrades in arms by covering Howard's retreat.

Whatever the truth, his defiance of the naval might of Spain has become one of the legendary feats of English history. For fifteen hours the *Revenge*, with only ninety of her crew fit to fight, endured an agony of cannonading and musket fire that could only end in total destruction. Surrounded by five immense galleons, at least two of which were three times the tonnage of the *Revenge*, Grenville fought his ship until it was a slaughterhouse, running red with blood, riddled by eight hundred cannon-balls, its mast and rigging shot away, and almost every man dead or wounded. The Spanish, in recognition of such valour, presented amazing terms of surrender: common seamen would not be sent to row in the galleys but were offered safe passage to England, while officers would be kept in honourable captivity awaiting ransom. Grenville would accept no such terms. The *Revenge* had already sunk two Spanish galleons, and "the Spaniards," he said, "should never glory to have taken one ship of her Majesty." He ordered the master gunner to blow up the *Revenge* with all aboard so that "nothing might remain of glory or victory to the Spaniards". Self-immolation may be a suitable death for heroes, but the crew, of a more pedestrian reasoning and more mortal clay, thought otherwise and insisted upon surrender. Grenville's scorn was classic, and he had to be forcibly restrained from falling on his sword to escape capture. Desperately wounded though he was, there was still fight left in the old seadog. The Spanish treated him with the respect due to the devil himself and did their best to save his life, but Grenville had no intention either of living on in captivity or of quietly dying of his wounds. In an act, possibly legendary and certainly unbelievable in any man except a Grenville, he deliberately crushed his wine goblet, and, while his horrified hosts watched, methodically chewed up the pieces of glass until his mouth dripped with blood. He died a legend, and his final words were true to character: "Here die I, Richard Grenville, with a joyful and quiet mind, having ended my life like a true soldier that has fought for his country, Queen, religion and honour." When, a few days later, a hurricane swept down upon both the treasure *flota* and Philip's galleons, and sank seventy ships including the hulk of the *Revenge*, the Spanish understandably thought that Grenville had been in league with the devil and had called upon the elements to revenge his death. Without passing judgment upon Sir Richard's relations with the satanic forces, the twentieth century can only surmise that the ferocious old mariner was more fit for a padded cell than a naval command.

The same wild fantasy surrounds the death of that literate Puritan and courtier-cum-adventurer, Sir Humphrey Gilbert, who was lost at sea in 1583 on his return from an ill-starred effort to explore and colonize the coast of Newfoundland. Elizabeth had already noted that Sir Humphrey was a particularly unlucky commander, and this last voyage, when one hundred colonists were lost in a wreck on the uncharted coast of Nova Scotia, again proved her judgment correct. Economic ruin faced Gilbert, for he had invested every penny in his vision of populating a New World, but his self-confidence never wavered. "Be of good cheer," he assured his men, for God had given him special knowledge of the inestimable good to be achieved from the expedition, and would help persuade the Queen to lend him ten thousand pounds for further discoveries in distant lands. The elected few, with whom Sir Humphrey counted himself, were men of iron purpose and conviction, and throughout the voyage Gilbert insisted that the Lord had given him a promise which should suffice to check any mutinous grumblings among his crew.

When the little flotilla, sadly reduced to two ships but still confident in God's favour, sailed home, Sir Humphrey transferred his flag from the forty-ton bark, the *Hind*, to the tiny ten-ton *Squirrel* because he feared that men might say he was afraid of the sea. Even his admirers thought this gesture excessively rash and wondered that he should "prefer the wind of a vain report to the weight of his own life". Heroes, however, must live up to their reputations, and the last that was ever seen or heard of the foolhardy commander was Sir Humphrey sitting in the stern of his cockleshell craft, with a book in his hand and the words "We are as near to heaven by sea as by land" on his lips. Hours later during a wild September storm, the *Squirrel* "was devoured and swallowed up of the Sea".

It is ridiculously easy to dismiss as mere madness the actions of heroes who behaved like a band of overgrown, if divine, juvenile delinquents, more suited for a house of correction than a hall of fame. Yet to do so is to miss the full flavour and true proportions of the age. Not only did Gilbert, Grenville, Essex and the rest take themselves and their reputations seriously but so also did the world in which they lived. Drake's ruddy and belligerent features and tublike frame hung in the portrait galleries of innumerable Protestant princes throughout Germany and Holland; the daredevil death at the age of thirty-two of Sir Philip Sidney, who rode into battle without his steel cuisse because his wounded commander was unable to wear armour, was held up as an act of daring and renown becoming a great poet; and Marlowe spoke for his generation when he wrote of the dreadful Tamburlaine that his honour consisted "in shedding blood".

The heroes of the sixteenth century were no deities fulfilling their boisterous destinies in Olympian isolation. Grenville and Gilbert were not exceptions to the Tudor rule; they were simply magnified examples of it. Individually their actions are grotesque, but placed within the context of an age where exaggeration and violence were the central characteristics of life, their feats become no more extraordinary than that of the indefatigable Robert Carey, who won a two thousand pound bet by walking from London to Berwick in twelve days, or that of the unnamed English soldier whose arm was shot off by a cannon-ball at the siege of Ostend. Nothing daunted, the young man picked up the severed limb, returned with it to camp and announced to his comrades: "Behold the arm which but at dinner helped its fellow." The sixteenth century, as did the eighteenth, believed in "bottom", the untranslatable word which united stoicism with enthusiasm, histrionics with conviction, and foppery with toughness.

Violence, cruelty and intensity were commonplaces of Tudor life. The endurance of Drake's tiny band which circumnavigated the globe in an epic voyage lasting three years must be set off against the discomforts and risks of normal existence. Imagine life as it actually was – a long agony of itches from skin diseases, lice and fleas, a steady procession of toothaches, gout, stones, rheumatism and pains, and the constant fear of smallpox, sweating sickness and the plague. Only the strong of body and stout of heart survived, and even they could not long withstand medical practices designed more to test the patient's fortitude than to cure his sickness. The surgeon's saw without ether, the barber's tooth-extractor without novocaine, and the physician's potions without understanding, were no less terrible than Spanish musket and cannon shot. The death of Don Juan, Philip's half-brother, from a horrible combination of syphilis and some variety of the plague, was just as frightful as that of Sir Richard Grenville. The suffering of poor Lady Throckmorton at the hands of Dr. Atslow must have been comparable to that of the wretches on the *Revenge*. Lady Throckmorton had had a haemorrhage after the birth of a daughter, and Sir Arthur Throckmorton carefully noted down in his diary the treatment with full clinical details. His good lady was wrapped in sheets soaked "in plantain water and vinegar of roses in equal quantities"; she was kept from all motion and both her arms were "tied very hard and sometimes loosed and tied again"; her diet was limited to "roasted meats without sauce and fish sometimes"; she had to "forbear all wines, salt and sharp waters, drinking as little as may be and that must be ale"; she was bled from both arms two or three times daily; and she was forced to "sit from her buttocks up to her navel in a deep bowl of cold water". The reader will be glad to know that not only did Lady Throckmorton survive her cure but that Dr. Atslow was later imprisoned for high treason and tortured on the rack; a mild punishment for what he prescribed for his patients.

The picture of Sir Francis Drake sitting cross-legged on a sea chest and enjoying himself hugely while lecturing his delinquent chaplain, who was chained and collared to the deck in front of him, is an example of ruthlessness and egotism unforgivable even in a demigod. The unfortunate Francis Fletcher had spoken disrespectfully and ill-advisedly of his captain and had intimated that the misfortunes of the *Golden Hind* had come as retribution for Drake's execution of one Thomas Doughty for witchery and disobedience. Sir Francis's simple Puritan soul was outraged by this fearful evidence that Satan had entered even into the heart of a minister of God, and calling his crew together he addressed the frightened and humiliated clergyman: "Francis Fletcher, I do here excommunicate thee out of the Church of God and from all benefits and graces thereof, and I denounce thee to the devil and all his angels."

In judging Drake's sadistic satisfaction, it is well to remember that in the sixteenth century Satan was a ubiquitous and awe-inspiring personality and that cruelty gave spice to life. Sir Francis behaved no worse than Tudor audiences who laughed at Falstaff's embarrassment on being thrown into the river in a basket of dirty linen, and Francis Fletcher's misfortunes can scarcely be compared to the degrading suffering of the poor devils who stood with their ears nailed to the public stocks, helpless targets for the mockery, jeers and pelting of every passer-by. Men wore a tough hide of inhumanity and callousness which inured them to the sight of blind beggars trying to club a pig to death, or to the agonies of the condemned poisoner writhing in a pot of boiling oil, of the witch suffering on the stake, and of the traitor strung up on the gallows and then, still living, cut down, castrated and disembowelled. Sensation, dulled by daily suffering equal to that brought by any executioner's axe or hangman's noose, required the stimulus of horror and cruelty. That good Christian gentleman, Phillip Stubbes, was loud in his indignation against the godless people who played football on the Sabbath, but he obviously felt that blinded eyes, broken necks, and noses that "gush out with blood" were injuries that justly befell sinners who profaned the Lord's day. Violence and pain meant little to this worthy defender of God's truth, and he thought death not too great a penalty for swearing. If such a punishment, he conceded, were judged too severe, then he wished that offenders "might have a piece of their tongue cut off, or lose some joint", and if the weak of heart could not stomach this, at the very least blasphemers should "be seared in the forehead or cheek with a hot iron [and] engraven with some pretty posie, that they might be known and avoided". Under the circumstances, the Reverend Francis Fletcher might be judged lucky to have escaped with injury only to his vanity.

Every city and court of Europe was exposed to brawling, duelling and histrionics. Raleigh delighted in the magnificence of his famous cloaks and his reputation for "perpetually differing"; throughout his life George Clifford, Earl of Cumberland, wore in his hat a glove dropped by Elizabeth; Sidney, as he lay dying of thirst and a broken hip, gravely presented his cup to a common soldier with the words: "Thy need is greater than mine"; and Essex, leaving his military post, rushed off through enemy territory to fraternize with Henry IV of France, and arrived in the French King's camp resplendent in orange velvet embroidered with gold and sprinkled with jewels, and with an entourage dressed in the same livery. As Raleigh said, it was style that made the man! Even in their personal

lives the heroes of Tudor England lived by standards more
suited to Valhalla than the banquet hall. The story is told
of how Raleigh and his son won immortality and coined
a bon mot by staging a family row at a dinner party. From
the start Sir Walter was doubtful about his son's table man-
ners but the young man had promised to "behave himself
mighty mannerly". The two Raleighs sat next to one another and half way through the meal young Walter suddenly remarked to the company: "I, this morning, not
having the fear of God before my eyes but by the instiga-
tion of the devil, went to a whore. I was very eager of her,
kissed and embraced her, and went to enjoy her; but she
thrust me from her and vowed I should not, 'For your
father lay with me but an hour ago'." Sir Walter was understandably outraged by his quarrelsome offspring's words
and struck him "a damned blow over the face". In
deference to his father, young Raleigh did not hit back but
turned instead to his unsuspecting neighbour and struck
the astonished gentleman, saying: "Box about: 'twill come
to my father anon." "Box about" became a proverb in
the seventeenth century.

Gilded youths with "fierce dragons' spleens", wearing a
lord's revenue on their backs, and buccaneers who were
mindful only of the vainglory of life must have been irritating beyond measure to the merchant immersed in his accounts, to the bureaucrat insensible of romance, and to a
Queen who counted her change and constantly inquired
into the cost of glory. The sixteenth century, however, forgave them their idiocies because they were great. Man's
fate on earth was boredom, pain and death, and those who
endured haemorrhoids and scrofula, and looked with dull
eyes upon a life of disease-ridden monotony, demanded
the chance to enjoy life vicariously. They thrilled at
Raleigh's boast that England would make the kings of
Spain "kings of figs and oranges, as in old times" or his
bragging that one of the Queen's warships was a match
for forty Dutchmen, for such words lent verisimilitude to
their dreams.

The cult of the individual was part of the European
heritage. Though Renaissance emphasis upon the worth of
man may have given new brilliance to the actions of man-

kind, the medieval world also had thought in terms of the individual. No one until the nineteenth century ever considered man to be a soulless nonentity, a mass statistic to go along with a world of mass production, mass styling and mass annihilation. Man remained unique; and individually, not collectively, he enacted the divine drama of salvation and damnation. The old Church had preached against pride and egotism and had besought Christians to do their duty to God and society, but it had done so in terms of the actions of individual men: the over-mighty magnate, the proud prelate and the grasping usurer. Greatness, whether it was the incarnate evil of Judas, the justice of St. Louis, the courage of Henry V, the piety of Henry VI, or the pride of Charles of Burgundy, fascinated the medieval mind. The feudal past had always been willing to make allowances for the uncommon man. Saints had traditionally been a breed apart; their folly had been judged by standards peculiar to themselves and had been found to be a higher wisdom. By the same token heroes and geniuses in the sixteenth century were not judged by the mores of normal men. Those proud, undisciplined and extravagant conquistadors, who single-handed carved out an empire for Spain, lived by a code unique to themselves and to the other pioneer-warriors of the Renaissance. Cortés persuaded his men on the beaches of Vera Cruz to burn their boats and forget about failure because, he said, such an act would be comparable to the "brave deeds done by heroes among the Romans". The boast of Bernal Díaz that he had won nobility by fighting in twice as many battles as Caesar was accepted as a valid achievement in life. Elizabeth forgave in Essex a degree of childishness and insolence which would have been ridiculed and punished in lesser men, and Pope Paul III thought it not unreasonable to excuse the boasted murders of Cellini because, as he said, "men unique in their professions, like Benvenuto, were not subject to the laws."

History, as the humble man knows, is reserved for the Titans, those extraordinary men and women who achieve immortality by impressing their feats upon the memory of mankind; the rest of us must make do with heaven. But even among the Olympian host, the historian must choose.

Not every warrior can be elected for salvation, and the remaining pages are reserved for the adventures of but two Elizabethan heroes – Sir Walter Raleigh and Robert Devereux, Earl of Essex.

Raleigh was fortune's tennis ball, a knavish, witty, boisterous fellow, proud as the devil and impudent as Puck, who was obsessed with the desire "to sway all men's fancies, all men's courses", and who was hated above all others "in court, city and country". Only Elizabeth could handle him, and she alone seems to have liked this "tall, handsome, and bold man" who suddenly appeared at her court in the early months of 1582. Yet even the Queen never gave him a chance to "sway all men's fancies"; she preferred to listen to his ready and persuasive tongue and to dress his shapely limbs in the orange uniform of the Captain of her Guard. The Council door remained closed, and Raleigh had to be content with the Queen's chamber.

Exactly how Raleigh came to Gloriana's attention is a mystery. He was born around 1552 and stemmed from an old and respected Devonshire family. Neither his carriage nor the company he kept endeared him to men in authority, for young Walter's insolent knowledge of his own genius was matched only by the impudent rowdiness of his associates. His servants were for ever brawling with the London constabulary. Raleigh himself was twice jailed in 1580 for disturbing the peace, and he won a measure of renown by silencing a noisy tavern bully by filling the fellow's mouth with wax and tying his beard to his moustache. Despite skirmishes with the law, he received a captaincy and the command of one hundred foot soldiers, and went forth to more glorious and bloody encounters against the Irish rebels. In Ireland Raleigh won notoriety by the violence and ruthlessness of his methods of waging war, and he seems to have spent considerable time and energy criticizing his superiors, writing over their heads to the Council in London, and earning the dislike of his commanding officer. By the spring of 1582 he was back in England and, probably through the favour of his half-brother, Sir Humphrey Gilbert, he was introduced to the Queen. A tart but silver tongue, a fine figure and a flair for the flamboyant were the qualities which won for him the Queen's bounty. If, as legend reports, Raleigh spent his last farthing upon a cape of wondrous grandeur which he extravagantly sacrificed to keep Elizabeth dry-shod, the investment paid off handsomely, for by May 1583 he had been granted the lucrative monopoly of licences to sell wine. This netted Raleigh the princely sum of twelve hundred pounds a year and permitted him to wear shoes said to have been worth "six thousand, six hundred gold pieces". Though real power as a stateman continued to elude Sir Walter, in 1587 he was given the coveted post of Captain of the Guard, a position that opened up the well-spring of the royal favour, the full depth of which the Captain seems to have sounded. Elizabeth once asked him in some annoyance: "When will you cease to be a beggar, Raleigh?" The answer was typical of the man. "When Your Majesty ceases to be a benefactor," was his barefaced but honest retort.

Sir Walter Raleigh was always something more than a piece of costly tinsel in Elizabeth's display of royalty. Gloriana doubtless admired her "Water", as she affectionately nicknamed him, for his dark beard, curly hair and foppish elegance, but quickness of mind and impertinence of speech, not a well-turned calf, won him her favour, and, much to the annoyance of the court, Elizabeth took him "for a kind of oracle, which nettled them all". There were few men in England who could gull their Queen, but Raleigh did so when he fatuously and provocatively mentioned that he knew his tobacco so well that he could actually weigh the smoke. Elizabeth rose to the bait and wagered him that he could not make good his boast. Sir Walter simply weighed the tobacco, smoked it in his silver pipe, weighed the ashes, subtracted one from the other, and presented the Queen with the answer. As she paid her debt, Elizabeth wryly remarked that she had heard of men "who turned gold into smoke", but Raleigh "was the first who had turned smoke into gold". The animosity so often directed at Sir Walter was largely of his own making. He was far too contemptuous of the shibboleths of polite society, and, though the Queen might find his barbed wit diverting, the ladies of the court could scarcely have been expected to take to their hearts a man who unflatteringly described them as witches who "could do hurt, but they could do no good". Raleigh knew well the proverb: "Slippery is the place next to kings," and he himself had written: "Whoso reaps renown above the rest, With heaps of hate shall be oppressed," but so long as Elizabeth smiled, angry tongues and envious glances could do him no harm.

For five years Raleigh stood guard at the Queen's door, hated by all who begrudged him his rich wardrobe and his closeness to the sovereign. In 1587, however, another star was born, and Sir Walter discovered he had to reckon with an impudent lad of nineteen, the young Earl of Essex, whose open face and soft sensuous smile touched the heart of a middle-aged Queen. Within the year, court gossip was reporting that Essex "hath chased Master Raleigh from the Court and hath confined him into Ireland". Certainly the young nobleman displaced the forty-year-old Captain of the Guard in his privileged position as royal confidant, but what ultimately destroyed Raleigh was his own insatiable conceit. Despite his virtuosity and imagination, Sir Walter lived and died a sublime egotist who had little but disdain for the foibles of mankind, nothing but insensitive and tactless criticism for convention, and only blindness for the feelings of others. In 1591 he made the serious mistake of shocking Elizabeth, who held strict and conventional views on the proper sexual behaviour of those attending upon a Virgin Queen. Rumour reported that Sir Walter had been "too inward with one of her Majesty's maids", and so he had, for Mistress Throckmorton had been undone and the unmistakable signs of pregnancy began to appear during the summer of 1591. In November Raleigh and his young mistress were secretly married, and on March 28th a son – Damerei Raleigh – was born. Incredible as it sounds, the Earl of Essex stood godfather to the boy.

If Raleigh hoped to escape the Queen's wrath by enlisting his rival's favour, he badly miscalculated. Despite the marriage and the blessing of Essex, Elizabeth took the view that one of her vestal virgins had been ravished. She withheld her fury for several months, but in August 1592 the brash couple were dispatched to the Tower to meditate upon the consequences of incontinence and the anger of a

Virgin Queen, who liked her Captains of the Guard unmarried and who took seriously her responsibilities as guar-
dian to her maids. Elizabeth was no prude, but she refused
to countenance the kind of sexual laxity prevalent at the
court of that amorous sovereign, Henry IV of France.
Raleigh had his Bess Throckmorton, and his stay in the
Tower lasted scarcely a month, but his career seemed to
be over; younger men and other heroes would fill the world
with their fame while he languished in the darkness of the
Queen's anger. No wonder he sadly wrote from the Tower:

> The flowers do fade, and wanton fields
> To wayward winter reckoning yields,
> A honey tongue – a heart of gall –
> Is fancy's spring, but sorrow's fall.

Long before Raleigh got Mistress Throckmorton "up
against a tree in a wood", and got both of them into
trouble, Elizabeth's affections had turned to that delightful
young aristocrat, Robert Devereux, Earl of Essex. The
Queen liked her courtly mannikins to be of noble birth.
With Raleigh she had made an exception, but in Essex she
found the perfect Harlequin to her ageing Columbine. The
Earl of Leicester, Essex's step-father and Elizabeth's exasperating but beloved beau of yesteryear, introduced the
young Earl to court in 1586. Romantically handsome, ir-
resistibly young, impetuously generous, carrying "on his
brow either love or hatred", and never able to "understand
concealment", the world stood at Devereux's feet. The
Queen sighed at the sight of so much promise and had to
have her Essex in constant attendance. Together they
played at cards and chatted until dawn, and Elizabeth put
up with more sulking and more dangerous nonsense from
this spoiled favourite than she had even from her "Robin",
the Earl of Leicester. Essex was "a great resenter". He complained about Raleigh and called him a knave, an upstart
and a vegetable of the court, and when Elizabeth still
showed fondness for her "Water", he tried to steal off to
the Netherlands to find solace in war. He petulantly insulted Charles Blount who was presented by Elizabeth
with a golden chess queen in recognition of his feats in the

tilt. Blount appeared at court with his token tied by a crimson ribbon to his sleeve, and on spying it, Essex sneered in a loud voice: "Now I see every fool must have a favour."

For all his trying ways, the Earl of Essex must have had great magnetism to have charmed Elizabeth into giving him real responsibility. With Raleigh she had correctly judged the true metal of the man – brilliant, conceited and unreliable. With Devereux she allowed her better judgment to be overridden by his passionate pleading to lead an expeditionary force in support of Henry IV of France. The tiny army landed in August 1591 with explicit orders to aid in the siege of Rouen and then return home after no more than two months. Rouen never fell; it was scarcely even attacked; and Essex had a glorious time. He outjumped the French King at a game of leapfrog, fell into ambushes, challenged the governor of Rouen to personal combat, and lavishly bestowed knighthoods upon twenty-four of his henchmen after apologizing for not having led them into battle where they could gain honour and earn their spurs. Elizabeth was understandably annoyed. She scornfully dismissed Essex's parading as "rather a jest than a victory", and peremptorily ordered the errant commander home. The Earl was amazed by such treatment and wrote bitterly that he "was blamed as negligent, undutiful, rash in going, slow in returning, undiscreet in dividing the horse from the foot, faulty in all things, becase I was not fortunate to please".

It is difficult to say where Essex was more dangerous: at court exercising his fatal charm and repairing his reputation in the Queen's eyes, or abroad, handling the serious concerns of war and diplomacy as if they were sports designed to display his virtuosity and daring. With Leicester's death in 1588, Elizabeth turned emotionally and politically to his stepson, so like him in his surly pride and winsome ways. She needed a counterbalance to the two Cecils – old Lord Burghley and his son Robert – and she had hopes of transforming her divine juvenile into a court politician. Essex, however, had neither the patience nor the sagacity to develop into a statesman. Like Raleigh, Drake and the other heroes, he lacked emotional stability and a sense of proportion. His idea of politics was to demand all sorts of offices and gifts for his friends, without regard for their qualifications or their acceptability by the Queen, and when she turned him down, he sulked and took it as a personal affront.

Essex must have been maddening and perplexing to his sovereign. At one moment he was dismissing politics with disarming candour, as beneath his dignity and intelligence; at the next, he was furious with Elizabeth for giving high offices to young Robert Cecil. Above all, the Earl desired a chance to excel – not at court but in war. "Soldiers in peace," it was said, were "like chimneys in summer", and being first and foremost a warrior, he called upon Gloriana to place the safety and honour of her realm in his inexperienced but eager hands. In June 1596 he finally got his opportunity, when the wind blew fair and the Queen's ships once again set sail.

Here was the chance to win glory, achieve immortality and relieve Philip of the fabulous riches of his empire. Seventeen of England's great galleons and largest merchantmen, accompanied by an armada of transports, pinnaces and flyboats, and a disciplined army of six thousand veterans from the Dutch wars were being sent for a second time to harass Spanish naval power by a strike at Cadiz. Lord Howard of Armada fame and the Earl of Essex were given joint command; Raleigh was restored to partial favour, made Vice-Admiral and placed on the five-man council of war authorized to advise the commanders. Such an expedition, led by the most famous captains of the older and younger generations, attracted an enormous number of volunteers; even John Donne went a-voyaging in quest, one imagines, of more than inspiration for his poetry. The fleet's destination remained one of the few well-kept military secrets of the century, but one and all knew that some great enterprise was being planned against Spain. Captains and sailors, generals and soldiers consciously put out of their minds the memory of a similar expedition under Sir Francis Drake which had set sail in 1589 with equally high hopes and had returned home a costly failure. It had netted one Spanish warship destroyed, a paltry plunder worth thirty thousand pounds, and eight thousand men dead out of an original company of fifteen thousand. Not even the

death of the old seadog himself in February 1596, a few
months before the new fleet set sail for Cadiz, dampened
enthusiasm for the expedition. Drake had perished fighting
an outdated kind of war, half-measures appropriate to
those wonderful and carefree days before Philip learned
to defend his treasure fleets and Caribbean ports. As always, the old warrior had relied on lady fortune and, for
once, she had played him false. His night attack on Puerto
Rico had been repulsed, his efforts to cut the Isthmus of
Panama had ended in a rout, and no gold or treasure galleons had been discovered. Rather wearily the veteran
pirate had assured his crew: "I will bring you to twenty
places far more wealthy and easier to be gotten," but he
never did; he died of dysentery instead, and true to form
he blamed his ill luck on traitors and rose up and donned
his armour saying that he would face death like a soldier.
Somewhere off Porto Bello his coffin was slipped into the
sea.

The new enterprise was no half-measure led by a tired
old captain who had seen better days. A fleet of one hundred and twenty sail under the daring Essex, the elegant
Raleigh and the veteran Lord Admiral Howard, and blessed
by every preacher within the realm, was a very different
matter. The volunteers who flocked to Plymouth thought
only of the 4,700 per cent profit made by those who had
invested in Drake's famous voyage around the world or
of the even more fabulous treasures seized only four years
before in 1592 when Sir Martin Frobisher captured the
sixteen-hundred-ton, seven-deck thirty-two gun Portuguese
carrack, the *Madre de Dios*, carrying five hundred
and thirty-seven tons of spices and priceless jewels, silks,
drugs, ivory, carpets, Chinese porcelain, ebony and "ele-
phants' teeth". The cargo, even after the crew had plun-
dered some hundred thousand pounds' worth of jewellery,
plate and gold was estimated at the impressive sum of one
hundred and forty-one thousand two hundred pounds.
The greatest galleon in the Queen's navy could be built,
fitted and manned for less than five thousand pounds: a
nobleman's estate could be purchased for seventeen thousand pounds; an entire army could be raised for forty
thousand pounds; and the total value of the *Madre de*

Dios was more than the yearly peacetime revenues of the Crown. The sailor who was lucky enough to find "three hundred and twenty sparks of diamond" and "a collar of a three-fold roll of pearl with six tags of crystal garnished with gold" had, if he could conceive the true value, a king's ransom in his pocket. It was the dream of such riches that filled the hearts of every officer, soldier and sailor when the fleet finally set sail on June 3rd, 1596.

The second Cadiz expedition came close to being the most extraordinary feat of the century, and for once heroism, rampant individualism and foolhardy histrionics paid off magnificently. From the start and against all reason, the gods were kind even to captains all of whom were inordinately touchy about rank and authority and obeyed orders only when obedience and honour happened to coincide. Even before the fleet sailed, Vice- Admiral Sir Walter Raleigh and Marshal of the Army Sir Francis Vere had a quarrel at dinner over precedence, and though the older men restrained themselves, younger and more hot-headed officers quarrelled so openly that one of them, Raleigh's brother-in-law, had to be ordered from the table. Howard and Essex were suspicious of Sir Walter because of the rumour that he had tried to persuade Elizabeth to give him sole command. The Lord Admiral was angered by the thought that the inexperienced Earl of Essex had been made joint commander, and when Essex inserted his own signature above that of Howard's in a report to the Queen, the Lord Admiral whipped out his knife and cut out the offending name because he "would have none so high as himself". "I see already," wrote one of the younger generation on board the fleet, "the fire kindled that must consume us inwardly," but the depressing prediction proved false, and the damnable pride, the braggadocio and endemic quarrelling which was so much part of Elizabethan life for once proved a source of strength and won an outstanding triumph for the Queen.

On Sunday morning, June 20th, while the church bells intermittently rang out the alarm and called the good people of Cadiz to mass the English sailed into the complicated and well-fortified harbour, and discovered King Philip's entire West Indian fleet at anchor. Thirty-six

loaded merchantmen were waiting to set sail for the Caribbean, their escorting galleons off refitting at San Lucar.
Only four huge galleons, known as the Apostles, and a
flotilla of galleys had been left behind to guard them. Cadiz
itself was located at the tip of a five-mile spit of land, the
ocean approaches defended by the high walls and cannons
of Fort San Sebastian and the bay side protected by Fort
San Felipe. The outer harbour lay slightly inland from
the city, and the inner harbour of Port Royal was another
six miles away and secured by an escape canal leading out
into the sea some ten miles below Cadiz. When the English appeared, the smaller of the merchantmen scampered
to the safety of Port Royal, and the four Apostles, accompanied by the galleys and a number of the larger merchantmen, anchored themselves, stem to stern, across the
narrow entrance to the outer harbour. After a great deal
of wrangling over where and how to proceed and who
should have the honour of leading the attack, the English
commanders accidentally stumbled upon the right strategy.
At one moment, however, it looked as if the whole enterprise was headed for disaster, when Howard refused to
risk the Queen's galleons against the combined fire of the
Apostles and the heavy artillery of the land fortifications,
while Essex was determined to wade ashore in the high
surf on the ocean side of Cadiz and storm Fort San Sebastian. For once both Howard and Essex listened to Raleigh,
who pointed out that no one had decided in what manner
to fight or "who should lead, and who should second". He
persuaded the two captains to launch their main attack
against the galleons guarding the entrance to the harbour,
and then proceed to attack Cadiz from the bay side of
the peninsula. A whole day was wasted over these discus-
sions, but on the 21st, with Raleigh in the van, since Elizabeth had issued explicit instructions that her Essex was
not to risk his precious person no matter how much honour
might be gained, the English fleet moved in upon the four
Spanish galleons – the *San Felipe,* the *San Andréo,* the *San
Mateo* and the *San Tomás.* The first two had been in at the
death of the *Revenge,* and Raleigh headed straight for
them resolved on retribution or, as he said, "to second her
with mine own life".

What followed was a fairy tale come true. As the English squadrons approached and the Spanish guns began to thunder, Raleigh ordered his trumpeters to answer each salvo with a blare of trumpets, "disdaining to shoot one piece at any one or all of those esteemed dreadful monsters". Once engaged with the Apostles, Essex, Raleigh, Vere and Howard vied with one another to manoeuvre closest to the enemy's fire and, for three hellish hours each commander kept as careful an eye on his rival as he did on the enemy. Raleigh ended this piece of mad daring, by warping his ship, the *Warspite*, close enough to the *San Felipe* to grapple and board her. Essex and Howard followed suit. When the Spanish saw the English closing in on them, they cut cable, intending to slip into the inner harbour at Port Royal, but wind, tide, fire and panic destroyed them. All four giant galleons drifted aground; two were captured and two others went up in an inferno of roaring flames and exploding cannons. Even the hardened Raleigh was horrified by the sight and wrote that "if any man had a desire to see Hell itself, it was then most lively figured".

The moment the four Apostles were routed, Essex ordered his men ashore to establish an advance bridgehead and prepare a bivouac for the rest of the army. With Essex in the leading boat, beating time on his drum, two thousand men made an unopposed landing. It was then discovered that the peninsula was only a half a mile wide at the point of landing and that Cadiz could be cut off and attacked without the help of the main army. The Earl led his troops at the double for three miles over soft sand to Cadiz, scaled the walls of the city at the head of a company of three hundred men, and with some fifty soldiers fought his way to the central square. Sir Francis Vere with a larger contingent preferred a more orthodox entrance, and broke through the gates of the city to join Essex in driving the Spanish forces into the citadel of Fort San Felipe. By nightfall, except for the castle, Cadiz lay at the mercy of English troops who, by the rules of war, could do as they pleased with the inhabitants and their possessions.

The usual indescribable scene of rape, wanton destruction and slaughter, which was the fate of most sixteenth-century cities unfortunate enough to be captured in war, did not take place, for honour required mercy as well as heroism, and the English captains kept their men under unusual control. The city fathers were allowed to ransom their lives for one hundred and twenty thousand ducats; more than one hundred of the wealthiest gentlewomen were personally ferried to safety by Essex and Howard, and were permitted to carry with them much of their jewellery and as many clothes as they could wear; and fifteen hundred priests, monks and women were escorted out of the city and to the mainland. Only the Dutch regiments were anxious to put the citizens to the sword and they were forcibly restrained by Raleigh and Essex. Even so Cadiz was pillaged, and contrary to the Queen's command, every man was allowed to keep whatever he could grab: diamonds, jewellery, gold, silks, and anything that glittered and caught the eye. Protestant sailors and soldiers strutted about in clerical vestments rifled from the Bishop of Cuzco; the streets were cluttered with furniture, books and bedding which had been cast out of windows in the frantic search for more portable and valuable loot; and everyone seemed to have forgotten the merchant fleet and the war galleys which lay huddled in the inner harbour. Troops assigned to guard the canal leading out of Port Royal hurried off to join the sack of Cadiz, and twelve of the galleys escaped into the open sea and made safely up the coast to Rota. The tradesmen of the city presumed that the English had already secured the merchant fleet and offered a ransom of two million ducats. Howard refused, demanding four million for the merchandise alone; but while the Lord Admiral and the Spanish haggled over maravedis, Howard's old enemy, the Duke of Medina Sidonia, had his revenge upon the English in a way only a Spanish grandee could have conceived. With a splendid disregard for mercantile interests and a nobleman's contempt for trade, he ordered the burning of the entire fleet and its cargo, valued at eight to twelve million ducats.

The destruction of the merchant fleet restored a certain degree of chilly sanity to the English ranks. The leaders were worried about Elizabeth's reactions to such negligence, and Raleigh, Essex and Howard each sent off special messengers in an effort to be first with their own highly-coloured and extravagant versions of the victory. The Lord Admiral and Essex quarrelled bitterly over whose fault the loss of the merchant fleet was, and they disagreed over the advisability of garrisoning and fortifying Cadiz. Essex was all in favour of staying on, and nominated himself as the new governor of the city. He gave up this scheme after being voted down by the council of war, but, as became his honour, he had the satisfaction of being the last Englishman to leave Cadiz before the fleet sailed home.

The returning heroes met with a very mixed reception at court. Elizabeth could not deny the magnitude of the victory: four of the largest galleons in the Spanish navy had been sunk or captured; fifteen immense merchant-men, three of which had been loaded with ordnance and cannon shot for the war in Holland, and an array of lesser craft had been burned with their entire cargoes: one hundred and twenty thousand ducats had been paid in ransom money and the English carried home the President of the *Contratación* of Seville in the mistaken expectation that he would fetch a handsome ransom. What irritated the Queen was the inexcusable loss of the merchant fleet, the irresponsible and dangerously regal fashion in which Essex had cheapened the honour of knighthood by creating over sixty knights, and the ill chance that two days after the fleet had left the Spanish coast the West Indian treasure fleet worth twenty million ducats sailed into Lisbon harbour. Moreover, Elizabeth was outraged by the cavalier disregard of her orders that all plunder was to be regarded as property belonging to the Crown and earmarked to help defray the cost of the expedition. Publicly she thanked her heroes: "Let the army know I care not so much for being Queen, as that I am sovereign of such subjects"; and she allowed a popular celebration of the triumph but limited it to London. Privately she raged at her military leaders and had her revenge upon Essex by forcing him to renounce most of his share of the plunder. Elizabeth was able to keep Raleigh's takings down to one thousand seven hundred and sixty-nine pounds, but she could do little about the fortunes quietly pocketed by soldiers and sailors and even by her own agent, sent with the fleet to look after the Crown's interests. Where, Elizabeth wanted to know, was the fifty thousand pounds she had invested in the venture? Essex, Raleigh, Vere and the rest had acquired glory but the Queen had only an empty exchequer, and as usual she did not like it.

Brilliant as Raleigh's role had been at Cadiz, he was never restored to full royal favour. In April 1597 he regained the Captaincy of the Guard, but it was Essex, despite the Queen's annoyance at his extravagant ways, who remained the hero of the voyage and the Queen's darling. Even so, the Earl was not satisfied. Court life did not become him. He lacked a graceful step both on the ballroom floor and in politics. He had had to share the honours with the old Lord Admiral, and, though the Queen loved him, she persisted in turning down almost every candidate whom Essex nominated for high office. Morosely he had to listen to the whispered truth that he could get anything for himself but nothing for his friends. The Essex of nineteen had been willing to sit at the feet of his Faerie Queene in attitudes of courtly adoration, but by 1596 the Earl had outgrown such love tricks. He sought power commensurate to his pride. He wanted a political party of his own, as independent of royal favour as that of the French Duke of Guise. The humiliating begging demanded by Elizabeth galled his dignity; her constant rejections insulted his ego. It seemed to Essex that only another brilliant feat of war could give him mastery at court, and he pestered Gloriana for a sole command in yet another blow against Spain. In July 1597 he received his wish: the leadership of a fleet almost as large as the Cadiz expedition, and this time completely in the hands of young heroes of "sweet conversation" and "greatness of mind".

Great was Lord Essex's optimism. One Dutch and three English squadrons totalling seventeen galleons, some seventy-five lesser vessels and a picked army of six thousand seasoned troops in twenty-four transports were assembled at Plymouth, with precise orders to destroy the Spanish fleet gathering at El Ferrol. Philip's naval might was apparently endless, and during the summer of 1597 he had been able to scrape together yet another armada, this

time under the experienced leadership of the Adelantado
Mayor of Castile, the nobleman whom Medina Sidonia
had once suggested as a captain more suitable than himself for the post of Admiral of the Ocean Seas. Essex was
instructed first to destroy the King's fleet and naval installations "with the least danger and loss of our people",
and then to sail for the Azores to intercept the treasure
flota, seize the island of Terceira and establish a permanent English base there. From the start Robert Cecil
anticipated nothing but evil for the voyage and gloomily
predicted that the fleet at El Ferrol would not be burned,
the treasure *flota* would not be captured, nor would the
Azores be taken, and informed opinion in England wondered whether the risk of so many lives was not more than
the King of Spain and all his riches were worth. Such pessi-
mism was quickly justified, for everything went wrong from
the start. Essex, Raleigh and young Lord Thomas Howard
commanded the three English squadrons. Sir Francis Vere
sailed as Marshal but was chagrined to discover that the
position of Lieutenant of the Land Forces had been given
to Charles Blount, Lord Mountjoy. Essex tried to mollify
his one really experienced army expert by blaming the
Queen for this appointment, but Vere suspected with reason that, since Blount belonged to the Earl's following at
court, he had been made Lieutenant at Essex's request. For
the first time the Earl was totally on his own; Howard
proved himself the better sailor but cautiously stayed in
the background; and Vere was by far the abler general but
sulkily refused to give advice.

The weather was as unreasonable and as unmanage-
able as the captains. On July 10th, after days of frustrating
delay, the fleet sailed with much fanfare only to limp back
a week later, having encountered heavy seas in which both
Raleigh and Essex came near to sinking. Howard rode out
the fury of the gale and provokingly swept down the
Spanish coast to the point of rendezvous off Corunna to
wait for his chief. He returned on July 31st to discover
Essex having a difficult time repairing his battered ships
and preventing discouraged and seasick gentlemen-
volunteers from deserting. Even Raleigh was moved to
compassion by the Earl's troubles, and wrote Cecil begging

him "to work from Her Majesty some comfort to my
Lord General, who, I know, is dismayed by these mis-
chances, even to death, although there could not be more
done by any man upon the earth, God having turned the
heavens with that fury against us, a matter beyond the
power, or valour, or will of man to resist."

Valour was of little avail against a perverse and maddening heaven. The wind continued to blow from the west
and the fleet remained harbour bound until August 17th,
when Essex hurriedly set sail leaving behind a large part
of the army. More than the weather was frustrating the
Lord General. The fact of the matter was, as Robert Cecil
suspected, that neither the Earl nor Raleigh wanted to
obey the Queen's explicit command to head for El Ferrol
and destroy the Spanish fleet. Both men, obviously prefer-
ring to combined glory with profit, had thir eyes on the
plunder of the treasure *flota*. The burning of the Spanish
fleet in port seemed to be out of the question the moment
Essex sailed without the major portion of his army, and
gales and contrary winds gave the captains a good excuse
for heading for the rich hunting ground of the Azores
without even looking in at El Ferrol. When the various
elements of the English navy reached the Azores, the
chimera of riches and honour remained always just over
the horizon. As for Essex, bad luck, nervous dread of
failure and constant slights to his pride seemed to be the
only realities of a venture in which he invariably guessed
wrong, failed to give adequate orders to his subordinates
and was for ever chasing after mare's-nests.

It was decided, while awaiting the treasure fleet, to attack the various islands of the Azores: Mountjoy was to
head for San Miguel, the Dutch for Pico, Howard and
Vere for Graciosa, and Essex and Raleigh for Fayal. The
Fayal encounter nearly wrecked the expedition even before the treasure *flota* arrived, because Raleigh monopo-
lized what little honour there was to be had and nearly
got himself court-martialled for his efforts. While Raleigh's
squadron was taking on water, Essex suddenly went rushing off to look for the Adelantado, who was reported as
having left El Ferrol to meet and escort the West Indian
fleet to the Azores. Hurriedly, the Earl ordered his Vice-

Admiral to meet him at Fayal, but he failed to mention the fact that he would not himself arrive for several days. When Sir Walter's squadron reached its anchorage off Villa Dorta, it found no Essex, and to make matters worse the people of Villa Dorta rapidly began to clear the town of all valuables and to disappear into the hills. For three days Raleigh waited, while his men watched the dream of plunder vanish before their eyes. The problem was again the sticky question of honour and command. Essex and Raleigh had been assigned together to seize the island. Moreover, the Earl was the senior officer of the fleet and was expected to assume command and have the first bid at glory. Raleigh, on the other hand, had been left without instructions, and he did not regard himself as being inferior in authority to Essex. As he put it, he was one of the principal commanders of the fleet and as such was not subject to the Queen's patents instructing captains to do nothing without the permission of the supreme commander.

If Raleigh's landing on Fayal had not so redounded to the Vice-Admiral's honour, Essex might not have been so infuriated. Sir Walter led his men ashore in the face of Spanish troops drawn up on the sand, forced his way into the town of Villa Dorta, and won immense renown by risking his life, first by walking nonchalantly across the field of fire without his helmet or armour and then by leading a reconnoitring party himself. In this second venture he had asked for volunteers but, when no one spoke up, he scornfully announced that he would go himself. Donning his headpiece and breastplate and accompanied by his cousin, Sir Arthur Gorges, he crawled forward against heavy Spanish musket fire. Both men were wearing gaily coloured scarves which attracted the enemy's attention; bullets tore at Raleigh's clothing and a shot scorched Gorges's leg, but neither of the heroes would remove the offending garments, thinking it unfitting "to honour the Spanish marksman by removing their colours". Raleigh's charmed life remained impervious to Spanish shells, and both men were highly esteemed for one of the more senseless performances of the entire expedition.

Next morning when Essex finally put in an appearance, everything except the fort above the town was in English hands, and a jubilant Raleigh rowed out to arrange with his commander for the final assault upon the citadel. He met with an icy reception, and some of the lesser officers around the Earl actually urged him to court-martial and execute his disobedient Vice-Admiral. Eventually, Thomas Howard made peace between the two men. Essex accepted a rather grudging apology from Raleigh for his unauthorized landing, and revenged himself by omitting all mention of Sir Walter's exploits in his official report to the Queen.

Tension between the two leaders was not eased by the discovery that the Spanish in the fort had made off while the English captains bickered, taking with them every scrap of plunder and leaving behind two Dutch and English prisoners with their throats cut. Further acrimony was forestalled by the sudden report of the approach of the treasure *flota*, and Essex spread a cordon about the island of Terceira with its heavily fortified port of Angra. The Earl, unfortunately, was so nervous that the Spanish fleet might elude him that he kept changing his position, and two hours after he had moved the main units of his squadrons, the entire West Indian fleet, rich with the treasures of the New World, majestically sailed into Angra through the very place that Essex had evacuated. There was not even to be a consolation prize. A huge eighteen-hundred-ton carrack, which was almost trapped by Raleigh, escaped capture by running itself aground near the city of San Miguel. The Spaniards rushed out in small boats and rescued most of the cargo and crew before burning the ship. Essex had gone off to seize the town of Villa Franca so as to approach San Miguel from the rear while Raleigh continued his blockade of the harbour. The army, however, discovered vast quantities of wine and melons at Villa Franca and failed to make the planned attack on San Miguel. Raleigh and the sailors all pointed out that if Essex and the army had done their part the plunder of the great carrack would have fallen to the English.

As Essex cruised disconsolately and aimlessly about the Azores, reluctantly making up his mind to return home *sans* honour, *sans* profit, to face the anger of the Queen and the secret smiles of all his ill-wishers at court, England lay exposed to invasion by the fleet that Elizabeth had

been so insistent should be burned at El Ferrol. Urged
on by a dying Philip, who sought one last chance to achieve
God's purpose against the heretics, the Adelantado Mayor
of Castile set sail from El Ferrol on October 9th with one
hundred and thirty-six ships, four thousand sailors and six
thousand soldiers. The Spanish planned to seize Falmouth
as a base of operations, deposit the army and then turn
and meet Essex's scattered and demoralized ships as they
limped back from the Azores. Whatever the merits or
demerits of such a scheme, and certainly it had the advantage of catching the English totally unprepared, once again
the heavens intervened: the autumn gales blew and the
winds that dispersed the Spanish fleet swept homewards
the English squadron, their captains frantic to be first with
their own versions of the miserable failure.

The Queen was thoroughly irked by her heroic children,
and with good reason. She blamed Essex for having left
her realm defenceless while he gallivanted without profit
about the Azores, and she showed unusual self-restraint
when she limited her criticism to the weary remark:
"When we do look back to the beginning of this action
which hath stirred so great expectation in the world and
charged us so deeply, we cannot but be sorry to foresee
already how near all our expectations and your great hopes
are to a fruitless conclusion." Evidently Elizabeth had
finally learned the true worth of her Essex. She had known
what to expect and had prepared herself for a "fruitless
conclusion".

While Raleigh periodically strutted like a peacock or enveloped his massive egotism in a mantle of cold contempt,
and Essex alternated between spells of boyish enthusiasm and petulant tantrums, old Lord Burghley, rheumy of
eye and gouty of leg, gave his deformed and hunchbacked
son, Robert Cecil, some sound if sententious advice on how
to succeed in the Elizabethan world. "Towards thy superiors," he warned, "be humble yet generous; with thy
equals familiar yet respective; towards inferiors show much
humility and some familiarity"; for "the first prepares a
way to advancement; the second makes thee known for a
man well-bred; the third gains a good report which once

gotten may be safely kept." Then the wise old Lord Treasurer drove home his lesson by examples from his son's generation. "Yet do I advise thee not to affect nor neglect popularity too much. Seek not to be E[ssex] and shun to be R[aleigh]."

The advice was well taken and carefully learned, for Robert Cecil rose to be the principal minister of both Elizabeth and James, while Essex and Raleigh consumed themselves, their fortunes and thei1 lives in the fires of their own megalomania. For all their daring exploits, the heroes of the Elizabethan age were dangerous egotists, indulging, like Essex, in brittle posing and playing to the populace, or disdaining, like Raleigh, to make the least concession to public opinion. Great stars, wrote Sir Edward Coke, "fall when they trouble the sphere wherein they abide". It was egotism that made both men magnificent but it was their pride that ultimately led to their destruction. Essex, like Coriolanus, so forgot himself and his ordained place in society that he endeavoured to usurp a function not properly his own   the right to rule. An inflated ego led him into treason during the twilight of the great Queen's reign, but that story is yet to be told.

Raleigh's destruction came more slowly. His fate was to be left over from the Elizabethan age, a fallen Lucifer whose pride could not be suffered by contemporaries because it was sustained by extraordinary talent. It was left for a Stuart king to strike off the head of the man who delighted in giving the lie to the very standards by which he chose to live. Society might have been willing to accept Sir Walter Raleigh's brilliant versatility – soldier and business man, sailor and scientist, explorer and poet, colonizer and musician, ship builder and historian – but it could not stomach the damnable laughter with which he dismissed a world that had permitted him to excel.

> Tell Potentates they live
>   Acting by others' action,
> Not loved unless they give,
>   Not strong but by a faction,
> If Potentates reply,
>   Give Potentates the lie.

Tell men of high condition,
    That manage the Estate,
Their purpose is ambition,
    Their practice only hate:
And if they once reply,
    Then give them all the lie.

Tell zeal it wants devotion;
    Tell love it is but lust;
Tell time it is but motion;
    Tell flesh it is but dust:
And wish them not reply
    For thou must give the lie.

Tell physic of her boldness;
    Tell skill it is pretension;
Tell charity of coldness;
    Tell law it is contention:
And as they do reply,
    So give them still the lie.

Doubtless there was a fundamental rottenness about the final decade of Gloriana's reign, an artificiality which the tinsel of the court could conceal no more than cosmetics could hide the fact that the Queen was growing old and ugly. Possibly Sir Philip Sidney, who gave his life to the creed of action, was correct when he wrote that there had once been a time when England had set her heart's "delight upon action and not upon imagination, rather doing things worthy to be written than writing things fit to be done!" Years later, after emotional exhaustion had set in and society had grown tired of the pettiness and childishness of heroes, Raleigh looked back upon the heroic age and sadly confessed that "all is vanity and weariness". But Sir Walter added one last nostalgic comment: it had been "such a weariness and vanity that we shall ever complain of it and love it for all that". It had been good to be alive in those days when men had lived like gods. Humanity had enjoyed even its weariness and had gloried in the vanity of life, because the great feats of heroism had not been done solely for seasons of greed and egotism. Insatiable

curiosity, the excitement of discovery, and above all the very
element that Sidney most deplored – imagination – had
urged Drake on round the world, had sustained Gilbert's
dream of colonizing a new land and had filled the heart of
Essex. Lust for glory, plunder and immortality drove them
on, but so did the wonderful romance and secret fear of
new worlds to conquer, new universes to comprehend, new
gods to worship and new horizons to lure them ever on-
wards to "the discovery of things which were hidden from
other men".

Eleven

New Horizons

On March 3rd, 1493, Christopher Columbus sailed the battered *Pinta* into Lisbon Harbour and demanded that the temples be filled with blossoms and boughs in his honour. In October of the same year, a Spanish humanist, Peter Martyr, wrote sceptically to a friend that the Italian adventurer was "back safe and sound, and declares he has found wonders". Sixty years later, any hint of incredulity had vanished, and another Spanish historian had only unqualified praise for Columbus and his achievement. The finding of a New World, he wrote, was "the greatest event since the creation of the world, apart from the incarnation and death of Him who created it". The magnitude of the exploit is difficult to comprehend; it cannot even be compared to the conquest of space, for the twentieth century is intellectually and emotionally prepared for almost any kind of discovery that may be made. It expects and even desires to be astonished. The sixteenth century had no such preparation or predilection for change. Authority, blessed by generations of churchmen and supported by the giants of classical scholarship, was the intellectual rock upon which medieval society rested. Authority was a little fanciful about the details, but the main outlines were clear and incontrovertible. Man lived on an earth which held the place of honour at the centre of the universe; it was "like the yolk in the middle of an egg," and around it the heavenly spheres rotated to the music of the firmament.

Medieval cartographers accepted the word of Ptolemy and recorded the earth's circumference as just under twenty thousand miles, and they followed the leadership of the Church in assuming that the human race was confined to the northern hemisphere and surrounded by an impenetrable torrid belt, which encircled the earth in the region of the equator.

Within two generations of Columbus's voyage of discovery, the medieval earth was smashed beyond recognition. The world suddenly expanded by some five thousand miles; two new continents were located; and Europeans had to accept the serious possibility of the antipodes, where people might live "foot to foot" with themselves. Even before the proportions of a new and enlarged earth had been fully realized, more unnerving discoveries were being made. It was bad enough that men should be deprived of their most cherished myths and be told to recast the map of the world, but worse was to follow. Within fifty years of Columbus's voyage to America, the shape of the heavens themselves was being called in doubt. Two revolutions of concept – the outlines of the earth and the spatial image of the universe – erupted at almost the same time, and between them they destroyed the intellectual underpinnings of the past and cast Adam and all his race out of the secure Eden of a scripturally intelligible world and an anthropomorphic universe. Rewriting geography caught the imagination, and Europe was soon swept up in the romance of discovery; recasting the universe, however, filled the mind with terror. Adventurers dared the unknown and went to test for themselves Raleigh's assurance that "there are stranger things to be seen in the world than are between London and Staines," but it took men of even stronger metal to risk their souls by venturing into the new cosmology in which the earth and her sister planets hurtled in senseless orbit about the sun.

Medieval man was not accustomed to thinking of the earth as a geographic entity. His horizons were those of his village, his landmarks were the ancient oak and the narrow footpath, and his unknown lay just over the neighbouring hill. The world that lay beyond sight and sound was hidden by a heavy fog of ignorance, so complete that men did not even possess the vocabulary necessary to think in global terms. Their world was not flat, as is so often suggested, but it was devoid of any idea of continents and was seen as a series of separate and uninhabitable zones (the Arctic, Antarctic, and Torrid), and as a single land mass, the *orbis terrarum* of Asia, Africa and Europe. The concept of an earth covered by an unbroken sea with occasional islands of land accessible by water was alien to the medieval mind, which visualized the oceans as lakes surrounded by land, considered Jerusalem to be the centre of the world, and thought of the Garden of Eden and other regions of Christian mythology as geographic realities.

What medieval geography lacked in accuracy it made up for in imagination. The East was a land of fantasy, where dwarfs and giants, griffins and unicorns, dog-headed demons and huge clubfooted men lived amidst marvellous wealth and endless commotion. The Indus, the Ganges and the Nile were associated with the Rivers of Paradise, and the mysterious land of Gog and Magog was always placed somewhere east of Eden. Africa and Asia were happily confused, and often the Indian Ocean was pictured as a lake bounded by India and Ethiopia. Fountains of youth and rivers of gold were always to be found in India and darkest Africa, and the Atlantic Ocean was generally regarded as populated with monstrous sea serpents that fed upon foolhardy mariners.

On one point learned cartographers and superstitious sailors were correct: the Atlantic Ocean was an almost insurmountable obstacle even to the most daring seafarer. The medieval adventurer faced "the green sea of darkness" with no means of navigation once he had lost sight of land, and he sailed in frail vessels that could make no headway against a contrary wind. The unknown of the fifteenth century, just as in the twentieth, gave way not so much to boldness as to brains. As the electronic computer and advanced mathematics have been the necessary prerequisites to the navigation of space, so the compass, the astrolabe, the quadrant and the compilations of Arab mathematicians and astronomers were essential to the technological conquest of the oceans. The first great discoverers were either able navigators themselves, or had with them pilots who could combine mathematical theory with experience at sea. By 1484 seamen could venture forth into the darkness of the broad Atlantic with a fair expectation of finding their way home again, and Vasco da Gama's triumph in rounding the Cape of Good Hope was possible only because he had the nerve and the scientific skill to stand two thousand miles out into the South Atlantic to pick up the favourable winds and currents that allowed him to clear the Cape and sail on to India.

In the conquest of the oceans, the shipwright was as important as the astronomer. The square-rigged and clumsy medieval cog, a ship that wallowed in the high waves of the Atlantic and, except in a tail wind, slipped sideways faster than it moved forwards, was redesigned and combined with the manoeuvrable Arab lateen-rigged *sambuqs*. The result was the Portuguese *caravela redonda*, the prototype for all sixteenth-century European sailing vessels. The *caravela* was a seaworthy craft that could hold its course in any but the most adverse wind, and was large enough to undertake voyages of three thousand miles without a landfall and carry the men silly enough to risk their lives in the romance of discovery.

Even when sailors and navigators had the necessary skills and the ships capable of taking them into the vastness of the north and south Atlantic, they required stout hearts to face the elements in vessels that were scarcely larger than small trawlers, to exist on a diet of salt beef, beans, biscuits, stale water, and an occasional ration of wine, and to endure months at sea with no sleeping accommodation except the bare deck. It is little wonder that crews mutinied, pilots were disobedient, and the life expectancy of captains was short. Even in the sixteenth century, when ships were stronger and wind and weather conditions better understood, the mortality rate was enough to discourage the most determined adventurer. Thomas Wyndham and one hundred of his crew of a hundred and forty men died of fever while sailing off the coast of Guinea in 1553; that same year Sir Hugh Willoughby and all his men perished when stranded north of the Arctic Circle; Richard Chancellor drowned in the autumn of 1556 while returning from Russia; Gilbert went down with all hands in 1583 in the

North Atlantic; Thomas Cavendish never returned from his second circumnavigation of the earth in 1591; John Davis was killed by Japanese pirates off the Malay coast; and Hawkins and Drake both died at sea on the same expedition.

Yet for every fatality, a dozen clamoured, as one Spanish conquistador put it, "to serve God and His Majesty, to give light to those who were in darkness, and to grow rich, as all men desire to do". Whether the wide harbours of the world were explored more for gain than for adventure and Christian zeal is not easy to say. Lust for the riches of India and Cathay encouraged Columbus to believe that San Salvador lay within the Japanese archipelago, urged Vasco da Gama to risk the voyage round the tip of Africa, and fostered the persistent search for a south-west route to the East and a northern passage up the St. Lawrence River or through Hudson Bay. "Spices and Christians" had been da Gama's answer as to why he had sought to reach Calicut in 1498. A single shipload of Ceylon cinnamon, Malabar pepper, Moluccas cloves, or East Indian nutmeg was worth countless lives and failures. Magellan started out in 1519 to circumnavigate the globe with five ships and two hundred and seventy-five men; only eighteen of his original crew completed the voyage three years later, but, in the eyes of the investors, the tiny *Victoria*'s precious cargo of cloves more than compensated for the death of the captain and so many of his men.

Europe's need to discover civilizations richer than itself in culture, luxuries and above all in spices may have been the source of the wind that scattered "young men through the world to seek their fortunes", but those same adventurers sailed with a double sense of superiority – the confident knowledge that they excelled in guns, ships and navigational techniques, and the even more comforting conviction that they were bringing Christian "light to them that sit in darkness". When Cortés's troops burned the priceless Mayan libraries of Yucatan, they did so because they knew that the books "contained nothing but superstitions and falsehoods about the devil". The search for the legendary kingdom of Prester John was as persistent as the dream of El Dorado and was almost as important in

Columbus's motivation as the search for the court of the Great Khan. Throughout the age of discovery, in Protestant as well as Catholic lands, avarice marched hand in hand with a sense of self-righteous superiority. Those most Catholic Majesties of Spain, Ferdinand and Isabella, voiced the sublime egotism of all Europe when they presented Christopher Columbus with an open letter of introduction to the princes of the unknown world.

> To King —
> We have heard that Your Highness and your subjects entertain great love for us and for Spain. We are informed, moreover, that you and your subjects greatly desire to hear news from Spain. We therefore send our Admiral, Christopher Columbus, who will tell you that we are in good health and perfect prosperity.

The Spanish Admiral of the Ocean Seas carried with him copies of a more sinister document: the authority to "discover and acquire islands and mainland in the ocean sea". What he encountered threw European cartographers into confusion and Spanish merchants into dismay. Painfully and dangerously, the coastline of an immense land mass began to emerge, an unknown and disturbing impediment to be got round in the important bussiness of reaching the Indies. For a full generation after the discovery of America, European eyes continued to look east and south, and the advice of the early sixteenth century was not "Go west, young man," but "To the south! to the south! They that seek wealth must go to the riches of the Aequinoctial; not unto the cold and frozen north." The outlines of two new continents were gradually revealed by mariners anxious to find an entrance into the Pacific, but when the westward route to India through the Straits of Magellan was finally located on the other side of the world in freezing Antarctic latitudes, the passage proved too dangerous to be of commercial value. By the time, however, that kings and merchants came to realize that China was indeed an eternity away and was not, as Columbus optimistically argued, only three thousand five hundred miles west of the Canary Islands, the imagination of Europe had been caught by the idea of a New World, capable of proving reality to be far more marvellous than even the most bizarre legends of the feudal past.

Medieval fables were transferred to the Americas – rivers of eternal life, fountains of youth, giant Amazons, hippogriffs and satyrs – and to them were added the wonders of reality: pyramids of skulls, human sacrifices, cannibalism, cities built on water, rivers so wide that they appeared like oceans, and above all, riches that seemed to confirm the wildest dreams about the land of Ophir and El Dorado. On Good Friday 1519 Cortés and four hundred Spanish desperados commenced the conquest of Mexico, and within the year they had sent home to the Emperor's court in Brussel unheard-of trophies of war; "a whole golden sun, a fathom in breadth, and a whole silver moon of the same size", and great piles of weapons encrusted with gold and silver, "altogether valued at a hundred thousand gulden". The artist Albrecht Dürer, when he viewed the collection, exclaimed that in all his life he had "never seen anything that so rejoiced my heart", and announced that the New World was indeed a golden land. Twelve years later came word of an even more spectacular conquest: Francisco Pizarro with sixty-two horsemen and one hundred and six foot soldiers had struggled over the top of the world and descended upon the rich and defenceless Inca civilization of Peru. News of the ransom which he demanded from the captured Inca Emperor, Atahualpa, became legend – a room twenty-two feet by seventeen feet filled as high as a man could reach with articles of silver and gold, a fortune estimated at four and a half million ducats. It was the vision of similar lands and treasures that led Jacques Cartier in 1541 ever deeper into Canada, as he sought the imaginary kingdom of Saguenay, which was always just beyond the great forest somewhere up the Ottowa River. Only disappointment awaited Cartier at the end of his journey, for he never found his phantom land, and the twelve barrels of gold which he brought back to France turned out to be iron pyrites or fool's gold. His precious stones were quartz, and sixteenth-century Parisians coined a new phrase for the counterfeit – *diamants de Canada*.

Though failure continued to dog the efforts of those who

sought a golden shower in the north, the south remained a fabulous hunting ground for riches and reputations. The silver mines of Zacatecas in Mexico and the Potosí lode in Bolivia were opened up in the 1540s, and started a rush of fortune hunters anxious to share in the flood of precious metals that for a hundred and fifty years poured 18,600 tons of silver and two hundred tons of gold into the coffers of the kings of Spain, and possibly as much again into the pockets of private prospectors. The world remembered that Francisco Pizarro, the illiterate and illegitimate son of a Spanish peasant, had won for himself a fortune and the title of marquis; it forgot that he was murdered in 1541 and that his brother Hernando died in a Spanish jail. So insatiable was the demand for adventure that the new continents were named, not after the man who discovered them, but after the explorer who most successfully advertised the largely fictional story of his enterprises – Amerigo Vespucci.

England's role in the drama of discovery remained until Elizabeth's reign that of a passive but avidly interested spectator, who begrudged Spain and Portugal their good fortune but lacked the energy to challenge their monopoly. English fishermen looked towards the Grand Banks of Newfoundland, the chimera of a northern passage to China took Richard Chancellor to Russia in 1553, and the profits of the slave trade led the cousins John Hawkins and Francis Drake first to Africa and then deep into the Spanish Caribbean during the 1560s. But it was not until Sir Humphrey Gilbert printed his *Discourse of a Discovery for a New Passage to Cataia* in 1576, and Drake sailed into Plymouth harbour in the *Golden Hind* on September 26th, 1580, with a 4,700 per cent profit in his hold, that England set the oceanic world ablaze and cast off her reputation for "sluggish security".

Of all the adventurers who went down to the sea in ships, putting "a girdle round about the earth" with their naval daring, the one most enthralled by the romance of the New World was Sir Walter Raleigh. "What shall we be," he asked, "travellers or tinkers; conquerors or novices?" In answer to his own question, he set out in 1595 upon an adventure, more fit for boys than elderly heroes in their middle fifties, to find the fabled land of El Dorado, where kings and commoners went clad in gold. Almost from the moment the first white man set foot in Central and South America, stories were heard of a city of gold. Its exact whereabouts was elusive and peripatetic, but one of the most authoritative reports located El Dorado, or what the natives called Manoa, in the upper reaches of the Orinoco, presumably on the assumption that if the city existed at all, it could only be reached by penetrating the most pestilent, inaccessible and jungle-ridden area of South America. For two generations the legend of an offshoot of the Inca civilization, located deep in the interior of Guiana, continued to grow, eventually blossoming into an extravagant saga which included humble household utensils cast in solid gold and gardens where every tree and flower had its replica in precious metals. For ten years Raleigh gleaned from Spanish reports and seamen every scrap of information about Guiana and the mystery of the Orinoco. When finally he set sail, a dozen distinguished persons had been persuaded by his silver tongue to invest in a dream or actually to join the expedition. Lord Burghley and Lord Admiral Howard gave money, and the sons of Sir Richard Grenville and Sir Humphrey Gilbert both sailed with the fleet on February 6th, 1595.

By chance, Sir Walter captured the one Spaniard who knew most about Guiana and who was himself obsessed with the legend of a fabulous civilization just round one of the endless bends of the Orinoco. Don Antonio de Berrio, last of the Spanish conquistadors, had been searching the area for fifteen years, and he communicated his zeal to his English captor. Encouraged by Berrio, Raleigh had one of the smallest of his ships fitted for river travel, and with one hundred men began the long ordeal of rowing up the Orinoco. For the first time, he began to appreciate the hell which De Soto, Champlain, Pizarro, Cartier, and the rest of the great adventurers had endured. He was forced "to lie in the rain and weather, in the open air, in the burning sun, and upon the hard boards", and conditions became so foul that "there was never any prison in England that could be found more unsavoury and loathsome". At fifty-three the gallant captain longed for the comforts of a feather bed and a decently cooked meal, but his vision kept him dry and fed, and he continued on into the labyrinth of tributaries that formed the Orinoco. Raleigh found no golden cities, but he saw wonders that inspired him, and made him all the more willing to believe the fairy-tales told by the Indian population. Three hundred miles inland he encountered "the most beautiful country that ever mine eyes beheld", a land rich in game and the fullness of the earth, where every pebble seemed to hold the promise of a fortune. Only the ugly crocodiles that swam in the wake of his ship, and to which one of his company fell victim, marred a demi-paradise. He beheld the great falls of the Caroni, a series of cliffs, each as high as a church steeple, over which the water rushed, sending up a mist so thick that the English "took it at the first for a smoke that had risen over some great town".

From the Indians Raleigh learned of wonders even more marvellous: of oysters that grew on trees; of kings who clothed themselves in gold dust; of giant men called Ewaipanoma with mouths in their chests and eyes in their shoulders; and of Amazons who on the twelfth month of each year invited the lustiest warriors of neighbouring tribes to stand on the borders of their territories while the damsels "cast lots for their valentines". The ladies enjoyed their men until the moon signified the end of a month of feasting and love-making. Guiana always remained for Raleigh "a country that hath yet her maidenhead, never sacked, turned, nor wrought".

The rainy season came, and Sir Walter's little band decided that they had had enough of hard boards and unsavoury victuals. They returned to the ships in the estuary and sailed back to England with no gold in their pockets but with visions of paradise in their heads. When Raleigh came to write of his adventures – in *The Discovery of the Large, Rich and Beautiful Empire of Guiana, with a Relation of the Great and Golden City of Manoa* – he captured for every European who could read the thrill of distant lands, the sense of adventure and the hope of El Dorado. By 1600 the New World had lost much of its newness, but there were always, then as now, readers avid for science fiction, and before the century was out Sir Walter's

Discovery had been republished four times in German, twice in Latin, innumerable times in Dutch, and once in French.

The surge of emotion that drove Englishmen from the comforts of their chimney seats to search "the most opposite corners and quarters of the world" was touched with something more than the love of adventure and the desire for gold. The New World was "a shelter and a hiding-place", where men of humble origin could carve out for themselves a new and more perfect home. At first the hope of planting a nation in the wilderness remained a myth, part of the imaginary trappings of the unknown world. Such a vision had inspired More's *Utopia*, that philosopher's paradise where reason and wisdom reigned triumphant, and the ills, horrors, and inequalities of the sixteenth century made way for the perfect harmony of an orderly, if sterile, semi-communistic state. Part of a spoof (the chamber-pots were made of gold), part a penetrating study into the social and psychological realities underlying human society, and part an idealized version of the medieval concept of a balanced, ordered and integrated society, the *Utopia* made a deep impact upon the Tudor mind. Throughout the century the idea persisted that somewhere in the New World there lay hidden a haven and refuge from the troubles of the Old.

Three men were responsible for the first efforts to transform such an aspiration into reality: the extraordinary Sir Humphrey Gilbert, who died in his futile endeavour to colonize Newfoundland, the ubiquitous Sir Walter Raleigh, and Richard Hakluyt, the propagandist who inspired all men with his magnificent collection of *Voyages*. From the start America was seen as a way of skimming the "milk of bitterness" from England, and Gilbert and Raleigh sought to persuade almost one hundred English Catholics to leave their hearths for a new start in life. When first the colonists and then Sir Humphrey were drowned, Raleigh worked alone in urging Englishmen "to take fast root and hold" three thousand miles away from home. Of the imperial powers, only England succeeded in transplanting her people and establishing small, tough and vital replicas of herself on the inhospitable shores and endless forests of an uncharted and virgin land. Spaniards went out by the thousands, but they sought gold to plunder and souls to save; Frenchmen ventured forth in far more conservative numbers to trade and trap along the St. Lawrence River; only the English sent out living offshoots – men to toil, women to be fruitful, children to ensure the future, and laws by which to live. The achievement was a miracle of advertising: persuading financiers to hazard capital on a long term investment, and enticing the industrious work-man and the thrifty housewife to the supreme folly of risk-ing all upon the fantasy of a better life. Religious hatred, economic privation and fear of the gallows eventually drove a multitude from their homes, but the New World could never have been successfully populated by bitterness alone. The indispensable role of Raleigh and Hakluyt was first to show by the failure of the Roanoke venture how not to plant a colony and then, with Hakluyt's *Principal Navigations, Voyages and Discoveries of the English Nation*, to charm Elizabethan society with the romance, not of discovery, but of colonization.

In March 1584 Sir Walter Raleigh received one of those wonderfully self-assured charters issued by European sovereigns; the Queen conferred upon him the authority "to discover barbarous countries, not actually possessed by any Christian prince and inhabited by Christian people", and "to occupy and enjoy the same for ever". Within a month two ships were sent out to reconnoitre the south-eastern coast of North America for a suitable location for a colony. Roanoke Island had no harbour, but its shores were loaded with grapes and it seemed to be reasonably secure from the predatory eye of the Spanish. In August of the following year, one hundred and seven colonists landed. From the start the experiment was an unmitigated failure. The English were a scruffy lot of undisciplined ex-soldiers and incipient buccaneers in quest of easy money, and when they found little but hard work and virgin forests they quickly lost heart. Most of their supplies had been lost at sea, and the landing had been made too late in the year to plant crops for the winter months. The settlers were thrown upon the generosity of the Indians, who had barely enough for themselves and who were soon antagonized by the white man's notion of justice. A silver cup was stolen from the colonists who immediately retaliated by burning an entire Indian village, and when the natives refused to supply further food, relations deteriorated to the point of open war. Very early in the history of America the white man evolved the theory that the only good Indian was a dead Indian. Raleigh had promised his settlers that new recruits and supplies would be sent out in March, but even had the reinforcements arrived on schedule, it is doubtful whether the colonists would have stayed on to plant a civilization in the New World. They were without heart and without women, and when Drake, who had been pirating in the Caribbean, appeared in July 1586, the colonists fled back to the security of the Old World.

Raleigh was bitterly disappointed by his settlers, but astute enough to perceive the cause of their failure. The first experiments in colonization had been financed on a shoestring and manned by explorers and exploiters, not by men and women who had the strength and vision to toil in the red earth of Virginia. It took Sir Walter two years to raise the necessary capital and find the volunteers for a second attempt. This time he was determined to ship out both sexes and to ensure their labour by offering each colonist five hundred acres of free land and a voice in the affairs of the colony. One hundred and fifteen settlers made the two-month journey to Virginia and arrived in July 1587 to find the original fort burned and the Indians still deeply resentful. Eighty-seven men, seventeen women and eleven children under Governor John White elected to make their homes upon the ruins of the old settlement, and all one hundred and fifteen vanished for ever. Raleigh had strained every financial nerve to supply his plantation, but even so the colonists were critically short of the essentials of life, and within a month of their landing they sent Governor White back to England to beg for seed and iron, livestock and cloth, and a multitude of other items necessary to transform a camp into an enduring community. Before Governor White left, there seemed to be a bare possibility that the settlement might live and take root; at least a child had been born in the New World, his grand-daughter, Virginia Dare. By the time he returned four years later nothing remained except a legend about a strange race of Indians with Nordic colouring and English features.

John White had sailed back to England to find Raleigh close to bankruptcy and the nation arming for the forthcoming clash with Spain. The fate of the colonists soon became a tragic by-product of the momentous struggle occuring in Europe, for there were no ships, arms or men to send to Virginia. Raleigh had already invested forty thousand pounds in the Roanoke experiment and was obliged to transfer a portion of his rights and authority to a joint stock company of London merchants, who contracted, in no great haste, to send out a relief expedition. Impatient as he was, it was not until August 18th, 1591, four years later to the month, that Governor White returned to Roanoke Island to be confronted with the ominous silence of the wilderness and the impenetrable mystery of what had happened to his colony. The fort still stood but the house and all their inhabitants had gone. The only clue to their fate was the code decided upon before White sailed for England. A Maltese cross was to be cut into the wood of the stockade in case of peril; a word was to be carved to indicate where the settlers might have fled. On one of the piles of the palisade was found the word "Croatoan", on a tree were cut the letters "C R O", but nowhere was there discovered a Maltese cross. The settlers had survived the first winter, for a Spanish frigate reported their existence in June 1588, but no hint remains of what terrible events occurred thereafter. Possibly, as the carved letters might indicate, the colony had moved to Croatoan Island or had gone to live with the Croatoan Indians. The most likely explanation, however, is that the settlers were surprised and massacred by Indians.

The tragedy of Roanoke was not without its blessings; one hundred and fifteen men, women and children had vanished, but their successors learned two vital lessons that eventually ensured the success of the Jamestown colony: first, that colonization, in contrast to plundering and gold prospecting, was immensely costly and no private individual could carry the burden alone; and second, that there was no real hope of ever discovering gold and gaining a quick profit in the areas open to English exploration. The settlers who followed after the Roanoke mystery, and the merchants who joined in the stock companies to supply and maintain the new colonies, did so with some, if not all, of the scales removed from their eyes. The settlement of the new continent was accomplished by realists who knew the odds and were willing to accept the heartaches and the labour necessary to conquer and civilize the New World. Raleigh initiated a tradition that ultimately bore fruit in 1607; Hakluyt kept the memory of Roanoke alive; and both men lived to see in North America "an English nation".

The shock of discovery, of finding the world a different and, in some ways, a better place than the one imagined by classical and medieval authority, undoubtedly weakened the grip of the dead hand of custom. Novelty was in the air. Everywhere there were "new and rare observations", as men discovered for themselves a host of fresh wonders. Peter Martyr announced the existence of the New World in his *De Orbe Novo* in 1530; new theories of medicine were propounded by Paracelsus in 1523; a revolutionary book on diseases was issued in 1541 by Johannes Baptista de Cavigliolis; André Thevet printed his *Les Singularités de la France Antarctique* in 1557; William Gilbert's *New Philosophy Concerning Our Sublunar World* was written well before the author's death in 1603; and Englishmen marvelled over Monardes's *Joyful Newes Out of the Newe Founde Worlde* on the subject of botany. Discoveries in every area of human speculation led to questioning and, if need be, to the putting aside of ancient truths for newer verities, based on empirical evidence. Not even the evidence of sight and sound could place limits upon man's fancy or on his enthusiasm for novelty. "Why then should witlesse man," wrote Edmund Spenser, "so much misweene that nothing is, but that which he hath seene? What if within the Moones faire shining spheare" there were unsuspected worlds and unimagined wonders? Men in the moon and incredible civilizations somewhere in the distant firmaments, however, bid fair to make the mind boggle and fill the heart with fear. New discoveries on earth and in the affairs of man were acclaimed even by a Church that somehow adapted the story of Adam and his expulsion from the Garden of Eden to the existence of human beings in the antipodes, who could not possibly be descendants of the original Christian man. But disturbing discoveries in the heavens and the recasting of God's domain were very different matters, and when Copernicus announced the existence of the new cosmology and published *De Revolutionibus Orbium Coelestium* in 1543, his ideas were dismissed by the common man as dull, unsettling and silly. It was ridiculous, dangerous and presumptuous to argue that as massive a body as the earth, which was the centre of God's universe, could revolve on its axis or hurtle in space around the sun.

The traditional view of the universe was too imposing, too secure, too deeply rooted in the most atavistic impulses of the human race to be denied. Not only did the wisest of classical philosophers vouch for the truth of the cosmos, not only was it proved by biblical evidence and by God's own voice speaking through His Church on earth, but also man's every instinct and his own eyes told him that he was the central and most important point around which the heavenly bodies marched. The dark of a winter's night provided indisputable evidence that moon and sun, planet and stars, Milky Way and the entire celestial display rose and set to the rhythm of the spheres. To the Elizabethan observing such wonders, it seemed clear and proper that he should be standing at the core of the universe, and that heaven and earth should have been created as the setting for a divine drama in which man was destined to play the leading role as God's special creation. The authority of Aristotle and the word of Scripture asserted only what any simpleton could see and reason for himself, and all but a tiny and suspect band of mathematicians agreed with John Donne that the "new Philosophy calls all in doubt".

> The Sun is lost, and th'earth, and no man's wit
> Can well direct him where to looke for it.

The much-acclaimed dogma that modern science is based on empirically observed data worked upon by reason is one of those uncritically treasured truisms that do nothing but befuddle the mind. The creed implies that old-fashioned, Aristotelian science was without observation, and was grounded upon improbable hypotheses, totally at odds with reason. Such an assumption is not only untrue, it also obscures the crucial point that the errors of Aristotelian science were rooted in too high a regard for what the eye sees and for what appears to be reasonable. Classical cosmology was founded upon four observed fundamentals of existence: the nature of all things is to remain at rest and therefore what must be explained is movement and motion; the earth is stationary; the world of man is composed of air, fire, water and earth; and the heavens are spherical and rotate about the earth every twenty-four hours. To the evidence of the senses classical philosophy added a number of suppositions about the nature of the universe: it was orderly, purposeful and ultimately intelligible; it was finite and consisted of ether; there was in the heavens a prime mover to account for celestial motion, and the physical principles that explained the actions of the firmament were not the same as those which operated on earth; and finally the heavens were free of flux and decay and were eternal and immutable. When translated into a cosmic design, classical theory and observation produced a convincing picture of a universe that was easy to comprehend, made excellent sense, and above all else, was comfortably anthropomorphic in its assumptions and cosmological starting-point. At all times man was assumed to be standing securely within an immense sphere, looking up from a central location at the inner surface of the firmament. All things were ultimately relative to a fixed point of observation – the human observer standing upon a stationary earth.

Aristotelian philosophy explained the existence of change and corruption in the world of man by the commotion caused by each of the four terrestrial elements, as it sought to find that location most satisfactory to its nature. Earth and water were for ever attracted downwards towards the centre of the terrestrial globe; fire and air moved upwards, aspiring to a higher and more perfect place in the heavens. Had the elements achieved their inner drive, the world would have died – it would have consisted of motionless and eternal layers of earth, ocean, air and fire – but since

the elements were mixed and constantly struggled to disentangle themselves they produced change, violence and
decay on earth. Outside the world of man, a different set
of physical properties operated, since the element of ether
had achieved its harmonic and natural place. Beyond the
sphere of the moon all was contentment, ageless and enduring. Like the layers of an onion, the firmament extended outwards in a series of rotating crystalline ethereal
spheres, to which were attached the various points of
celestial geography. First came the circle of the moon, next
that of the two lesser planets, then the sphere of the sun,
followed by the three outer planets, and finally the circle
of the firmament where in endless incomprehensible numbers resided the fixed stars. Two more spheres remained,
one classical, the other Christian: the invisible orb of the
prime mover, which was thought to be the cause of all
heavenly movement and the source of the music of the
heavens; and, even farther out, the empyrean, the abode
of God and His heavenly hosts. There was scarcely an
Elizabethan who had not been taught all or part of the
Aristotelian cosmos, and long after Copernicus, Kepler and
Galileo had destroyed for ever the music of the spheres,
educators were still indoctrinating young gentlemen with
the ancient view of the universe. In 1622 Henry Peacham
assured his young readers in *The Compleat Gentleman*
that:

The celestial bodies are the eleven heavens and spheres.
The eleventh heaven is the habitation of God and His
  angels.
The tenth, the first mover.
The ninth, the crystalline heaven.
The eighth, the starry firmament.
Then the seven planets in their order, which you may
  remember in their order by this verse.

Would you count the planets soon,
Remember S I M S V M and the Moon.

The first letter S for Saturn, I for Iupiter, M for Mars, S
for the Sun, V, Venus, M, Mercury, lastly, the Moon.

Such a scheme of things was tidy, picturesque, intelligible, and above all else, activistic. The classical world had always assumed that the heavenly spheres, so filled with harmony and virtue, could affect the destinies of men. Fortune and fate resided in the stars, and not even the Elizabethan introduction of such highly active and interfering inhabitants of the sidereal world as Intelligences, Potentates, Dominations, Cherubim, Seraphim, Angels and Archangels could deprive the classical cosmos of its influence upon the affairs of man. If, argued Sir Walter Raleigh, God had given "virtues to springs and fountains, to cold earth, to plants and stones ... why should we rob the beautiful stars of their working powers?" From time out of mind astronomers had been astrologers, supporting their scientific labours from the profits of casting horoscopes and reading the message of the stars. The sixteenth century was a busy period for those versed in the interpretation of the heavenly movements, and the year of the Armada was regarded by astrologers in every capital of Europe as an ominous date. Even the most unskilled viewer of the skies could see that Saturn, Mars and Jupiter were in prophetic conjunction, and that such a combination should occur during a year in which two solar and two lunar eclipses were scheduled to take place made the portent all the more alarming.

Such was the cosmic scheme of things, and to it Elizabethans added the human conceit of believing that the celestial display had been created for their benefit. Man might live upon an earth which one sixteenth-century Frenchman described as being "so depraved and broken in all kind of vices and abominations that it seemeth to be a place that hath received all the filthiness and purgings of all other worlds and ages", but it was also clear that the heavens declared the glory of God and that the stars had been set in the skies for exactly the same purpose as that for which the butterfly had been created: "to adorn the world and delight the eyes of men". It was accepted by all that the sun, moon and other stars had been ordained "for no other purpose but to serve the earth". The horse, it was said, had been "brought forth for the use of man"; the soil produced grain so that the horse might live and labour; and the skies had been instructed to water the grain. Any scientific wizard who denied such a satisfying and obvious totality of earth, man, God and heavens, was not just a fool but a dangerous fool, and Martin Luther voiced the common sentiment of all Europe when he said of Copernicus: "The fool will overturn the whole art of astronomy."

The Aristotelian fetters that held fast the sixteenth-century mind were so stout that even the greatest of English medical scientists, William Harvey, confessed, after a lifetime of disproving classical medicine, that Aristotle "has always such weight with me that I never think of differing from him inconsiderately". Such bonds could not be broken without a total revolution within the mind of man. Answers are determined by the questions asked, and, before the old physics and astronomy could be displaced, men had to pose questions that were profoundly disturbing and darkly heretical. In the face of every accepted authority, a Pandora's box of doubt and inquiry had to be opened: what if motion were natural and rest had to be explained? what if the mental picture of a universe with the earth as its centre was wrong? what if mankind did not look out from the middle but stood instead on the outside and looked in? what if the cosmos were not finite but infinite with no centre at all? what if the firmament moved only because the earth rotated? and finally – the most seditious question of them all – what if every celestial body were rushing through boundless space in a fashion describable only in terms relative to other moving objects? If such propositions were true, then where was certainty, where coherence? where was man's God-given place of honour in a universe of soundless, senseless motion *sans* time, *sans* measurement, *sans* purpose? Such notions did not come easily even to men of great genius, and the sixteenth-century scientist, though he had his moments of inspiration, was only human, a normal mixture of erudition, quackery, enthusiasm and blindness.

Nowhere was the ambivalence between medieval and modern so apparent as in science. Scientific truth was a strange composite of the old and new, chemistry and alchemy, astronomy and astrology, mathematics and numerology, medicine and magic, science and sorcery. A bold mind might lift a corner of the curtain of ignorance and glimpse the truth, but the man who dismissed astrology as nonsense might himself be a helpless devotee of cabalistics and occultism. Paracelsus announced that "the sick should be the doctor's books", but he believed in the *"electrum magicum"* of charms, and prescribed for his patients doses of ground-up jewels on the hypothesis that the more precious the stones, the more efficacious the remedy. Sixteenth-century doctors were, by modern standards, expensive and learned charlatans, who talked knowingly about choleric and melancholic influences within the body and killed their clientele with "comfortable potions" of crabs' eyes, powdered human skulls, Egyptian mummy's dust and live spiders. Yet the greatest of sixteenth-century surgeons, Ambroise Paré, for the first time made amputation an operation through which the victim had a reasonable chance of survival, and he was wise enough to say of his prowess as a doctor and surgeon: "I treated him and God cured him." The distinguished mathematician, Blaise de Vigenère, argued that no one should "study the divinely beautiful proportions of numbers in order to make them serve the computations of a bank", yet Thomas Digges, one of the most famous of Englishmen versed in "cunning Calculations", was an expert in ballistics and went to sea to test his theories about compass variations.

Of all the scientific figures of the Elizabethan age, the most extraordinary example of intellectual brilliance combined with mental obtuseness was Dr. John Dee of Mortlake. That "arch-conjurer of the whole kingdom" was the admired confidant of royalty, the adviser of mariners, the friend of the learned Dutch cartographer, Gerard Mercator, the defender of Copernicus, the author of an imaginative and ambitious scheme to reorganize the English fishing industry, the translator of Euclid's *Elements*, the Queen's astrologer, and by his own confession an unswerving believer in occultism, spirits, apocalyptic numbers, cabalistic formulas and magic inscriptions. When a mutilated and stabbed wax effigy of Elizabeth was found in Lincoln's Inn Fields, Dr. Dee was called upon to assure his alarmed sovereign that the doll was nothing but the work committed to spiritualism that he maintained a private medium by the unlikely name of Edward Kelley, to whom he paid a yearly salary of fifty pounds. The good Dr. Dee was possessed of a magic mirror, a polished stone of mystic properties, and a "gazing table" which stood on a square of red silk, with each of its legs resting on a wax seal inscribed in Hebrew.

The liberation of the human mind from superstitions, preconceptions and traditional habits of thinking is such a painful and disturbing process that it is surprising that Kepler, Dee, Copernicus and William Gilbert were not burned at the stake along with Giordano Bruno. They escaped persecution primarily because they were the high priests of a mystery that very few people understood. Copernicus's view of the universe may have been as clear as "sunne beams" to Thomas Digges, who pronounced in 1576 the heliocentric system to be so self-evident that "any reasonable man that hath his understanding ripened with Mathematicall demonstration" must accept it, but until well into the seventeenth century *De Revolutionibus* remained the concern only of a few trained scholars. Copernicus's mathematical hypotheses did not come to the attention of the public or the ecclesiastical authorities until they had been enlarged by Bruno, Kepler and Galileo into a cosmic system of new and dangerous dimensions and unChristian implications.

The first step of the new cosmology was built upon the weakest point of the old. Classical and medieval astronomers had long been aware that the planets did not behave with proper Aristotelian regard for a spherical, immutable, and harmonious universe. They wandered in a mystifying manner, usually moving in a stately and proper path across the sky in an east to west direction, but occasionally turning about in a contrary fashion. Various theories were propounded to explain these bothersome celestial exceptions, but they all had one weakness in common: the mathematics required to explain such erratic movement was so elaborate that it contradicted the Aristotelian concept of a universe of marvellous simplicity and perfection. From the start, mathematicians found the planets – especially Mars – aesthetically disturbing, and Copernicus turned to the absurdity of assuming that the earth rotated and the sun was the centre of the universe for reasons more aesthetic than empirical. It seemed to him that the medieval mathematics of the heavens were too complex, and that symbolically the sun, as the source of all light, should hold the place of honour at the centre of the universe. Copernicus could take the first giant stride of imagining an earth spinning in space and a sun round which all else revolved, but he could not jump the next intellectual hurdle of seeing that the crystalline spheres of the classical cosmos were unnecessary, once the assumption of a rotating earth had been accepted. Copernicus had lifted the curtain and peeped under it, but he continued to stand on the medieval side and view the heavens in terms of Aristotelian orbs.

The heliocentric system made a deep stir within the brotherhood of astronomers, even though it was offered only as a mathematical hypothesis and not as an accurate description of the firmament. In suggesting that the earth turned, Copernicus had concluded his argument with the statement: "You will find, if you think carefully, that these things occur in this way." In the second half of the sixteenth century, two sidereal events occurred that caused scientists and laymen to think more carefully about the great astronomer's views and to reconsider the structure of the universe. In 1572 a new star appeared in the skies, the first since the one that had shone over Bethlehem. For seventeen lunar months it blazed so brightly that it could be seen even in daylight. Then it vanished as mysteriously as it had arrived. Astrologers, clerics, philosophers and kings were thrown into confusion, for surely such a brilliant sign betokened some extraordinary event in the affairs of man: the death of Elizabeth, the outbreak of the plague, the approach of war. What, in fact, the new celestial body did foretell was the demise of classical astronomy, for anyone could now perceive that the star was located in a sphere of the heavens that, by Aristotelian and medieval reckoning, should have been sublime and immutable and should have contained no such alien and transcendental body. Five years later another exception to classical cosmology put in an appearance and presented further proof that the firmaments were themselves capable of change and corruption. In 1577 a comet raced across the sky in the area where no comet should have been.

Slowly the old concept of rigid and immutable crystalline spheres, complete with heavenly music, was set aside. Thomas Digges, when he saw the star of 1572, announced that he now hoped to "discern by exact judgment whether the earth lies quiet and immovable in the centre of the World". He was disappointed, for no one could give visual evidence that the earth moved and no one could think of any kind of sidereal motion except a circular one. An extraordinary mind such as Giordano Bruno's was capable of an imaginative leap into space, and of conceiving of an infinite universe which possessed countless worlds and incarnations of Christ, but Bruno's *Del Infinito, Universo, e Mondi* was condemned almost the moment it was published in 1584, and the author was burned at the stake for the grossest kind of heresy in 1600. Until the seventeenth century, scientific evidence weighed against Copernicus. If an immensely heavy earth really did rotate at a thousand miles an hour, then an object dropped from a high cliff should land well to the west of its starting-point, and a cannon-ball should carry farther when shot in a westerly direction than when pointed to the east. Moreover, if the world moved about the sun, then the fixed stars should move slightly, relative to the earth's position on either side of the sun. The stars remained constant, cannon-balls refused to co-operate, and stones dropped from towers showed no signs of a spinning earth.

It was not until Johann Kepler broke through the sixteenth century's mystical preoccupation with spherical motion, and Galileo Galilei expounded the doctrine of inertia, that the map of the heavens was rewritten and religious authority rose up in alarm. The stumbling-block to Copernicus's heliocentric thesis lay in the fact that the mathematics required to describe the circular movement of the planets about the sun was almost as intricate as that of the old system, which used the earth as its centre. In proving an elliptical orbit for the planets, Kepler brought to the heliocentric cosmos the great advantage of mathematical elegance and simplicity. Galileo did much the same thing for medieval astrophysics. The weightiest argument in favour of Aristotle's crystalline spheres had been the fact that they accounted for heavenly motion and gave a plausible explanation of why celestial bodies remained for ever in the skies. Galileo liberated the sixteenth century from the myth that an object will move only when impelled by the continuing force of a prime mover. He advanced the theory that motion, not rest, was normal and that all heavenly elements moved in orbit at a speed proportional to their original impetus.

Though the modern concept of inertia and motion did not receive its final formulation until Descartes and Newton, the cosmology described by Galileo and Kepler was already depriving God of an active part in its operation. The universe was becoming a perfectly ordered but quite mechanical clock, created by a benevolent deity who was satisfied with the role of celestial mechanic and impetus giver. In 1610, a year after Galileo first used his telescope to see for himself evidence of phenomena already mathematically expounded, Sir Henry Wotton wrote to James I a letter even more sceptical than the one Peter Martyr had sent to his friend on Columbus's return from the New World. He had, he said, the strangest piece of news to report: the mathematical professor of Padua had "discovered four new planets rolling about the sphere of Jupiter, besides many other unknown fixed stars". Also the Italian astronomer had viewed the moon and found it not to be "spherical but endued with many prominences, and, which is of all the strangest, illuminated with the solar light by reflection from the body of the earth". The author of these wonders, concluded Sir Henry, "runneth a fortune to be either exceedingly famous or exceedingly ridiculous".

Few Elizabethans before 1600 had passed far enough over the threshold of modernity to conceive of the new and godless cosmos of endless space and mechanical motion as anything but ridiculous, but in every field of human observation the veil of myth was being drawn back. In morality, Sir Francis Bacon was writing that his century "was much beholden to Machiavel and others that wrote what men do, and not what they ought to do". In the study of history, Sir Walter Raleigh was ready to remove God from the formula. "To say that God was pleased to have it so", he said, "were a true but an idle answer (for his secret will is the cause of all things) ... Wherefore we may boldly look into the second causes" and understand history in terms of human motivation. In politics, Sir Thomas More voiced in the *Utopia* the proposition that the commonwealth should be designed to help people lead happy lives. In charity, rich merchants gave more to benefit education than to ensure their souls' salvation. In science, men were wondering with Galileo whether God really had "designed so many vast, perfect and noble celestial bodies ... to no other use but to serve this passible, frail and mortal earth". If the theological justification for the heavens were doubtful, might not the ultimate heresy be correct after all? The universe might not have been created as a backdrop for the drama of man's salvation, but as a kingdom to be conquered and ruled by man's intelligence. The destiny of man, said Francis Bacon, was "to extend the power and dominion of the human race over the Universe". Human happiness, scientific usefulness, a mechanical cosmos, all these, as Pascal complained, had turned God into a first cause who "set the world in motion by a twist of his finger and thumb", and who thereafter left heaven and earth to man's tender mercies and ruthless exploitation.

Steadily the face of Gloriana's England began to change. It was not so much that the features became, with each passing year, more Jacobean than Elizabethan; the metamorphosis was more profound and enduring than that. Imperceptibly the scientific mind, the secular frame of reference and the mechanical universe appeared, like an ugly stepdaughter, unwanted but always present. The medieval profile receded; the image of modern man with his self-confidence and his mania for definitions and categories began to emerge. Men of imagination breathed the intoxicating scent of change and announced with Jean Fernel that "our age is doing today things of which antiquity did not dream", but most Europeans were unaware of where questioning and doubt were leading. Elizabeth would have been as shocked as the cardinals of the Roman Church by Bruno's pantheistic and infinite universe. Her age may have been edging out of the feudal past, but the Queen herself remained what she had always been – no

modern, but the greatest Elizabethan of them all. Gloriana
had always detested newfangledness; she liked her society
and her heavens to be orderly, anthropomorphic and
solidly divine. Though the world was passing the old lady
by, she was not yet dead; and such was her magic that history seems almost to have slowed down to wait for Elizabeth to leave the stage. Yet before she turned England and
Europe over to James of Scotland and Henry of Navarre,
to Galileo and Montaigne, and to the harbingers of intellectual inquiry and political revolution, she had a few
medals left to display.

Twelve

Epilogue
"Dead But Not Buried"

ELIZABETH was growing old, and not even rooms divested of their mirrors could conceal the truth that she and all her generation were mortals "whom time had surprised". As age crept silently into court, management and artifice, rouge pot and wig became all the more essential to her reign. Pageantry and adoration, pomp and stateliness stood alone, devoid of the light-hearted gaiety and exuberance with which the young Princess had mounted the throne. There were still moments when the Queen could conjure up the spirit of those earlier days. At the age of sixty-six she danced the Spanish Panic to a whistle and tabor, but she did so in the privacy of her closet, "none being with her but my Lady Warwick". Her tongue remained as sharp as ever, her laughter as cutting, and her anger as majestic. When, in front of the entire court, the Polish ambassador accused her in polished Latin of unneutrality and threatened war, she stormed at him in impromptu Latin, so vital and colourful that all England delighted at the Ambassador's discomfort and their Queen's brilliance.

After four decades, the charm still worked, and her people continued to talk of "her mind of gold, her body of brass", but with each passing year, Elizabeth depended more and more on artful staging to achieve her effect. As the Queen's face became wrinkled and her body grew stiff, ceremony waxed all the more lavish. Her table, reported a foreign traveller in 1598, was set out with carefully arranged solemnity.

A gentleman entered the room bearing a rod, and along with him another who had a table cloth, which after they had both kneeled three times with the utmost veneration, he spread upon the table, and after kneeling again, they both retired. Then came two others, one with the rod again, the other with a salt-cellar, a plate, and bread; when they had kneeled as the others had done, and placed what was brought upon the table, they too retired with the same ceremonies performed by the first. At last came an unmarried Lady (we were told she was a Countess) and along with her a married one, bearing a tasting-knife; the former was dressed in white silk, who, when she had prostrated herself three times in the most graceful manner, approached the table, and rubbed the plates with bread and salt, with as much awe as if the Queen had been present: when they had waited there a little while, the Yeomen of the Guard entered, bare-headed, clothed in scarlet, with a golden rose upon their backs, bringing in at each turn a course of twenty-four dishes, served in plate, most of it gilt; these dishes were received by a gentleman in the same order they were brought, and placed upon the table, while the lady-taster gave to each of the guards a mouthful to eat, of the particular dish he had brought, for fear of any poison.

During the tasting and laying out of the meal,

twelve trumpets and two kettledrums made the hall ring for half an hour together. At the end of this ceremonial, a number of unmarried ladies appeared, who, with particular solemnity, lifted the meat off the table, and conveyed it into the Queen's inner and most private chamber, where, after she had chosen for herself, the rest goes to the Ladies of the Court. The Queen dines and sups alone, with very few attendants; and it is very seldom that anybody, foreigner or native, is admitted at that time.

Elizabeth supped alone with her memories, while her

people made do with ceremony. Old Burghley was content that it should be so, for he had been arranging the pomp and circumstance for as many years as Gloriana herself had reigned. The Queen knew her servant's worth and her own indebtedness. In his final sickness, she came to his bedside to feed him with her own princely hand, and the old man was so moved that he told his son that in heaven he hoped to continue to be "a servitor for her and God's Church". There were, however, younger men who were not so willing to serve God by bowing low before a bejewelled and bewigged Virgin Queen, whose harried worshippers never knew from one day to the next whether she fancied herself as a coquette or a school-mistress. The time for change was approaching, and Lord Burghley's death on August 8th, 1598, at the age of seventy-eight, was the signal for a younger generation to begin a struggle for succession which tore the veil of ritual to shreds.

Two men bid for the old Lord's Treasurer's powers and titles and looked ahead to a day when Elizabeth must step down and her cousin of Scotland sit in majesty upon the Tudor throne. One was Burghley's second son, Robert Cecil; the other was my Lord of Essex. Even the most wanton of the gods might have hesitated to arrange so uneven an encounter. Essex was thirty-one in 1598, Cecil thirty-five; one had been trained as a peacock of the court and was obsessed with the vanity of his species; the other had been carefully and lovingly educated by his father in the art of government. Robert Cecil was a member of Parliament at twenty-one, on diplomatic mission at twenty-five, knighted and admitted to the Privy Council at twenty-eight, and at thirty-three made Principal Secretary, a post he had already been administering without title for five years. In a world which jibed cruelly at his hunchbacked deformity and spindly legs, Cecil made his way, partly by his father's influence but more by his own industry. Almost alone of the second generation, he could match his sovereign's attention to detail. There were few secrets that the Cecils, father and son, did not possess; there was little stirring at court or elsewhere in the land to which they were not a party; but both Cecils were content to operate in the shadows, to exalt the cult of royalty and to possess the substance of power behind the glitter of a goddess queen. Burghley, her "Spirit", and Robert Cecil, her "Pygmy", were indispensable to Gloriana's reign, and she knew it.

In contrast, Essex was loved, pampered and treasured, but he was always expendable, and this Elizabeth also knew. Not all the vitality of his youth nor the virtuosity of his Renaissance heritage could altogether obscure his ugly egotism, made doubly sinister by the presence of deep-rooted baronial pride. Robert Devereux claimed power as his due, as his forefathers had done, because he had been born to the ermine; he was an earl and one of the natural leaders of society. But joined to anachronistic feudal pretension was a more dangerous quality: he demanded a place beside his Queen because he was Essex, a hero and a man. Etiquette required that he dance attendance upon a goddess and mouth the formula that transformed a capricious and crusty old woman into a semi-deity. No one knew better than the irresistible Earl how to speak to perfection words that his secret heart denied. "When your Majesty thinks that heaven [is] too good for me, I will not fall like a star, but be consumed like a vapour by the same sun that drew me up to such a height."

Elizabeth was too much of a realist to judge her courtiers by their honeyed phrases, but she believed in artifice and she knew her authority to be of God. The regal rank in which heaven's favour had placed her was divine, and royalty was an inviolable association of equals to which birth alone gave entrance. She could swallow her anger as a woman and forgive her handsome Essex his melancholic brooding and petulant outbursts, but when he publicly questioned her divinity as a queen, and announced that he could see upon the throne of majesty only an ageing and cankered female whose mind was "as crooked as her carcase", then he passed beyond the pale and committed a crime not just against her sex but against "God's immediate minister on earth". "Those who touch the sceptres of princes," she warned, "deserve no pity."

As long as Burghley lived, the conflict between Essex and Cecil was contained. Devereux glittered at court and sought to satisfy his thirst for honour and popularity by

feats of heroism at Cadiz and in the Azores; Cecil remained
discreetly behind the scenes "with his hands full of papers
and his mind full of matters". Very early a pattern began
to emerge, one that augured ill for the unstable Earl and
drove him to ever greater acts of frenzy and hysteria. Essex
could touch Gloriana's heart but never her mind. He could
block Cecil's advance so long as he remained close to the
Queen, but the moment he left for adventures upon the
high seas, Elizabeth quietly gave political office to his rival.
When Essex was strutting in front of the walls of Rouen,
Cecil was placed on the Privy Council; when in 1596
Devereux was off in search of military laurels at Cadiz, Sir
Robert was made Principal Secretary. By 1598 it was painfully clear that my Lord of Essex was gaining all the honours
and Sir Robert Cecil was winning all the offices. It was bad
enough that the Queen should have rewarded hard-working Cecil, but it was even worse when she honoured Charles
Howard, Essex's old military rival, by creating him Earl of
Nottingham. The new title plus his office of Lord Admiral
gave Howard precedence over Essex. Enraged and mortified that his Queen could possibly recognize military service in someone other than himself, Essex sulked, feigned
sickness and refused to appear at Court until Elizabeth had
rectified such an insult to his honour. On December 18th,
1597, she gave in and created him Earl Marshal of the
Realm, the highest military post in her gift.

Essex was extremely pleased; his honour had been satisfied and his rank sustained. Elizabeth had acceded to his
demand, and that was only proper since she was a woman
and he was a man. But as always, Devereux had no sense
of proportion and no idea when to stop. He insisted that
all men should be either with him or against him. He never
realized that parties did not belong to him but to the Queen,
and he wrote to Lord Grey to demand that he should present his colours and declare himself to be a friend or an
enemy. When Grey refused to commit himself, Essex darkly
hinted that he would do well to remember that the Earl
Marshal controlled all military promotions. In answer Lord
Grey posed an issue that Elizabeth could not long ignore.
The Queen, he said, could not permit men of the sword
to owe their advancement to the whim of a party leader

and court favourite. If she did, she would endanger her throne, and her faithful nobility would "languish under the despised yoke of one of their own "rank". The truth of Grey's observation became apparent in July 1598, when the Queen and her Earl Marshal clashed over the appointment of a new Lord Deputy for Ireland. Trouble had been brewing in Ireland for over a decade, and strong military action was required in that graveyard of English reputations, but no one wanted the post of Lord Deputy or the chance to rescue English honour. Elizabeth favoured Essex's uncle, Sir William Knollys. The Earl urged the appointment of his old enemy, Sir George Carew. The Queen grew weary of Essex's pleading and angrily told him to have done with it. In a fury of contempt, he turned his back on his sovereign, and received a box on the ear for his discourtesy and the order to get him gone and be hanged. At that moment, Essex lost what little self-control he possessed and his hand reached for his sword. Nottingham stepped between prince and subject, and Devereux in a blind rage stormed out of the presence chamber. Wiser and more dispassionate heads reminded him that "there is no contesting between sovereignty and obedience", but Essex would have none of it. "I owe her Majesty," he said, "the duty of an Earl and Lord Marshal of England ... What! Cannot princes err? Cannot subjects receive wrong? Is an earthly power or authority infinite? Pardon me, pardon me, my good Lord; I can never subscribe to these principles." The mirror of majesty had been smashed. The principle that would some day pull monarchs by the dozens from their thrones, and for which in later centuries men the world over would gladly die, unexpectedly appeared in the unpleasant mouth of a fatuous and empty-headed sixteenth-century egotist.

Matters between the Queen and her difficult Earl were patched up when Devereux fell ill in September 1598, but reconciliation failed to bring a respite in the jungle warfare of court politics. With Burghley dead, trouble immediately broke out over the inheritance of the old man's most coveted and lucrative office, the Mastership of the Court of Wards. Essex felt that he must have it, both for honour's sake and to save himself from bankruptcy. As early as

1589, scarcely two years after his arrival at court, he was at least twenty-two thousand pounds in debt. On the Earl of Leicester's death he had been granted the income from the customs on imported sweet wines and had been able to borrow heavily on the strength of this, but his household was steadily growing in size and expense, and his political influence depended on his ability to place his friends at court and in his own house. Control of the Court of Wards carried with it immense patronage and wealth, and the moment that Burghley died, a hopeful patron-seeker wrote to Essex: "I pray that we may hear that you are Master of the Wards, for then I shall hope that you will bestow a male or female upon me." The Queen's solution was, as usual, to take no irrevocable step; she delayed and presented the prized office to no one, telling the Earl she would be her own master.

Deprived of one of the richest plums of political life, Essex did the expected: he wrote the Queen a hot, almost threatening letter, demanding that she think again of his suit, and when she continued to refuse him, he announced that he deemed it "the fairer choice to command armies than honours". He forced Elizabeth and the Council to select him as Lord Lieutenant of Ireland, where Hugh O'Neill, the Earl of Tyrone, was successfully harrying the English out of the land. Elizabethan Ireland was a restless, primitive country, where English influence managed to maintain itself only in the Pale, a small area to the west and north of Dublin, and in occasional English coastal ports further to the south. Elsewhere the Queen exercised nominal control through the leading chieftains – O'Neils, O'Donalds, O'Briens, O'Connors, Desmonds, Butlers, and the like. For most Elizabethans, Ireland was a damp, disease-ridden bog of barbarism into which the English poured men and money without profit. In 1596 the Queen had sent three thousand five hundred soldiers to fight; within a year fifteen hundred were "either dead, run away or converted into Irish". For much of her reign, the Irish clans disliked one another so ferociously that they had little time to hate the English and less occasion to unite against them, but in 1594 Ireland found in Hugh O'Neill something approaching a national leader. O'Neill's rebellion was serious, but to make matters worse behind him stood the Spanish, always waiting, always hoping that Ireland would become Elizabeth's Dutch ulcer.

Into this land of rebellious clans, where witches and unseasonable weather abounded, marched the Earl of Essex with the strongest force Elizabeth had ever sent into Ireland – sixteen thousand foot soldiers and thirteen hundred horsemen at a cost of a thousand pounds a day. Everything now depended on success. As one observer cautiously put it: "If the Lord Deputy performs in the field what he hath promised in the council, all will be well; but though the Queen hath granted forgiveness for his late demeanour in her presence, we know not what to think thereof," and he wisely concluded that under the circumstances "danger goeth abroad, and silence is the safest armour". If Elizabeth was giving her Essex enough rope to hang himself, she must have been well satisfied with the results. In early April 1599 he set out with carefully drawn plans to attack Tyrone in his Ulster fastness. Moreover, he had stringent orders from the Queen not to promote his worthless crony, the Earl of Southampton, to the post of second-in-command as General of the Horse, and to use his authority to create knights only with discretion. Instead of searching out O'Neill, Essex went off on a series of wild-goose chases into Leinster and Munster, which cost five thousand men to no purpose except the capture of a decrepit Irish castle "from a rabble of rogues". Instead of destroying Tyrone, he negotiated peace with him, and to make matters still worse he made Southampton General of the Horse, and lavishly, nay treasonously, bestowed knighthood upon thirty-eight henchmen with little to recommend them except that they were loyal to Essex.

As might be expected, Elizabeth was furious, but she was also frightened by conduct that smelled of treason. In letter after letter, the sting of her invective lashed at her Deputy. Why had nothing been accomplished after so many loud boasts and so great a financial effort? "If sickness of the army be the reason, why was not the action undertaken when the army was in better state? If winter's approach, why were the summer months of July and August lost? If the spring were too soon and the summer that followed

otherwise spent, if the harvest that succeeded were so neglected as nothing hath been done, then surely we must conclude that none of the four quarters of the year will be in
season for you . . ." The miserable Essex sat in his tent and
complained that nothing came from England except "discomforts and soul's wounds". He had cause to feel bitter;
ridiculous failure confronted him in Ireland, and behind his
back the Queen had given the Mastership of the Court of
Wards to Robert Cecil.

At what point treason entered Essex's mind is difficult
to say. Possibly the notion had been lying dormant ever
since he dared deny the divinity of kings. Still more probably he spoke treason when he and Tyrone discussed
secretly terms of peace. Surely the thought was father to
the half-formed plan to throw caution to the wind and
return to England at the head of three thousand men. Even
in rebellion, however, Essex proved himself too egotistical
to be successful. Instead of arriving at court with an army
to give weight to his treason, he chose to travel light with only
a select company to guard him from arrest, and he depended
upon his fatal charm to confound his enemies and renew
the Queen's love. He sought only to exercise his male prerogative to rule over womankind and to demand his historic
due as the barons of Runnymede had required of King
John, but, as he sadly confessed, he spoke either "a language that was not understood or to a goddess not at leisure
to hear prayers". When, on the morning of September
28th, 1599, he strode unannounced and covered with filth
into the Queen's chamber at Nonsuch Palace, he encountered a goddess in no mood to hear prayers spoken by a
subject teetering on the brink of treason. For once Elizabeth was caught totally unprepared, with the adornments
of her divinity and the trappings of her vanity put aside.
Possibly had Essex found a Queen attired in regal splendour, and not a wrinkled old woman without her wig or
make-up, the meeting might have been more dramatic.
As it was, the disobedient Earl thought he had again
won the day, for the Queen was strangely quiet and deceptively gracious. Not until she had donned the adornments of royalty, put on the face of a queen and talked at
length with Sir Robert Cecil, did the storm descend,

and Essex was called upon to explain his insubordination.

As the days passed, Gloriana's anger increased, and she recalled Lord Grey's warning. "By God's son," she stormed, "I am no Queene. That man is above me: who gave him command to come here so soon? I did send him on other busynesse." Essex was imprisoned two days after his return, but the Council hesitated to bring him to public trial. He was the darling of the London rabble and the leader of a dangerous band of impecunious soldiers, disappointed office-seekers, disgruntled noblemen, and lawless and landless knights of his own creation: in fact, all the outcasts of Tudor society whom the Queen had been unable to charm by her artistry or satisfy by her patronage. The walls of Tudor popularity were being assaulted for the first time since the rising of the northern earls in 1569, and cautious councillors urged Elizabeth to curb her fury and cancel the trial. Against her better judgment, she allowed Essex to escape the consequences of his idiocy, but it was clear that she had neither forgotten nor forgiven, and she turned a deaf ear to "shaming, languishing, despairing Essex" and his pleas to be allowed to return to court. Gloriana had learned that "affection is false", and in September 1600 she forced into the open the treason that she knew still lay within an unrepentant heart. She refused to renew the Earl's lease of the customs on sweet wines, and Essex's entire financial structure collapsed, forcing him to gamble all on an act of political madness.

Nemesis had long withheld her hand, but from November on she moved swiftly to prove the truth that "character is man's fate". By the time Essex turned to treason, the deterioration in his character had passed beyond the point of hysteria; it was bordering on an insanity which led him to confuse the fantasies of his own sick brain with reality. He "shifteth from sorrow and repentance to rage and rebellion so suddenly," reported Sir John Harington, "as well proveth him devoid of good reason or like mind." Essex's house was turned into an arsenal and the headquarters for rebellion, and in early February 1601 the conspirators drew up their final plans to seize the court, the Tower, and the city of London. On Sunday morning, February 8th, Essex and Southampton, with a company of two hundred henchmen, rode into the city to raise the apprentices with the cry: "For the Queen! For the Queen! a plot is laid for my life." A few of the citizenry cheered but no one stirred, and when a royal herald proclaimed Essex to be a traitor, his own following began to melt away. The throngs watched but made no move to help their darling Essex, the victor of Cadiz, and by evening the farce had been played out. Essex's Sunday parade was over, his senseless rebellion dead, and retribution swift and decisive. On February 18th, Essex and Southampton were brought from the Tower to appear before a jury of their peers. For a time the Earl's dark pride and obsession with honour sustained him. At his trial he was magnificently scornful and, like Mary of Scotland, his dramatic instinct was superb. When Raleigh was sworn in as a witness against him, Essex wanted to know "what booteth it to swear the fox?" To the court he proudly disdained to speak "to save my life, for that I see were vain: I owe God a death". Essex persistently denied that he had been disloyal or "ever wished to be of higher degree than a subject", but the evidence against him was overwhelming. It was manifest to the court, as Cecil remarked, that the Earl had "a wolf's head in a sheep's garment", and Tudor society agreed with Bacon when he said of Essex's behaviour: "Will any man be so simple as to take this to be less than treason?" When the terrible sentence was read – "to be laid on a hurdle and so drawn to the place of execution, and there to be hanged, cut down alive, your members to be cut off and cast into the fire, your bowels burnt before you, your head smitten off, and your body quartered and divided" – Essex answered back that he thought it only fitting that his "poor quarters, which have done her Majesty true service in divers parts of the world, should now at the last be sacrificed and disposed of at her Majesty's pleasure". Again, however, Devereux was posing; he knew full well that his mistress would never expose her Essex to such an indignity. The hangman would be cheated, and he would die as became his rank, by the axe.

Elizabeth had won the battle, and in the end she won the war, for Essex's defiance did not long withstand the teaching of a lifetime: "He that nameth rebellion, nameth ...

the whole puddle and sink of all sins against God and man." Conceit had brought him to such a pass, and every Christian knew that unrepentant pride must inevitably lead to eternal damnation in the fires of hell. Before the day of execution, Essex made confession of his faults, and when he faced the axe on February 25th, 1601, he did so "in humility and obedience", and prostrated himself before his "deserved punishment". "A nature not to be ruled" had finally been tamed.

With Essex's passing, something disappeared from sixteenth-century England and from Elizabeth's life. The ramparts of Tudor popularity held firm; the Queen had triumphed, but the Essex tragedy had clearly shown that the cult of a virgin queen could not for ever satisfy all manner of men and that her system of government was not immune to attack. Elizabeth never really got over Essex's treason or his disloyal words about her mind and heart being "as crooked as her carcase". Sir John Harington reported in October 1601 that "the many evil plots and designs have overcome all her Highnesse's sweet temper. She walks much in her privy chamber, and stamps with her feet at ill news, and thrusts her rusty sword at times into the arras in great rage". Still later he described her as reduced to a skeleton, altered in her features and even her taste for dress gone. It was pathetically clear that Gloriana knew her sword to be rusty and felt "creeping time" to be at her gate.

More and more the Queen remembered what used to be and grieved for what was past. Old, sightless Blanche Parry, who had rocked the Princess in her cradle, died in 1590. Leicester, her Robin, had already gone, and soon stiff, hardworking Walsingham and Chancellor Christopher Hatton, her "Mutton", would face their turn. Essex and Parker, John Knox and John Calvin, Drake and Hawkins, Catherine de Medici and Henry III of France, William of Orange and Suleiman the Magnificent, Ivan the Terrible of Russia and Mary Stuart of Scotland – Elizabeth outlived them all. Even the oldest of her enemies, Philip her brother-in-law, died in '98, in the forty-fourth year of his reign. When the bells of the Escorial tolled their message of grief, they rang out an era that both Elizabeth and

Philip had known and respected: a century of divine-right monarchs and paternalistic governments, of a Europe where men still paid respect to the fiction of religious unity and dressed their thoughts and motives in proper Christian platitudes, of a universe that was intelligible and tidy, and of a world which cherished the medieval concept of subjects born with divinely prescribed duties and kingdoms ordained by God.

Internationally the old and well-understood configurations were passing. Spain remained a great power, but by the time of Philip's death Spanish belief in miracles was sadly shaken, and the old crusading zeal so dim that most Spaniards were ready to make peace with the heretic Jezebel in England and to accept Dutch independence. Pride, not religious conviction, kept the war alive, and within a decade of the King's death it was clear that Spain could no longer afford to maintain her honour. Peace with England in 1604 and with Holland in 1609 were the inevitable consequences of economic and spiritual exhaustion. Spain's misfortunes were partly, as Philip sadly explained, the work of God who had granted him many kingdoms, but not "a son fit to govern them", but the blame rested as much with Philip as with his worthless heirs. His empire was withering away from within. The gold of the New World stayed just long enough to inflate the economy and destroy Spanish industry before passing into the pockets of heretical Dutch merchants, who supplied Philip's fleets with the hemp and tar of the Baltic and the salt herring that his Hieronymite monks ate on fast days. Philip had inherited a kingdom richly diverse in culture and tradition, and like Elizabeth he sought the unity of his realm, but the final irony of his reign was that he succeeded too well. He imposed upon his subjects an intellectual and spiritual straitjacket, so tight that one Spanish ecclesiastic said he "deemed it better to be damned for frivolity than for heresy". In 1598 Spain still looked imposing, but intellectual and economic sclerosis was already well advanced. Wealth and confidence were moving northwards to Holland, and the weight of military power was slowly but surely shifting to the side of France.

The tides that flowed into the estuaries of the Dutch

coast carried on their crest the riches of the entire globe, and merchant-princes in their counting houses stood elbow-deep in gold. At Amsterdam the acquisitive spirit was permitted full rein; the economic freedom to buy and sell without regard to religious belief, state policy, social welfare, or the soul's salvation gave the city a position un-equalled in Europe. The Dutch provinces could send out ten thousand ships and more men-of-war than England and Scotland combined, and at least half those sail made their port on the Amstel river. Antwerp died, but Amsterdam flourished; the southern provinces bled, but the northern cities prospered; and baffled observers noted the strange riddle of the beleaguered Dutch towns and ports: "It is known to all the world that whereas it is generally the nature of war to ruin land and people, these countries on the contrary have been noticeably improved thereby." In 1600 it seemed to many Elizabethans that it had been the junior partner in the war against Spain who had profited from the decline of Spanish seapower and had taken to heart Raleigh's advice that "whosoever commands the sea, commands the trade; whosoever commands the trade of the world, commands the riches of the world, and conse-quently the world itself." While famine, inflation, and com-mercial recession plagued Elizabeth's England, and dreary guerrilla warfare in Ireland absorbed her revenues, Dutch merchant-princes waxed fat on the profits of both war and peace. Holland stood on the threshold of fifty years of economic and cultural pre-eminence, her Golden Age, during which Amsterdam would be rechristened "the crowned queen of Europe".

In France the shape of the future was evident to those who could discern the realities of international power. By 1600 a new Bourbon dynasty under Henry IV was recasting and revitalizing Valois France. When the last Valois was mur-dered at St. Cloud on the morning of August 1st, 1589, the first reaction had been shock that God could have permit-ted such a deed and could have turned the kingdom over to a heretic. Only later came the angry determination that Henry of Navarre should never live to make good his claim. Those about the dead monarch pulled their hats

down over their eyes and vowed that they would die a
thousand deaths before accepting Henry IV as king. At
thirty-five the new King of France dubbed himself "a
King without a country, a soldier without money, a husband without a wife". Henry, like Elizabeth Tudor, was a
master of the well-turned phrase, but his situation was not
quite as desperate as he mockingly portrayed it. As a king,
time and history were his indispensable allies. The exhaustion of over thirty years of intermittent war eventually
silenced even the most vocal bigot and salved the most
tender conscience, and despite papal excommunication and
satanic blessings, his claim to the throne remained inviolate.
No one had a better right to the Valois crown than Henry
of Navarre. Nor was he a soldier totally without resources.
Queen Elizabeth would have been the first to point out the
error in his mathematics, for in 1599 by her own meticulous calculations she reckoned that he owed her £401,734
6s. 5½d. The Catholic League might have the consecrated
banners of the Pope to sustain its candidate for king, and
the gold of Spain to pay its armies, but Henry had Valois
and Capetian blood in his veins and English silver in his
pockets. Only the final witticism was true – he was indeed a
husband without a wife. His marriage to Margaret Valois
in 1570 had proved to be the preliminary to the blood bath
of St. Bartholomew's Day, and their connubial life continued to be as tumultuous as its start, vacillating wildly
between bouts of sensuous reconciliation, mutual promis-
cuity and bitter recriminations. By 1587 the breach was
complete, and Margaret Valois sided with the Catholic
League against both her brother and her husband. Even
after Henry of Navarre made good his right to the throne,
they continued to live apart; and she remained Queen and
wife in name only until these slender ties were dissolved by
divorce in 1599.

Henry IV is as much a legend as Elizabeth – saviour of
his realm, apostle of sanity, reason and tolerance, archi-
tect of French greatness, benevolent king and patriotic
monarch who sought the welfare of the peasantry and the
prosperity of the commercial classes, and above all a royal
lover from whose lusty caresses no woman was safe. As with
Elizabeth, the myth becomes the historical figure, and pos-

sibly Henry spoke no more than the truth when, towards the close of his life, he wrote: "France is deeply indebted to me, for I worked hard for her!" Certainly he laboured long to outwit Philip of Spain, foil the fanatical designs of the Catholic League and secure his throne. The great strength of the League was that it represented all good Catholics who were horrified at the thought of a Protestant monarch; its great weakness was its dependence upon Spanish money and troops and its bafflement over who was the legitimate sovereign if Henry were barred from lawful inheritance. As long as Cardinal Bourbon, Henry's Catholic uncle, lived, the Cardinal could legitimately be recognized as Charles X, but when he died in May 1590, the League was torn apart by contending candidates. Fat Charles, Duke of Mayenne, brother of the murdered Henry of Guise and leader of the League, aspired to the throne. But Philip of Spain planned to bestow the crown upon Isabella Clara Eugenia, his daughter by Elizabeth Valois, and Mayenne never dared push his own claims too hard, since Spanish arms and money seemed to be the only barriers capable of keeping Henry of Navarre out of Paris.

For four years France endured the horrors of a war to which there seemed to be no possible solution nor recognizable victor. Isabella Eugenia was unacceptable because she was Spanish, Mayenne had little support because he was a Guise, and Navarre was detested because he was a Protestant. At first it appeared as if God, after all, might be on the side of legitimacy, when Henry IV's starving, ill-paid and desperate little army routed Mayenne's superior force at the Battle of Ivry in 1590, but Paris, without which no victory could be permanent, remained stubbornly and violently Catholic and withstood a siege of five hellish months. The aristocratic and commercial classes of the city might have capitulated, but the rabble, who suffered the most, were strongest in their determination to resist a heretic king even unto death. Monks and priests, thirteen hundred strong, donned breastplate and helmet and marched the streets as a sign that the spiritual sword of Christ was not without its fighting edge. As the months slipped by, dogs, cats, even rats, began to disappear from the cellars and alleys of Paris, sacrifices to the city's

determination to remain alive and to add a little variety to a
diet of oatmeal and water. Grim stories were reported as
hundreds starved and died. Flour for bread, it was said, was
mixed with human bones; cases of cannibalism were suspected; and the revolutionary Council of Sixteen announced that it was preferable in God's eyes to eat children than
to recognize an apostate monarch.

Just when it seemed as if the city must surrender, the
Duke of Parma came to its rescue and marched his invincible Spanish legions out of Brussels to the relief of Paris.
Fanatical Catholics celebrated with solemn *Te Deums* of
thanksgiving, but artisans and peasants, moderates and
sceptics, and the party of the Politiques wondered whether
such a miraculous eleventh-hour reprieve were worth the
price of three more years of bloodshed and confusion.
Henry of Navarre, for all his flamboyant courage, was no
military match for Parma, and Paris remained adamantly
determined never to accept a Protestant sovereign. The
Catholic League was paralysed by quarrelling within its
own ranks when the Duke of Mayenne and the left-wing
Council of Sixteen clashed over the leadership of the
League and the control of Paris. Philip II annoyed his
Catholic supporters by sending as his representative the
Duke of Feria, undoubtedly the sixteenth century's most
tactless diplomat, and the King antagonized all Frenchmen
by putting his Spanish historians to work to prove that
France's cherished Salic Law, limiting the succession to the
male line, was a myth. Only the wolf and the bandit took
heart and multiplied in a land where law and moderation
seemed to be dead.

If France were to be spared further agony, and if Henry
of Navarre were ever to possess a kingdom commensurate
with his exalted title, it was evident that he must renounce
his Protestant faith and turn Catholic. Such a solution had
been voiced as early as 1589, but it took the King four
years to realize that he had no other choice. On July 25th,
1593, dressed in white and escorted by the highest dignitaries of the realm, Henry made formal recantation at the
abbey church of St. Denis. A minority remained unconvinced and regarded his conversion as "supping with the
devil", but most Catholics jumped at the chance to end

forty years of chronic war and return to their pigs and crops, their ledgers and accounts, and the serious business of civilized existence. Paris voluntarily opened its gates on the morning of March 22nd, 1594, and when Henry rode through the streets, the crowds, which a year earlier would have torn him limb from limb, greeted the King with ecstasies of joy.

Like his royal cousin in England, Henry preferred mercy to revenge and realized that diplomacy was a surer weapon than war. He won over the regional governors and the noble magnates of France with fat gifts and expensive titles, and when his council complained about the price, he explained that "the things they are delivering up to us would cost us ten times as much if we had to take them by force". Even for the Duke of Mayenne he demanded no punishment. The Duke was made governor of the Ile de France, and his many debts were assumed by the crown. Henry was content to walk his obese and rheumatic old adversary, for whom every step was a torment, at a brisk pace through the gardens of Montceaux during the heat of the day, and the King happily whispered to a friend: "If I lead this fat lump a long enough dance I shall have my revenge."

Catholics could be won to peace by honours and silver. Protestants, however, proved more difficult, and Henry was forced to give up a portion of his sovereignty and to recognize the legal existence of a Calvinistic state within a Catholic kingdom. By the Edict of Nantes in 1598 Huguenots were allowed to practise their faith in all towns except Paris and the episcopal cities. They were made eligible for all government offices; a special law court was established to handle cases involving their faith and their persons; and for a period of eight years they were given control of two hundred towns where they were permitted to maintain armed garrisons at the King's expense. The practice of religious toleration in a century that absolutely denied the principle was established by a monarch who had deemed Paris to be worth a mass, had been the friend and disciple of Montaigne, and, like his master, agreed that, were something possible, 'twere better than if it were true. Peace and prosperity were possible only at the price of sacrificing spiritual truth, and when conservative lawyers tried to block the edict by arguing that it violate the historic laws of France and the Holy Church, Henry assured them that they stood in far greater danger of being declared heretics for not obeying him than for sanctioning an act which might be displeasing to God.

Henry worked hard for France, checking the resurgence of feudal anarchy, cooling the heat of religious ardour, profiting from the discredit of old ideas and institutions which seemed capable only of producing further war and disunity, and rebuilding a land that was potentially the richest and most powerful in Europe. By 1600 the essential condition which had made Spanish hegemony possible and had been the major consideration of Elizabethan foreign policy had disappeared: France was no longer a weak and divided realm to be sacrificed at the bidding of another state. She was once again the senior kingdom of the continent; and before the century was out, England would again view France, not Spain, as the enemy.

At home, too, the world was passing the old Queen by. For a few brief decades Renaissance egotism, religious zeal, the acquisitive spirit, the thirst for adventure, and even lingering medieval chivalric posing and love of display had been harnessed and put to work by an organic and ordained Tudor state. The result had been a perfectly balanced yet wonderfully buoyant and sensitive society. Elizabethans wrote with the boisterous grace of a Shakespeare; they were glad to be alive, yet profoundly aware of their own mortality, and just a little afraid of the life to come. Even the Puritans, though they thundered warnings about God's punishment upon the wicked, enjoyed the world in which they lived; if they had not, they would not have been so anxious to improve it. But as the years passed, the static and ordered society grew rigid and unwieldy, and Renaissance confidence and vitality slipped into self-satisfaction and treason. By 1600 landed country gentlemen, religious zealots and city merchants were growing restive under a divinely proportioned and paternalistic regime.

After Elizabeth died and the irritating element of Stuart

personality was added to a dangerously unstable political, religious and economic situation, elderly Elizabethans looked back with nostalgia to a golden age and remembered far more than had in fact existed. "During her life, what peace in her country! What plenty in her land! What triumphs in her court! What learning in her schools! What trades in her cities! What wealth in her kingdom! What wisdom in her counsel, and what grace in her government!" Alas, the image was untrue, for the final decade of Good Queen Bess's reign saw neither plenty in her land nor grace in her government. Between 1594 and 1597 the harvests failed for three consecutive years and the poor starved. In the popular mind hoarders and usurers, those medieval caterpillars of the commonwealth, were to blame, and Elizabeth's government was severly criticised for doing little about them. As the price of food soared, the buying power of wages dropped to an all-time low, and Oxfordshire peasants took up arms against the Queen's sheriffs and justices of the peace.

A paternalistic government was not completely devoid of ideas on how to handle the economic crisis, and the most revolutionary of all Elizabethan poor laws was enacted in 1601 by a secular government which for the first time recognized that poverty was a social not a spiritual or individual ill. Humane as were Elizabeth's economic views, her policy remained essentially medieval and anachronistic in an age that was casting off its feudal and religious approach to economics. The Tudor state believed in curtailing cut-throat competition, fixing wages and prices, licensing all production under grants of monoply, to achieve a stable and contented society and a fair living for all. Unfortunately, medieval guild economics applied to the entire kingdom did little to curb the recession, and they antagonized the most vocal and wealthy elements of the population. If peasants and apprentices censured the Crown for failing to keep wages and prices in reasonable accord, and for its inability to appease a wrathful God who had brought unseasonable rains for three summers in a row, landlords and merchants were irritated by a paternalistic state that strangled free enterprise, failed to recognize the dynamism of an expanding commercial and industrial economy, and raised the cost of living by issuing monopolies to favoured courtiers in order to finance their lavish and uneconomic ways.

Tudor England was changing. A few great peers might continue to maintain households of two or three hundred retainers, but iron smelters might employ as many as four thousand workers. During Elizabeth's reign coal production increased sevenfold, and iron production was up fivefold. By 1600 it was noted that a London merchant might be worth a hundred thousand pounds, as much as the greatest peer in the realm. Slowly but surely, Englishmen began to perceive that the search for the black combustible earth of Yorkshire was more rewarding than the quest for silver, and that the mining of iron might be more profitable than the digging of gold in the New World. The wealth, prosperity and domestic peace with which Elizabeth had blessed her people produced within the landowning and commercial groups a new sense of their own social and political importance. In 1500 Erasmus had described the prince's threat as an eagle's scream before which all men and interests gave way; by 1600 a new note was heard, the idea of service to the state as a public and landed obligation and not as a duty to the sovereign. Elizabeth's loyal Commons were evolving a new and revolutionary conceit, viewing themselves as legislators, not as humble petitioners, and demanding a share in the government of the realm. Members of the lower house, though as yet they hesitated to answer the question, had heard and recorded Essex's fateful outburst: "What! Cannot princes err?"

To merchants anxious to search out new avenues of trade, to country gentlemen groaning under a decade of wartime taxation, to entrepreneurs with clever schemes to improve production and reap a quick profit, and to a realm that was suffering from the long trade depression of the 1590s, government monopolies regulating and licensing almost every item of life from buttons to tobacco seemed to be an immoral and unwarranted interference into the rights and economic activities of the individual. It was over the abuse of such monopolies that in 1601 the most serious and concerted attack upon the structure and theory of Tudor government broke with a fury that alarmed

Elizabeth almost as much as had the Essex rebellion. Three vital issues were at stake: the royal prerogative which stood above earthly criticism, the right of the Crown to interfere in the actions of subjects in order to ensure the welfare of all, and finally the role of the Commons as humble advisers to the Crown, not as arrogant initiators of policy. During the controversy over monopolies, the Commons listened in hostile silence to the efforts of Privy Councillors to explain the royal prerogative and the Crown's right to license and control trade and production. When one of the Council suggested that in theory all men's estates belonged to the sovereign, he was shouted down by land-owners who had long since forgotten their feudal obligations and viewed their lordships and manors as private property. Worse yet, when at the close of the first meeting the Queen passed through the parliament chamber, the traditional cry, "God bless your Majesty," was weak and half-hearted. Gloriana was thoroughly alarmed, for the mortar of her entire governmental edifice – her precious and indispensable popularity which she wisely treasured even above her constitutional prerogative – was turning to dust.

Elizabeth had fought long and hard to conserve her subjects' resources and to win victory in the war against Spain with the least loss of English blood and the least expenditure of English money, but the war had been long, the cost heavy and her kingdom belaboured by famine and war-weariness. She had sacrificed to the war effort almost her entire inheritance from her father's confiscation of the monastic lands, and as her capital dwindled, her income declined and her dependence upon parliamentary subsidies mounted. Gentry and merchants, who more and more paid the royal piper, sought to call the governmental tune. As yet they demanded only the redress of evils and the reform of monopolies, but in so doing they implicitly championed the doctrine of economic liberalism, and by seizing the initiative and forcing their views upon the Crown, they raised economic and constitutional problems that were unsolvable within the structure and theory of the Tudor state.

Elizabeth's sense of political survival was matchless. She

realized that should the Commons present its demands in statute form, a dangerous precedent might be established for a further assumption of the legislative initiative by Parliament. Consequently, she promised immediate and complete redress of wrongs and the reshaping of the entire system of monopolies. By surrendering and admitting the existence of abuse, she saved her royal prerogative from being made the subject of a constitutional debate. As always Gloriana was willing to stoop to save what she held most high – her reputation and the unity of her kingdom. In her Golden Speech to parliament in November 1601 she told her loyal Commons that "I was never so much enticed with the glorious name of a king or the royal authority of a queen, as delighted that God hath made me His instrument to maintain His truth and glory and to defend His kingdom from peril, dishonour, tyranny and oppression". With unerring political sense, Elizabeth knew when to present her divinity dressed in the guise of utilitarianism.

At the conclusion of her address, Gloriana bade each of the gentlemen present approach and kiss her hand. It was the final farewell: sixteen months later the Queen was dead. In a strange, disturbing way she died, as she had ruled, when her "own great judgment advised", for Elizabeth elected death when she realized that she had no further reason to live. Throughout the winter of 1602 she had been suffering from bouts of melancholia, and had visibly begun to age. She seemed to have no care for her health, almost inviting pneumonia by wearing summer clothes. For days on end she sat looking into a past which no one at court could share. She must have known that Cecil, Raleigh and the rest were more mindful of what they were soon to get than of what they were shortly to lose, and the Queen allowed Cecil to rehearse her Scottish heir and to arrange the details of the succession behind her back. She saw, but said nothing, except to sigh that "her authority among the people [was] sensibly decayed". In early March a "heavy dulness" seized her, whereby she could neither sleep nor eat, and she sat waiting to leave an England to which she had nothing more to give and in which she no longer took interest. Years before, she had said that she had no desire to live if her life and reign were no longer of profit to her subjects. In March 1603 Elizabeth knew that moment had arrived, and the time for a new master had come. Like everything she did throughout the sixty-nine years of her life, she died with quiet dignity and perfect timing. Gloriana slipped rapidly from apathy into speechlessness, coma and death; and on March 24th, 1603, she turned her head to the wall and her eyes to God.

The magnitude of Elizabeth Tudor's success is baffling; the historian may record it but he can scarcely explain it. With failure, the dark necessity of circumstance and personality stand out and the chain of events leading to despair, death and perdition can be traced back to the first false step. But success is too mercurial, too volatile, to be disciplined by causality. It seems to possess no roots, no history; it merely exists, blooms and dies. What, after all, is success? Is it really what it appears to be, or is it a trick of historical hindsight? Elizabeth was successful in doing what? In bequeathing to her Stuart heir problems of state beyond his, or possibly any king's, ability to solve? In holding time at bay and allowing a later generation to pay the price? In concealing by her feminine guile the mounting pressure to have done with benevolent paternalism and "degree, priority and place"? Elizabeth was a success, but might not another sovereign have been more successful? What wonders might have taken place had she acted with the resolution of a Henry VIII? What might she have achieved? The answer, very likely, is catastrophic failure. And there's the rub. Gloriana rarely did the things mankind most admires, yet she is judged pre-eminently successful. She contrived to elevate inconsistency into a virtue, turn vacillation into wisdom and translate half-measures into policy.

Where there appears to be no cause there must be magic. The secret of Elizabeth's art was that she was blessed with ambitions commensurate with her abilities. She demanded no windows into men's souls, she coveted not her neighbour's lands, and she sought not to carve out an empire. She was content to preserve the unity of her kingdom and earn the devotion of her subjects. In the months before

she died, the Queen had occasion to speak of her life's
achievement, and she told her loving and loyal people that
"though you have had, and may have, many mightier and
wiser princes sitting in this seat, yet you never had, nor
shall have, any that will love you better". Alone among
her royal contemporaries she possessed the skill and the
means to achieve her end. Philip of Spain consumed himself and martyred his kingdom in demanding that absolute
truth be shared by all men. No matter how estimable his
vision it was doomed to failure, for not all the gold of
Raleigh's El Dorado, let alone the resources of the Spanish
empire, could have transformed such a dream into reality.
Catherine de Medici's purpose was simple and domestic –
palaces and sceptres for herself and all her brood – but
historic circumstance and the shallowness of her own
mind made a mockery of even such modest ambitions.
The same was true of Mary of Scotland and of Essex;
their hot desires took no account of reality. Only Elizabeth succeeded. She was no modern woman, but at least
she was an adult and a realist free of obsessions. "She only
is a king. She only knows how to rule!" was Henry of
Navarre's tribute.

Gloriana achieved her life's ambition: "To do some
act that would make her fame spread abroad in her lifetime, and after, occasion memorial for ever." In this she
was supremely successful, for the century that produced
Shakespeare, Harvey, Drake and Bacon bears her name –
the age of Elizabeth.

> Even such is time, that takes in trust
> Our youth, our joys, our all we have,
> And pays us but with earth and dust;
> Who, in the dark and silent grave,
> When we have wandered all our ways,
> Shuts up the story of our days;
> But from this earth, this grave, this dust,
> My God shall raise me up, I trust.

The words are Raleigh's, but the conceit belongs to Elizabeth and her golden heroes.

Index